UNION INTERNATIONALE DES SCIENCES PRÉHISTORIQUES ET PROTOHISTORIQUES
INTERNATIONAL UNION OF PREHISTORIC AND PROTOHISTORIC SCIENCES

PROCEEDINGS OF THE XVI WORLD CONGRESS (FLORIANÓPOLIS, 4-10 SEPTEMBER 2011)
ACTES DU XVI CONGRÈS MONDIAL (FLORIANÓPOLIS, 4-10 SEPTEMBRE 2011)

(Session XXXV)

VOL. 6

uispp

# Traceology Today: Methodological Issues in the Old World and the Americas

Edited by

## Maria Estela Mansur
## Marcio Alonso Lima
## Yolaine Maigrot

BAR International Series 2643
2014

Published in 2016 by
BAR Publishing, Oxford

BAR International Series 2643

Proceedings of the XVI World Congress of the International Union of Prehistoric and Protohistoric Sciences
Actes du XVI Congrès mondial de l'Union Internationale des Sciences Préhistoriques et Protohistoriques

Secretary of the Congress: Rossano Lopes Bastos
President of the Congress National Commission: Erika Robrhan-Gonzalez
Elected President: Jean Bourgeois
Elected Secretary General: Luiz Oosterbeek
Elected Treasurer: François Djindjian
Series Editors: Luiz Oosterbeek, Erika Robrhan-Gonzalez
Volume title: Traceology Today: Methodological Issues in the Old World and the Americas
Volume editors: Maria Estela Mansur, Marcio Alonso Lima and Yolaine Maigrot

*Traceology Today: Methodological Issues in the Old World and the Americas*

ISBN 978 1 4073 1282 8

Contacts: General Secretariat of the U.I.S.P.P. – International Union of Prehistoric and Protohistoric Sciences
Instituto Politécnico de Tomar, Av. Dr. Cândido Madureira 13, 2300 TOMAR Email: uispp@ipt.pt

BAR Publishing is the trading name of British Archaeological Reports (Oxford) Ltd.
British Archaeological Reports was first incorporated in 1974 to publish the BAR
Series, International and British. In 1992 Hadrian Books Ltd became part of the BAR
group. This volume was originally published by Archaeopress in conjunction with
British Archaeological Reports (Oxford) Ltd / Hadrian Books Ltd, the Series principal
publisher, in 2014. This present volume is published by BAR Publishing, 2016.

Printed in England

# BAR
PUBLISHING

BAR titles are available from:

BAR Publishing
122 Banbury Rd, Oxford, OX2 7BP, UK
EMAIL    info@barpublishing.com
PHONE   +44 (0)1865 310431
FAX      +44 (0)1865 316916
www.barpublishing.com

# Table of Contents

## List of Figures and Tables

### *H. De Angelis*: Microwear formation on glass: an experimental and archaeological study

### *N. Kononenko*: Use-wear and residues on obsidian artefacts from Melanesia

### *M. Leipus*: The functional analysis of heterogeneous raw materials and their application to different varieties of quartzites from Pampean Region (Argentina): experimental and archaeological results

### Y. *Maigrot* et al.: From bone fishhooks to fishing techniques: the example of Zamostje 2 (Mesolithic and Neolithic of the central Russian plain)

### J. *Rodet* et al.: The production of beads and lithic pendants in the Salobo river basin, Pará, Brazil

### V. *Parmigiani* & M.C. *Alvarez Soncini*: Wear traces on beaver teeth: the use of teeth as tools

# List of contributors

**Márcio Alonso Lima**
UFMG – Setor de Arqueologia do Museu de História Natural, SETE – Soluções e Tecnologia Ambiental, Brasil
mg.alonso@gmail.com

**Myrian Álvarez**
Centro Austral de Investigaciones Científicas – CADIC CONICET, Laboratorio de Antropología, B. Houssay 200, 9410 Ushuaia, Tierra del Fuego, Argentina
myrianalvarez@gmail.com

**Maria Celina Alvarez Soncini**
Centro Austral de Investigaciones Científicas – CADIC CONICET, Laboratorio de Antropología, B. Houssay 200, 9410 Ushuaia, Tierra del Fuego, Argentina
mcalvarezson@gmail.com

**Ignacio Clemente Conte**
Departament d'Arqueologia i Antropologia, Institució Milà i Fontanals, CSIC, Egipcíaques 15, 08001 Barcelona, Espagne
ignacio@imf.csic.es

**Marcondes Lima da Costa**
Prof. Dr. at Universidade Federal do Pará, Museu de Geociencias da Universidade Federal do Pará, Rua Augusto Correa, 01, Guamá, Belé, CEP 66075-110, Brasil
mlc@ufpa.br

**Hernán De Angelis**
Centro Austral de Investigaciones Científicas – CADIC CONICET, Laboratorio de Antropología, B. Houssay 200, 9410 Ushuaia, Tierra del Fuego, Argentina
hernandeangelis@yahoo.com.ar

**Evgeny Gyria**
Laboratory for Experimental Traceology, Institute for the History of Material Culture of the Russian Academy of Science (IHMC RAS), Dvortsovaya nab. 18, 191186 St. Petersbourg, Russie
kostionki@yandex.ru

**Nina Kononenko**
The University of Sydney, Australia
kononenkonina@hotmail.com

**Marcela Leipus**
Facultad de Ciencias Naturales y Museo, Universidad Nacional de La Plata, 1900 La Plata, Argentina
mleipus@hotmail.com

**Olga Lozovskaya**          Laboratory for Experimental Traceology, Institute for
                             the History of Material Culture of the Russian Academy
                             of Science (IHMC RAS), Dvortsovaya nab. 18,
                             191186 St. Petersbourg, Russie
                             olozamostje@gmail.com

**Vladimir Lozovski**        Department of Archaeology, Sergiev-Possad State History
                             and Art Museum-Preserved, pr. Krasnoï Armii 144,
                             141300 Sergiev Possad, Russie
                             zamostje68@gmail.com

**Yolaine Maigrot**          UMR 8215 du CNRS – Trajectoires De la sédentarisation
                             à l'État, MAE. 21, allée de l'Université,
                             92023 Nanterre cedex, France
                             yolaine.maigrot@mae.cnrs.fr

**Maria Estela Mansur**      Centro Austral de Investigaciones Científicas – CADIC
                             CONICET, Laboratorio de Antropología, B. Houssay 200,
                             9410 Ushuaia, Tierra del Fuego, Argentina
                             estelamansur@gmail.com

**Elizângela R. de Oliveira**  Master-Visitor Reseaecher at Museu Paraense Emilio
                             Goeldi, Departamento de Ciências Humanas, Avenida
                             Magalhães Barata, 376, São Braz Belém – PA,
                             66040-170, Brasil
                             elisoliveira@yahoo.com.br

**Nélida Pal**               Centro Austral de Investigaciones Científicas – CADIC
                             CONICET, Laboratorio de Antropología, B. Houssay 200,
                             9410 Ushuaia, Tierra del Fuego, Argentina
                             nelidapal@yahoo.com.ar

**Vanesa E. Parmigiani**     Centro Austral de Investigaciones Científicas – CADIC
                             CONICET, Laboratorio de Antropología, B. Houssay 200,
                             9410 Ushuaia, Tierra del Fuego, Argentina
                             veparmigiani@yahoo.com.ar

**Maria Jacqueline Rodet**   Profa. Dra. at Universidade Federal de Minas Gerais
                             (UFMG), FAFICH end Museu de Historia Natural-
                             UFMG., Rua Gustavo da Silveira, 1035, Santa Ines,
                             CEP 31080-010, Brasil
                             jacqueline.rodet@gmail.com

**Maura Imazio da Silveira** Doctor- Researcher Holder at Museu Paraense Emilio
                             Goeldi, Departamento de Ciências Humanas, Avenida
                             Magalhães Barata, 376, São Braz Belém – PA,
                             66040-170, Brasil
                             maura@marajoara.com

**Déborah Duarte-Talim**     Cooperator Researcher at Museu de Historia Natural –
                             Setor de Arqueologia,
                             Rua Gustavo da Silveira, 1035, Santa Ines,
                             CEP 31080-010, Brasil
                             delsduarte@hotmail.com

TRACEOLOGY TODAY

METHODOLOGICAL ISSUES IN THE OLD WORLD

AND THE AMERICAS

*Figure 1 – Selknam family in the central forest, Tierra del Fuego (Photo C. Furlong, 1908)*

# INTRODUCTION

## Maria Estela MANSUR

Centro Austral de Investigaciones Científicas CADIC-CONICET, Laboratorio de Antropología,
B. Houssay 200, 9410 Ushuaia, Tierra del Fuego, Argentina
estelamansur@gmail.com

## Márcio ALONSO LIMA

UFMG – Setor de Arqueologia do Museu de História Natural; SETE – Soluções e Tecnologia Ambiental, Brasil
mg.alonso@gmail.com

## Yolaine MAIGROT

UMR 8215 du CNRS – Trajectoires. De la Sédentarisation à l'État. MAE. 21,
allée de l'Université, 92023 Nanterre cedex, France
yolaine.maigrot@mae.cnrs.fr

The volume that we have the pleasure to introduce is the result of a selection of papers presented at the thematic session "*Traceology today: Methodological issues in the Old World and the Americas*" that was held at the XVI Congress of the SAB and XVI International Congress of the UISPP, which took place in Florianopolis in 2011. This was the second time that a UISPP Congress took place in America. In part for that reason, we thought that this event would be an excellent occasion to organize a session devoted to functional analysis in which American researchers could be represented. But before we refer to it, we would like to make some reflections regarding the title, scope and general theme of this Session.

Since it was established as a formal discipline, use-wear analysis has acquired the position of a routine practice in archaeological research. Its methods have become ever more sophisticated, with improvement in optical equipment, new observation as well as analysis and recording techniques, better photography of use-wear, etc. Besides the study of stone implements, similar analysis methodology and procedures are now applied to tools made on other materials, like bone, horns, ivory, glass, wood, and sometimes on metal. The temporal and geographical ranges of use-wear analysis have also widened to include assemblages from every period, and from all over the world. But besides methodology and techniques, it is important to mention progress done concerning the explanatory possibilities of microwear analysis: these have been widely discussed, considering their basis on ethnographic analogy, as a source for explanatory hypothesis, and experimentation.

Considering this wide scope of use-wear analysis, some years ago a group of colleagues headed by Natalia Skakun (Russia) and Laura Longo (Italy) proposed to form a specific commission of the UISPP devoted to this discipline. It was preliminary established in the XV UISPP Congress, in Portugal, and registered as Commission 33: *Tools function and socio-economical reconstructions of the past*. According to their proposal,

during the last decades, the development of the discipline had split somehow leading to two slightly different approaches in archaeological tools functional interpretation. One of them, usually called "Traceology", was led by the Russian school while the other, called "Wear Traces analysis" or "Functional analysis", was led by European and north American scholars. In Latin America, this last orientation gave birth to "Análise Functional" or "Sinais de Desgaste" in Portuguese, and "Análisis de rastros de uso", "functional" or "microdesgaste" in Spanish and more recently "Análisis funcional de base microscópica".

Anyhow, since the beginning of the 3rd millennium, five international conferences held two in Russia (1999, 2003), one in Spain (2001), one in Italy (2005) and one in Portugal (2012) have strengthened the debate and exchange of ideas between scholars and showed that new winds were starting to blow. Nevertheless, almost all the conferences or congress sessions on our discipline have taken place in Europe, sometimes in North America, and never in South America.

With this spirit in mind, the XVI UISPP thematic session "*Traceology today: Methodological issues in the Old World and the Americas*" was proposed. We believed that it could be an excellent occasion to meet scholars from all over the world who are devoted to Functional Analysis. We encouraged participation of Latin American researchers, who have developed original lines of research but have seldom be represented in meetings in Europe.

The main goals of that thematic session, as we stated at the beginning of the congress, were to explore, discuss and possibly merge the particular approaches of different scholars involved into use-wear analysis and its application to different raw materials. We also proposed to discuss about the current state of our discipline, the delineation of basic directions of investigation, new technologies and their correct application, in order to get reliable results for modelling technological processes and paleoeconomical reconstructions. And as a corollary, to explore, in particular, the differences between European and recently developed Latin American lines of research.

These objectives were also present in the articles forming this book. As you will see, the contributions include a variety of topics, with different raw materials as lithics, glass, bone, teeth. Their interest is principally methodological; most of them concern South America, but there are also communications concerning sites in Russia and Australia.

In the first paper, Márcio Alonso Lima presents the micro-wear analysis of lithic industries from Central Brasil. This communication is the result of research for a Dissertation concerning microwear analysis of lithic archaeological assemblages of this region. It includes the analysis of experimental tools used to work distinct substances of animal, vegetal or mineral origin, as well as of archaeological tools manufactured with different lithic raw materials (flint, quartz crystal and quartzite). The archaeological series analyzed consisted in 472 artifacts, coming from four sites of different parts of Minas Gerais State.

The second paper, by Myrian Alvarez, María Estela Mansur and Nélida Pal, presents the results of an experimental research on techno-functional analysis on bone tools. The study of bone tools represents a key-element for the investigation of many hunter-gatherer-fisher societies. In the case of those that inhabited the extreme south of America, bone technology had a particular importance considering both the frequency and the diversity of tools design. Consequently, the identification of the uses to which bone artifacts were devoted is relevant in order to understand their socio-economical dynamics. The paper presents an experimental program aiming at characterization of microscopic traces produced by three different processes: manufacturing of various types of bone artifacts, their utilization, and the alterations resulting from taphonomical processes. They were analysed by means of different optical devices and magnifications (stereomicroscope, reflected light microscope and scanning electron microscope). Its results let discuss their implications for microwear analysis of bone tools.

The third paper, by Hernán De Angelis, concerns an archaeological and experimental study of micro-wear formation on glass. As the author states, glass has been extensively exploited as a lithic raw material by the hunter-gatherer populations of Tierra del Fuego. This material started being used even before the concrete settlement of European "estancias" in the island, due to the fact that fragments of glass proceeding from shipwrecks were arriving to the shores since the Seventeenth century. From the functional point of view, glass has always been seen as a very fragile raw material, in which traces of use could hardly be preserved. Nevertheless, experimental and archaeological studies on glass tools demonstrate that this is not always the case. In this paper, De Angelis presents an experimental program, which includes the techno-morphologic analysis of all the microdébitage produced by manufacture of two series of tools made of glass, followed by the microscopic-functional analysis of experimental tools used on different materials. The results are used in order to interpret the archaeological assemblage from a ceremonial hunter-gatherer's site.

The fourth paper, by Nina Kononenko, presents the analysis of Use-wear and residues on obsidian artefacts from Melanesia. It is the result of a research where microscopic use-wear analysis and residue analysis are integrated. The study proposes diagnostic sets of wear attributes resulting from working eight categories of tropical plant and non-plant materials. Experimental results are used to study series of middle and late Holocene obsidian artefacts from 18 sites in Melanesia. This study has significantly extended the range of tool functions particularly in relation to tropical resources. The duration of use of prehistoric artefacts was also estimated through comparisons with experimental data providing important insights into the expedient pattern of use of flakes as single purpose tools in daily activities of prehistoric peoples.

The fifth paper, by Marcela Leipus, concerns the functional analysis of heterogeneous raw materials and its application to different varieties of quartzite for the Pampas region (Argentina). It presents experimental and archaeological results, obtained from application of microscopic functional analysis methodology to quartzitic raw materials from the Pampas. The experimental study enabled to characterize qualities of the different quartzite edges when they are used in different utilization processes. Analysis of archaeological series concerns three hunter-gatherers sites. Microscopic analysis revealed that they were used on diverse materials and with different kinematics. It was concluded that there was not a specific relationship between utilization and raw material or tool type. This variability suggests that quartzites could have been selected to make versatile and durable artifacts, as a part of a conserved technologic strategy.

The sixth paper, written by Yolaine Maigrot, Ignacio Clemente Conte, Evgeny Gyria, Olga Lozovskaya and Vladimir Lozovski, is titled "From bone fishhooks to fishing techniques: the example of Zamostje 2 (Mesolithic and Neolithic of the central Russian plain)". The authors say that fishing played a fundamental role in the subsistence economy of the Mesolithic and Neolithic inhabitants of Zamostje 2, a site located on the Russian plain (Sergiev Possad, Moscow). The abundant ichtiofaunal remains and the tools found at the site (harpoons, needle nets, weight nets, fishhooks and scaling knives) corroborate this importance. In this article, they focus on the consumption of fishhooks through an analysis of the wear traces observed on their surfaces. They compare the usewear observed on the archaeological fishhooks with that seen on experimental fishhooks used to capture different fish species. They show how some attributes (disposition, quantity and hardness of the fish teeth) influence the nature of the use wear, especially the striations, formed on the surfaces of the fishhooks.

The seventh paper, by Maria Jacqueline Rodet, Déborah Duarte-Talim, Maura Imazio da Silveira, Elizângela R. de Oliveira and Marcondes Lima da Costa, concerns the production of beads and lithic pendants in the Salobo Riverbasin, Pará, Brazil. The research is a part of the "Archaeological rescue in the area of Salobo Project", developed in the city of Marabá, State of Pará, where lithic industries from hunter-gatherer and ceramists groups were studied in archaeological sites of the left bank of the Itacaiúnas Riverbasin. The ceramic material has technological, morphological and stylistic features that refer to Tupiguarani Tradition. In this study, the authors present the technological analysis of lithic beads produced on silicified kaolinite of Flint type, for each of the sites, and then compare them with each other. The objects are in varied technical stages, what allowed the reconstruction of the different production stages.

The eighth paper, by Vanesa E. Parmigiani and María Celina Alvarez Soncini, explores the use of teeth as tools and includes an experimental microwear analysis of use on beaver teeth. As we all agree, the dental pieces constitute an important part of the archaeological material recovered in numerous sites and with different chronologies. They are a first degree taxonomic indicator but also, at the same time, an excellent raw material for ornaments and tools. This last aspect is the one presented in this work. The authors carried out an experimental study with teeth of *Castor canadiensis*, where incisors were used as tools, for scraping and cutting on different materials. Analysis was carried out by means of stereomicroscope and metallographic microscope, and it

let to identify traces of use, which differ from natural traces on teeth.

To conclude, the last paper, by María Estela Mansur, Marcio Alonso Lima and Hernán De Angelis, presents a short reflection about microscopic use-wear analysis in Latin America and its contribution to new problems, raw materials and taphonomic contexts. As authors say, since the publication of S. Semenov's Prehistoric Technology in Europe in 1964, microscopic analysis of archaeological materials has developed continuously, although it has followed an uneven rhythm, sometimes more rapid and sometimes slower. In Latin America, microscopic analysis started at about the same time -and developed in a parallel way- as in Europe and North America. Nevertheless it had its own course to follow, as it tried to solve different methodological problems, mainly concerning raw materials used, depositional contexts, etc. But besides methodology, it was also singular because of its theoretical-methodological approach in relation with the type of ethnographic and archaeological problems investigated. Different reasons led it to be little known, not only in the Old World but also in North America. The objective in this paper is to present a preliminary bibliography of the principal investigations and lines of research developed up to now.

We are pleased by the quality of communications presented and discussions engaged during the session. As we said, we believe that this UISPP congress in Florianopolis constituted an excellent opportunity to explore, in particular, the differences between European and recently developed Latin American lines of research, which have seldom been presented in Europe. We need to thank the organization of the conference for their support, as well as all the authors who worked in elaboration and reviews of papers of this book.

*Figure 2 – Waiwai woman, making a manihoc scraper*
*(Photo Arquivos do Setor de Arqueologia do Museu de História Natural da UFMG, Brasil)*

# MICROWEAR ANALYSIS OF LITHIC INDUSTRIES OF CENTRAL BRAZIL

Márcio ALONSO LIMA

UFMG – Setor de Arqueologia do Museu de História Natural, SETE – Soluções e Tecnologia Ambiental, Brasil
mg.alonso@gmail.com

**Abstract**: *This communication is the result of a Dissertation concerning a microwear analysis on archaeological tools manufactured with different lithic raw materials (flint, crystal quartz and quartzite). Use-wear traces differ when the tools are used to work on distinct substances of animal, vegetal or mineral origin. So in this case, starting from the special attributes of each raw material, we tried to identify which were the substances worked with the archaeological tools and with which kinematics. The archaeological series analyzed belong to four sites of different parts of Minas Gerais State. In all, this represents 472 artifacts.*

**Key-words**: *functional analysis, raw materials, traces of use*

**Résumé**: *Cet article présente les principaux résultats d'un Mémoire de Master concernant l'analyse tracéologique d'outillages lithiques fabriqués à partir de différentes matières premières lithiques (silex, quartz et quartzite). Les traces d'utilisation observées sur les outils varient en fonction des matières travaillées, qu'elles soient d'origine animale, végétale ou minérale. A partir des caractéristiques propres au silex, au quartz et à la quartzite, nous avons essayé de déterminer les matières travaillées à l'aide des outils lithiques ainsi que leur cinématique. Les séries archéologiques étudiées proviennent de quatre sites de différentes parties de l'état de Minas Gerais au Brésil. En tout, cela représente un total de 472 pièces.*

**Mots-clés**: *Tracéologie, outils lithiques, matières premières*

## 1. INTRODUCTION

The analysis presented in this article consists of fragments of a dissertation submitted to the Department of Sociology and Anthropology at the Federal University of Minas Gerais (PPGAN), being the first work on the topic conducted in Brazil (Alonso 2008). It brings together the results of the functional analysis of lithic industries of Lapa do Boquete and Grande Abrigo de Santana do Riacho, archaeological sites located in different regions of the state of Minas Gerais – Brazil: northern and central regions (Fig. 1).

The Lapa do Boquete was excavated between 1981 and 1998 and the Grande Abrigo de Santana do Riacho from 1976 to 1979, by archaeologist A. Prous and the team of researchers from the Archaeology Department of the Natural History Museum/UFMG.

These sites are important due to their chronology (with occupations that come to 12,000 years BP), and tithe technological diversity of the lithic industry, which has mainly flint (Boquete) and quartz (Grande Abrigo de Santana do Riacho) as its base. These sites have also retained, besides burials/interment/entombment, many artifacts made of various materials (AMHN XII 1991 Fogaca 2001 Prous *et al.* 1984). Each of these attributes stimulated the investment of a thorough analysis of the whole lithic assemblage. Functional microscope-based studies here applied consist of a type of analysis designed to assess both the activities on the sites and the technology decisions adopted (Alonso e Mansur 1986/90), Mansur 1986, Plisson 1985, Poirier 2004, Semenov 1964).

## 2. FUNCTIONAL ANALYSIS OF THE LITHIC ASSEMBLAGE

### 2.1. Development of experimental reference collections

The raw materials selected for the assemblage of the reference collection come from the same region of the sites (Boquete, Grande Abrigo de Santana do Riacho) and are similar to those used to fabricate the archaeological instruments exhumed from them. They are: Flint (fine and coarse), hyaline quartz (in its crystalline variety) and quartzite, especially silicified.

92 experimental pieces were made out of the three raw materials: 32 out of flint, 30 out of hyaline quartz and 30 out of quartzite. Flint was the only one with two varieties, one fine-grained and the other coarse-grained.

The matters to be worked with during the trial were selected according to the material found and/or possibly consumed in the respective archaeological sites: wood, non-wood plants, bone, skin, leather, meat, fish, cassava and ocher.

Three movements were performed during the work, in order to perform every action under pressure: longitudinal linear motion, linear and punctate transverse pressure (Fig. 2).

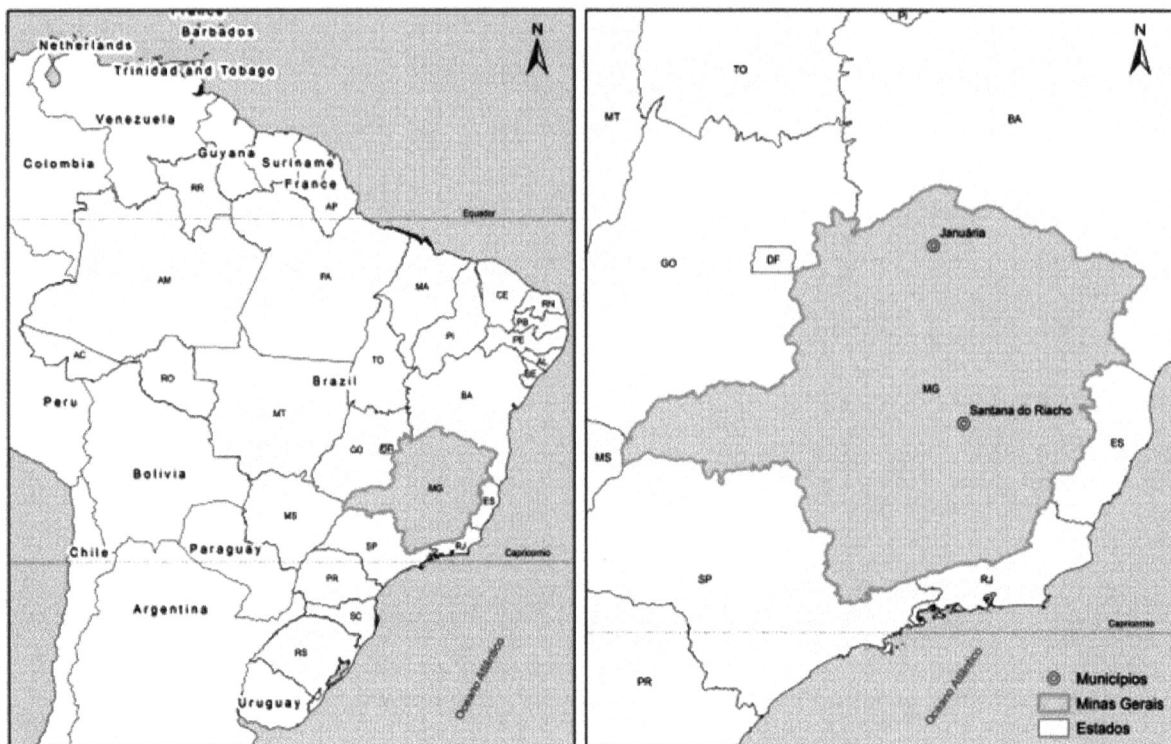

*Figure 1 – Map of Brazil with location of state of Minas Gerais and municipalities where the studied sites are*

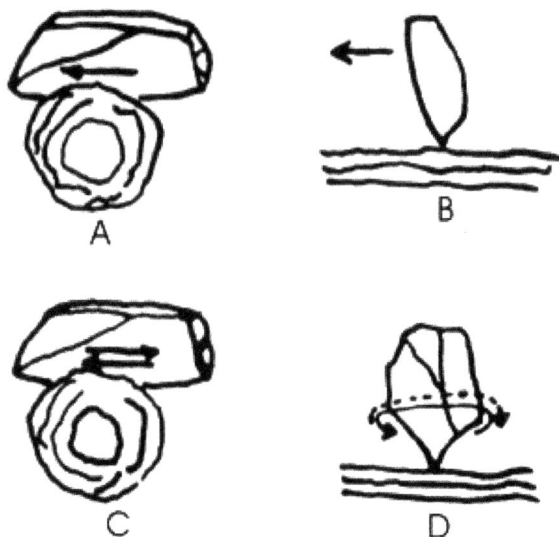

*Figure 2 – Types of action: Cut (A), Shaving (B), Sawing (C) and Punch (D). Source: adapted from Mansur-Franchomme, 1984*

Time of use is one of the variables that influences the development of usage traces, ranged between 5 and 60 minutes.

## 2.2. Preparation of the parts for observation

### 2.2.1. Drawings of the parts to be analyzed

The drawing, in this case, is a simple figurative view, which reproduces one or more sides of the original piece. Thereafter, the specific graphic conventions were indicated beside the margin of each drawing (Mansur, 1986).

### 2.2.2. Cleaning of the material

Every material must be clean, free of impregnations that may prevent its observation or create false traces. Soap and water were used in most cases to clean them. To remove the organic materials resistant to these two substances, we used cold or hot hydrogen peroxide ($H_2O_2$). The fat, including the grease left by hands, could be removed with alcohol or acetone.

When mineral crusts that made cleaning difficult covered the pieces, an ultrasound bowl was used to remove them. The working principle of the bowl is the vibration, which facilitates the removal of dirt.

The use of ultrasound was "taken on loan" from the work of Briker and Stahl (1991), who successfully used it to remove the encrustation of carbonates in fossil bones and teeth. The chemical solution adopted by the researchers was a dilute solution of acetic acid ($CH_3COOH$). In our case, we used only water, pure or mixed with household detergent.

The major limitation of the ultrasonic device (Fig. 3) is its tank size, which restricts cleaning to few pieces at a time, so they do not touch each other.

### 2.2.3. Methods of observation

The functional analysis of the lithic instruments was made through a binocular magnifying glass

8

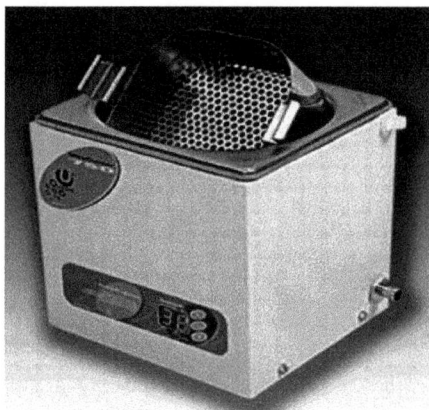

*Figure 3 – Ultrasound bowl used for cleaning parts*

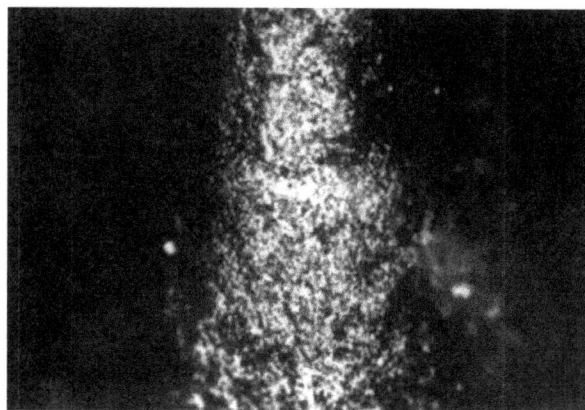

*Figure 4 – Rounding with intense glosses in flint*

Micronal/Olympus and an Olympus metallographic microscope with reflected light. The magnifying glass was used for the observation of macro-remains (shattering, rounding and shines). The metallographic microscope provides increases of 100, 200 and 500x. It is noteworthy that the increase of 100x is the most frequently used, as it appears to be sufficient for the clear observation of traces.

### 2.2.4. Photography

The device used for the photographic record was an Olympus camera (C – 35DA – 2) attached to the microscope. Currently, digital systems are more efficient for this purpose.

## 3. THEORETICAL BASES OF THE FUNCTIONAL ANALYSIS

The microwear analysis of archaeological material points to a number of traces that are formed on the instruments as a result of the different processes they have undergone over time: manufacture, usage, natural changes, accidental and post-depositional changes, etc.

### 3.1. Classes of usage traces on flint

According to ME Mansur (1986/1990), traces of use identified on the edges of lithic pieces from the work of S. Semenov (1964) can be classified as the following: chipping and rounding of edges, microscopic grooves, and microscopic residues micro polished.

### 3.1.1. Shattering of the edges

The shattering of edges can be observed with low magnification binocular loupe (macro-remains). Micro flakes are unintentional formations, which are accidentally loosed due to usage, natural and/or accidental factors. Thus, they may appear alone or in clusters, with various sizes and shapes. They may produce negatives very similar to those left as a result of usage and, in most cases, are impossible to be differentiated.

### 3.1.2. Smoothing and rounding of edges

These are perceptible, in the majority of cases, under magnifications over 100x. These can also be caused by natural actions, which can produce a rounding followed by a shine, which are called glosses (Fig. 4).

Depending on the degree of development, rounding may indicate the presence or absence of abrasives during use.

### 3.1.3. Microscopic striations

Can be observed from magnifications over 100x. Consist of linear markings formed by the dragging of abrasive particles composed of sand or even of micro particles that were loosed during use on the surface of the stone tools. There is a relationship between the amount of abrasive elements and grooves. In turn, the length and depth of the grooves depend on the pressure over the material being processed and size of the abrasive elements.

When followed by micropolish, can be considered reliable indicators of use and direction of the work, due to its orientation (Semenov, 1964).

The grooves are not formed in all cases of use and are, in general, uncommon on heterogeneous rocks.

### 3.1.4. Micropolish

The micropolish are described, initially only when it occurs on flint. These are necessarily interpretable under magnifications over 100x. They come as a result solely of use, which makes them diagnosable.

Can be defined as aspects of the edges of the surfaces which were used, that reflect incident light differently from areas of the flint that were not used (Keeley, 1980).

The hypotheses on the mechanisms of formation of the currently accepted micropolish takes into account the properties of silica and its different forms, crystalline or amorphous. The mechanical actions are important to trigger the process, through the disruption of the surface structure, which facilitates chemical attack. They may also, in certain cases, cause the amorphization of the cryptocrystalline surface of the flint (Mansur, 1986/1990).

The micropolish vary in its brightness or opacity, the regularity or irregularity of the surface and the presence or absence of certain topographical marks, such as comet-shaped depressions, hemispherical depressions, irregular contour depressions, among others. It is the presence of these or other microtopographic marks that define the micropolish (Mansur, 1986/1990).

The micropolish, even when they reach the last stage of development, hardly ever reach a 1 mm width from edge to edge (Mansur, 1986/1990). This reinforces the importance of careful treatment of lithic pieces, for any accident can affect the portion of the edge with micropolish.

The different types of micropolish that result from works on different materials can be found (Mansur 1986/1990).

### 3.1.5. Microscopic residues

Consists of traces on the worked matter that may be included in micropolish formed in the used edge (Anderson-Gerfaud, 1981).

### 3.2. Traces of use on quartz and quartzite

The microwear use are produced by structural modification of the surface of the instrument, which comprises the dissolution of a portion of the silica that makes up the superficial structure in specific areas of the edge, due to friction and the movements produced by the work, and also to the moisture from the working equipment (Gerfaud-Anderson, 1981; Franchomme-Mansur, 1981, 1986).

### 3.2.1. Quartz

Functional analysis of the quartz pieces began with the observation of their surfaces, whether they are natural or fresh, created by chipping (Fig. 5). Were also studied crystals of natural quartz, in order to understand their condition and natural changes that may occur (Alonso Lima and Mansur, 1986/1990; Mansur, 1999). Since this is a homogeneous material, the appearance of the natural surfaces and of those surfaces modified by use is comparable to other homogeneous materials, like obsidian (Mansur, 1999).

### 3.2.2. Quartzite

This is a rock composed of quartz grains (crystals), attached to cement, typically cryptocrystalline. Therefore, in order to study parts of the quartzite, a model that includes separate analyses of quartz grains and matrix or

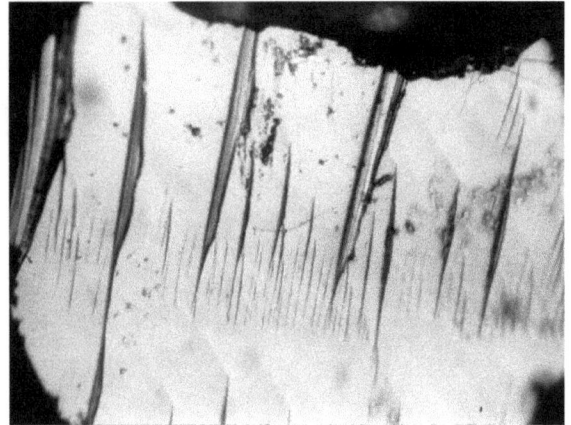

*Figure 5 – Stigma (striation) technology in fresh quartz surface (100x)*

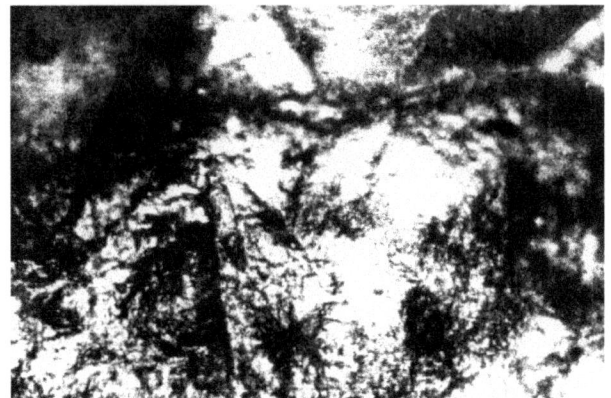

*Figure 6 – Grain quartz altered / rounded during use (Quartzite-100x)*

cryptocrystalline cement (Mansur, 1999; Alonso Lima and Mansur, 1986/1990) has been proposed.

Submitted to use, edged pieces of this rock produce little shattering and are more likely to round off by the detachment of grains.

When it comes to quartzite, it is necessary to examine the entire surface of the quartz grains (Fig. 6) (Mansour, 1999).

On cement, micropolish, when well developed, is, in itself, natural in the material being processed.

### 3.3. Disturbances and pseudo-traces

The state of preservation of archaeological pieces can compromise the results of the microwaer analysis. There are three main groups of factors that cause changes in stone tools:

1) Technological – are formed during the chipping (Fig. 7);

2) Natural – always follow the archaeological pieces, are formed by post-depositional actions (taphonomic), either above the surface or buried;

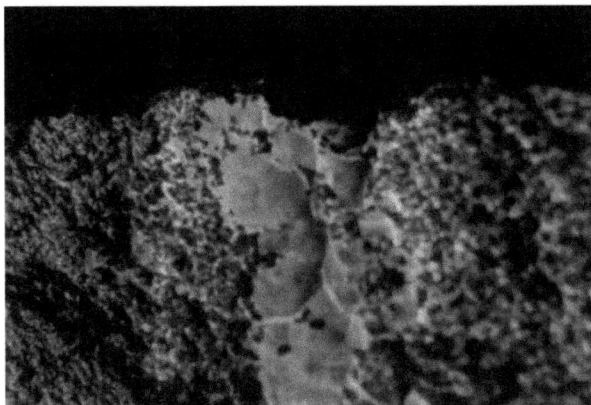

*Figure 7 – Percussion striations (Flint-100x)*

3) Accidental – are formed basically by handling and transportation of stone tools by archaeologists.

Such changes often produce similar marks to those that result from use.

Every archaeological piece presents, to some degree, changes and/or pseudo-traces (Keeley, 1980; Franchomme – Mansur, 1987).

The post-depositional process usually erases, partially or completely, the traces. The failure to observe micropolish, for example, does not therefore mean that there was no use. It becomes necessary, thus, the observation of other traces, like rounding, to indicate the possibility of use.

A common post-depositional alteration between parts is analyzed is what we call glosses, a result of the movement of a part of the sediment. It begins in a specific spot, and may extend throughout it when in an advanced stage of development.

Due to reasons that may cause an underrepresentation of the instruments used, we adopted here, for the functional designation of archaeological tools, categories created by Alonso Lima and Mansur (1986/1990), transcribed below:

1) Pieces definitely used (S): show signs that allow for the identification of the type of material, the movement made during work or both.

2) Pieces not used (N): present clear evidence that were not used (fresh edges etc...).

3) Pieces probably used (PR): Demonstrate traces that suggest that they have been used, followed by superficial changes that modify them in a way that makes it hard to attribute its use to a specific type of work, or a particular movement. It is estimated that the possibility of use is 80%.

4) Pieces not determinable or possibly used (PS): Present rounding feature, shine, etc., which may indicate a possible use, but do not present clear evidence of being used.

## 4. STUDY OF ARCHAEOLOGICAL MATERIAL

The sites of Lapa do Boquete and Grande Abrigo de Santana do Riacho and its insertion regions present characteristics that influenced the search and procurement of raw materials used in the manufacture of instruments of labor by the prehistoric man.

These are two geographically distinct regions of central Brazil, both in the state of Minas Gerais: in the north and in the center of the state.

### 4.1. Archaeological pieces for analysis

The selection of the material analyzed followed a tecnomorphological criteria. We selected the instruments that displayed a heavier technical investment in its making (scrapers – "grattoir/end scraper" – scrapers – "racloir / side scraper"-, knives, awls, etc.) as well as the non-retouched objects, that at first glance display edges that are possibly used, rough when it comes to the debitage and without any change, either to cut or to pierce (sharp end).

Besides the objects that were retouched or that displayed proper morphology, we selected residues of edge freshener once its butt could contain evidences of use from activities prior to the freshening.

### 4.2. Results of the microwear analysis for each raw material

In the chart below we present the analysis results of each raw material that was used in the making of the working tools found at the selected archaeological sites.

#### 4.2.1. Flint Pieces

We've denominated flint every cryptocrystalline siliceous rocks, which encompasses Flint in itself, and chalcedony, all of these have as $SiO_2$ as their formula.

#### 4.2.2. Quartz Pieces

Quartz is a silicon dioxide ($SiO_2$) in the crystalline state (Vieira, 1975).

#### 4.2.3. Quartzite Pieces

Quartzite is basically composed of quartz grains and accessory minerals whose presence depends on the location of occurrence and the environmental conditions during the formation process. In general, the cement and the grains have the same chemical composition.

This raw material is analyzed by observing the quartz grains and the cement the aggregates the grains separately.

The chart below presents the archaeological material analyzed.

*Table 1 – Summary of the analysis of the archaeological material*

| Raw-Material | Boquete | | | G.A. Santana do Riacho | | Total |
|---|---|---|---|---|---|---|
| | R | WR | Occasion | R | WR | R+WR+Occasion |
| Flint | 121 | 113 | 126 | 0 | 0 | 360 |
| Used | 33 | 8 | 2 | 0 | 0 | 43 |
| Quartz | 0 | 0 | 1 | 81 | 0 | 82 |
| Used | 0 | 0 | 0 | 64 | 0 | 64 |
| Quartzite | 6 | 4 | 4 | 16 | 0 | 30 |
| Used | 3 | 0 | 0 | 11 | 0 | 14 |
| Total Used | 36 | 8 | 2 | 75 | 0 | 121 |
| Total Analized | 127 | 117 | 131 | 97 | 0 | 472 |

R: Retouched – WR: Without Retouching

## 5. CONTRIBUTIONS TO THE INTERPRETATION OF THE ACTIVITIES CARRIED ON THE SITES

### 5.1. Archaeological site Lapa do Boquete

#### *5.1.1. Description of the site and its surroundings*

This site is located in the municipality of Januaria, in the northern part of the state of Minas Gerais. Region characterized by its caves and shelters Karst landscape.

##### *5.1.1.1. Karst*

The banks of the river Peruaçu are covered with vegetation, composing the riparian forest.

Outside the floodplain, but still on the banks of river Peruaçu, we notice the formation of semi deciduous forests composed of large trees and shrubs.

In the highest parts, on top of the limestones and dolomites, where cracks preclude the retention of moisture, we found species very well adapted to extremely dry climates, Caatinga species. Where there is some retention of moisture, deciduous forests are formed (Moura, 1997).

##### *5.1.1.2. Outside the 'karstificada' landscape*

Within a radius of 5.0 km around the site, various rocks can be found: flint shaped in blocks and pebbles, quartz in small fragments and pebbles, limestone is present in the formation of caves and in other chambers inside the canyon, sandstone also in blocks, among other of less importance under the eyes and the preferences of the prehistoric men.

This is a dry cave, long before the arrival of the first human groups to the region (Moura, 1997).

The sediment overlying the floor reaches, in its greatest depth, 1.5 m. All of the sediment deposition at Lapa do Boquete keeps traces of human occupation from the time when man first arrived there (around 12,000 years ago) until the recent historical period.

#### *5.1.2. Analyzed Material and results of the analyzes*

##### *5.1.2.1. Retouched materials*

121 instruments in flint and 6 instruments in quartzite have been analyzed, all of them retouched. They came from a 44 m² area, consisting of eight layers and levels of all polls conducted in the sheltered area of Lapa do Boquete (Fig. 8) were analyzed. It is important to describe that these layers form a thick Holocene stratigraphic package, which kept successive records of human occupation from 12,000 BP (layer VIII) through much of the twentieth (layer 0) century.

#### *5.1.3. "How" and "where" the instruments were used*

##### *5.1.3.1. Flint Instruments*

Among the 21 instruments retouched in flint, 18 show traces that they have been certainly used. Nine were used to scrape and three used to cut wood. Another instrument was also used in wood, but it is unclear whether to cut or to scrape.

Only one tool showed signs of having been used in the processing of the bone without showing striations that indicate the movement of the labor.

In four other instruments, the traces were not sufficient to determine the material in which they were utilized, but it was possible to tell that they had been used to scrape, as the stretch marks were preserved.

In another group of 15 instruments likely used (PR), the traces were obliterated and it could not be confirmed how and where they were used.

Most retouched edges that have been used have a slightly convex shape. If the shape of the edges is relatively homogeneous, its angles vary according to the action performed. The edges of the pieces used to scrape wood

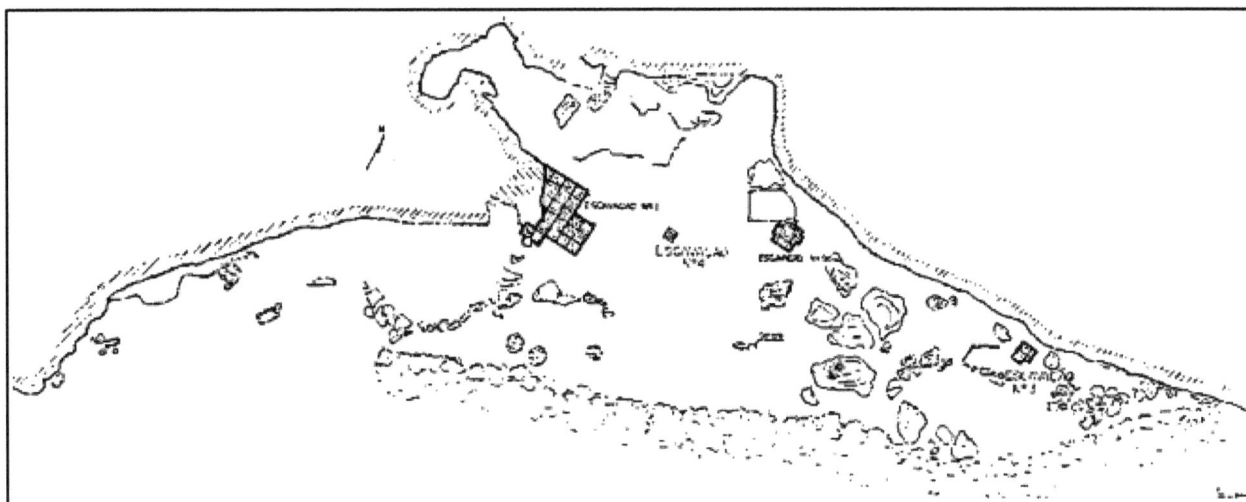

*Figure 8 – Plant of the Lapa do Boquete, with indication of excavated areas*

and those that the use and movement were not determined, are, in most cases, steep (over 70°).

Pieces used to cut wood have an active, semi-abrupt edge (between 45° and 60°), except for one of the pieces, that is more abrupt than what is usually expected. Only one of the pieces presents an acute angle, and the movement in which it was used could not be determined.

The piece that was used on bones, despite not having streaks that would indicate the direction of the movement, presents, on both edges, angles of 40 and 50° (semi – abrupt), inefficient for the action of cutting.

### 5.1.3.2. Quartzite Instruments

The two retouched tools that were certainly utilized (S) were used on different materials, one on wood and the other on skin, both for shaving/scraping.

Would the instruments made of quartzite be the first choice to work on skin? Only one piece of quartzite was classified as probably used (PR).

### 5.1.4. Distribution of instruments in the excavated areas and their position in the stratigraphy

#### 5.1.4.1. Retouched Instruments made of Flint

The set of instruments of flint used and retouched is distributed in blocks and their stratigraphic packages excavated.

The main concentrations (even if reduced) of "typical" pieces with traces of use are in contiguous blocks in the older layers. The most crafted material was wood, and the action was to shave/scrape.

Besides wood, the only material that was also worked on is bone, which was crafted by an instrument found at a distance of almost 10 m away from the concentrations described above, in block L18. This arrangement suggests a compartmentalization of labor within the site.

#### 5.1.4.2. Instruments of occasion of flint

In this category, we analyzed 131 pieces, that came from an area of 26 m².

Only two displayed traces of use, both designed to work on skin. One of them came from court JK9, level of contact 7/8, and the other came from block M11 block. Like many others found at the site with traces of usage, the ones in this category also came from level 8, or were very close to it.

The angles of the edges of these pieces are often abrupt. The low number of utilized pieces that belong to this category may be an indicative of the fact that their type is not exactly one that was systematically sought for by the prehistoric man who inhabited Lapa do Boquete.

#### 5.1.4.3. Non-retouched Instruments made of flint

The non-retouched instruments form the largest set of pieces of the whole lithic industry of Lapa do Boquete. It is composed of remains from the making of different kinds of artifacts and/or from the debitage of nuclei, and meant to serve as a prop on which the artifacts conceived by the prehistoric man would be materialized. We randomly selected 117 pieces from distinct layers within an area of 22 m². From this set, only five pieces presented clear indications that they had been definitely used, and three others evidences that they were probably used.

#### 5.1.4.4. Quartzite Instruments

There seems to be no clear preferences regarding the use of any raw material or specific technical work to the employment of work on wood, but instead, there were preferences regarding the specific local at the site in which this activity was performed; some of the retouched flint tools were found on the same block and layer as the retouched quartzite tools, all of them with traces of use on wood.

### 5.1.5. Comments on the use and position of the instruments in the stratigraphy

The oldest layers, 7 and 8, carry the highest number of pieces with traces of use, primarily on wood, and in various industries.

From this set of pieces, it was brought to our attention the advanced stage of development of the remains found in those used to cut wood.

The angles of the edges of the pieces of this set are divided in acute (around 30°) and semi-abrupt (around 50°) sharp, but resistant.

### 5.2. Archaeological site Grande Abrigo de Santana do Riacho

### 5.2.1. Description of the site and of its surroundings

This site is located within the municipality of Santana do Riacho, at Serra do Cipó, Minas Gerais (Malta and Kohler, 1991).

The geological characteristics of the region provide predominantly two types of rocks, suitable for use by prehistoric groups for chipping and for the production of most of their artifacts: quartzite and quartz. The latter can be found both in the milky or hyaline varieties (Prous, 1991).

Flint was also identified in much a smaller proportion in the excavations, but its known source is located at a great distance from Grande Abrigo de Santana do Riacho, which explains its rarity in this site.

The occupation of the site dates back to 12,000 years ago, and it has been almost constantly occupied by humans up to the historical period (Fig. 9).

### 5.2.2 Analysis results by category

From this site, all of the lithic material analyzed (97 pieces) is retouched: 81 pieces of quartz and 16 of quartzite. Among the quartz pieces, 22 presented vestiges that they had been definitely used. Other 43 showed changes that make it impossible to say how and in which material they were used. Twelve pieces present more intense alterations that prevent us from affirming whether they have been used or not. Four pieces were identified as surely unused.

Quartzite are 16 pieces, but only six of them displayed evidences of being used (Fig. 10). In six other pieces, the vestiges, despite the alterations, indicate a possibility, but not enough to determine the material that was worked on, or the motion carried. In three other pieces, the possibility of use is of 50%, that is, some changes identified prevent us from determining with certainty if they were not used. Only one piece has an edge with a 'fresh' aspect, which allows us to affirm that it had not been used.

### 5.2.3. "Where" and "How" instruments were used

#### 5.2.3.1. Quartz Instruments

The instruments were used to transform various materials, and in some cases, the same instrument worked on different materials. The actions were also diversified, which indicates a greater number of processing activities undertaken at the site.

17 pieces were identified and being of 'simple use'. These were used on a single material and with a single action/purpose for each instrument. Three of them were used on dye (two for scraping and one for cutting), seven used on wood (all for shaving) and seven on skin (six to scrape and one to pierce, in a semicircular motion).

One of the pieces (scraper) presents marks of being used in a perpendicular position to the edge on wood and leather, in different edges. Another displays evidences of

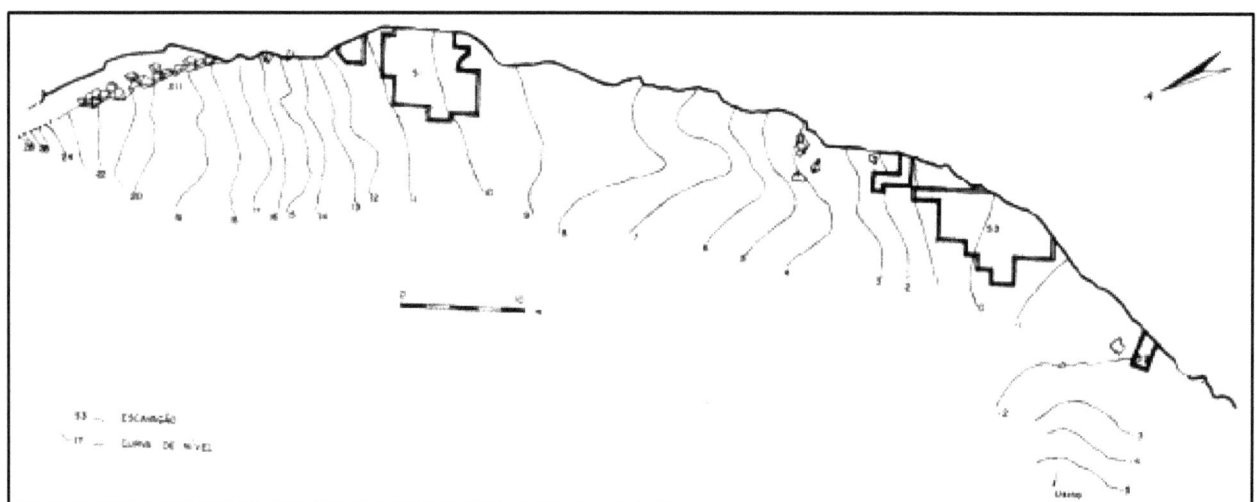

*Figure 9 – Plant of the Grande Abrigo de Santana do Riacho (See the site of the excavations)*

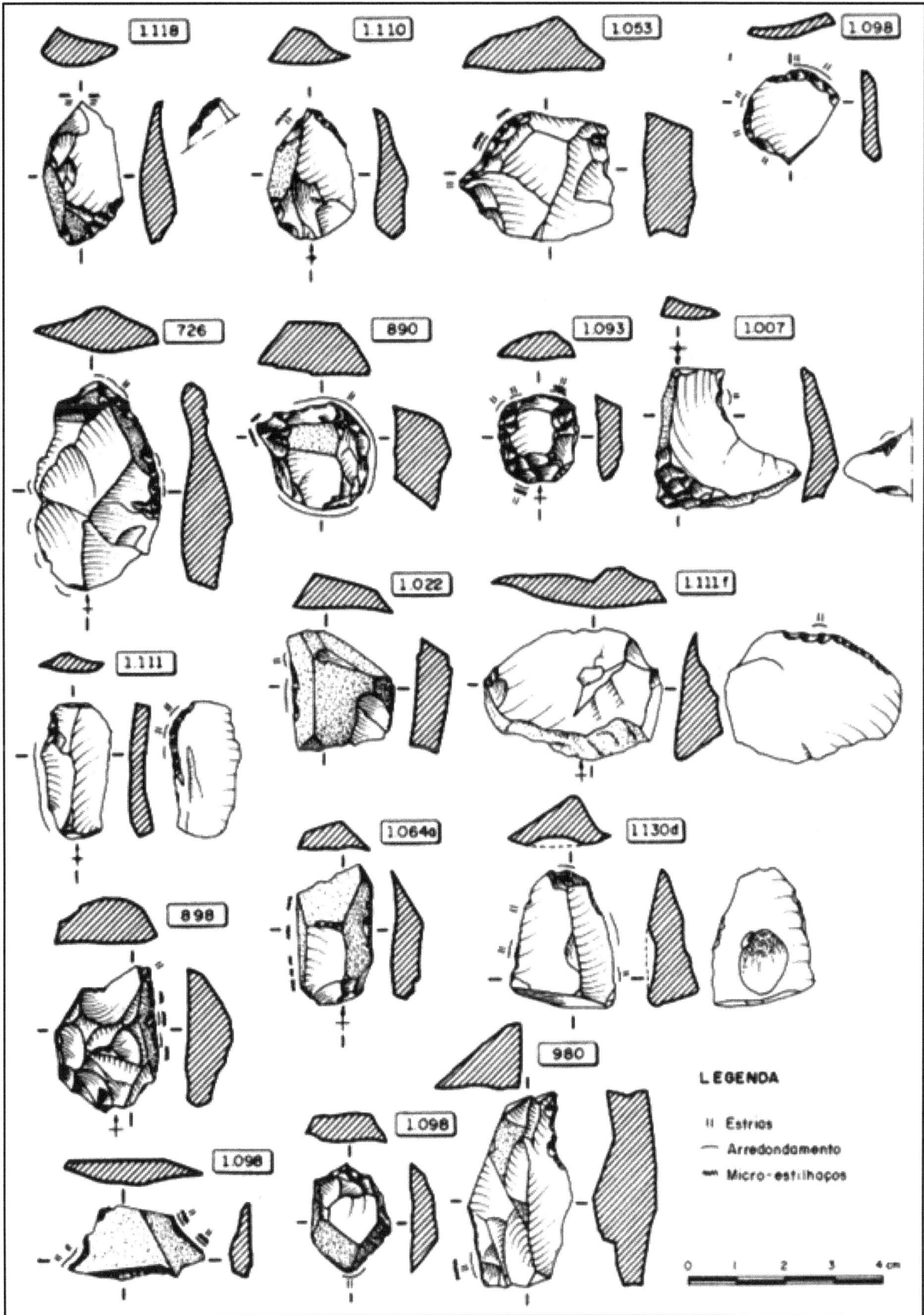

*Figure 10 – Pieces of quartz with traces of use (S.A. Grande Abrigo de Santana do Riacho).*
*Source: Adapted from Alonso Lima, 1991*

having been used to shave/scrape dye and skin, activities that leave similar traces.

The last three pieces had no marks that could indicate which material was processed with them, but the motion

15

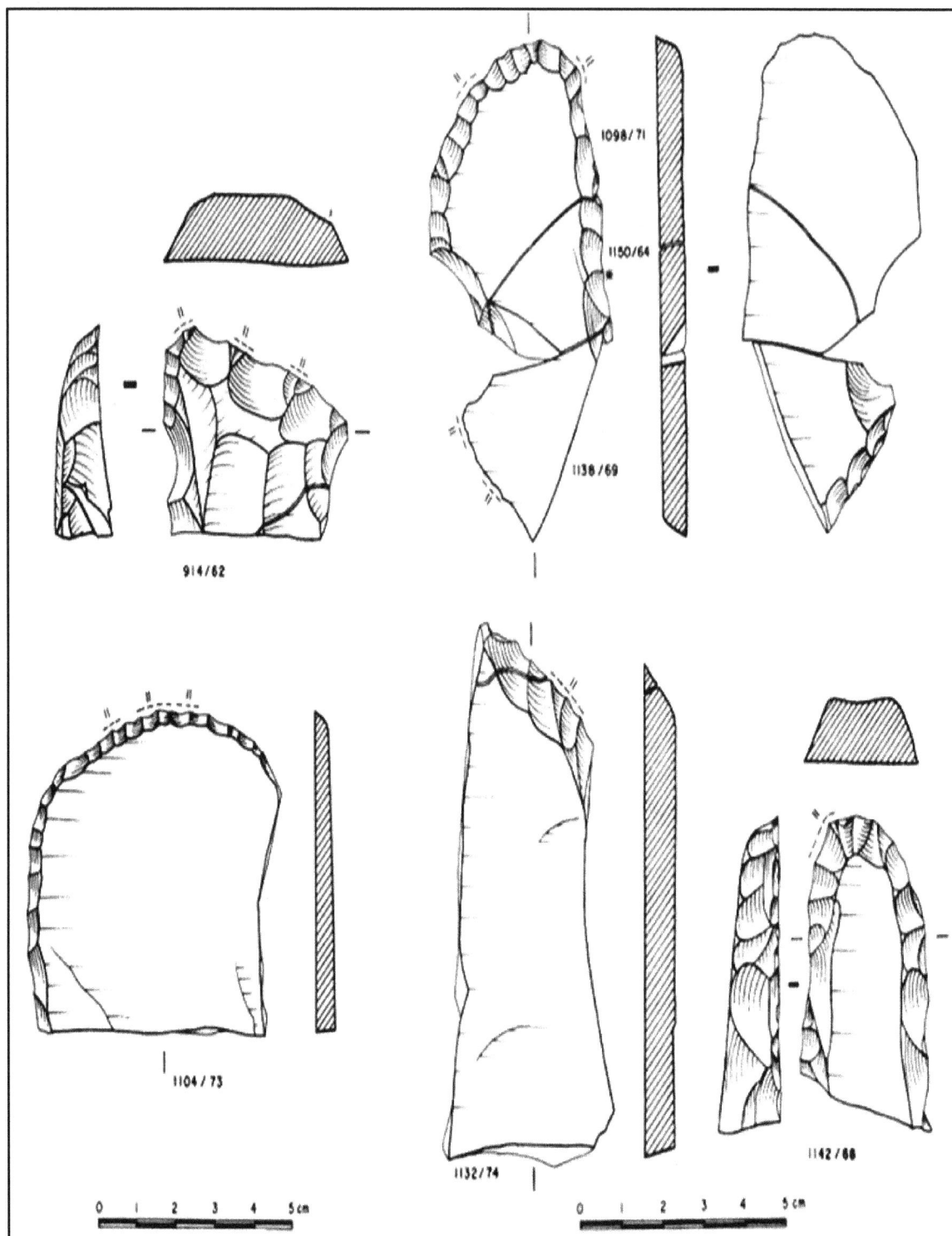

*Figure 11 – Pieces quartzite with traces of use. Source: Adapted from Alonso Lima, 1991*

is perpendicular to the edge and stretch marks were present.

### 5.2.3.2. Quartzite Instruments

Instruments of this raw material with marks that show that they were definitely used were produced for use with a motion perpendicular to the edge, but only one retained the traces left by the wood in which it worked. The others have not preserved diagnostic traces of use (Fig. 11).

### 5.2.4. Distribution of instruments with vestige of use in the excavated areas and their position in the stratigraphy

#### 5.2.4.1. Quartz Instruments

The material with marks of use came from the blocks of one of the three surveys (SRIII) performed. This set of pieces was found in a single package of sediments, "Layer 3":

Pieces with traces that show that were definitely used were concentrated close to the wall in a well-lit and sheltered area of the site.

Parts with traces of probable use (80% chance), were also clustered on the south-end courts of the site, on the opposite side to that where the burials were.

### 5.2.4.2. Quartzite Instruments

The clusters of this raw material are also in rows Q and R:

– Pieces definitely used: one piece in O27, one in Q26 and four in R25.

– Pieces probably used: one piece spatially shifted relative to the concentration near the quartzite wall in Q31, two pieces in Q25, and three in R25.

## 6. FINAL CONSIDERATIONS

The results of this research served to confirm the feasibility of the functional analysis of the lithic material from archaeological sites in Central Brazil, surpassing the analysis of changes in raw materials, but also providing important information about the relationship between raw materials, types of instruments and use of artifacts.

In the first instance, from the results of functional analyzes, we observed that there is a relationship between intensity of use and technological investment, and percentage confirmed by numerical superiority of retouched pieces with traces of use, although no specific preference to a type of use for a particular type of raw material has been perceived.

The prevalence of the marks of usage on the edge of the instruments worked on wood in relation to those that worked on other materials, such as skin and bone, can be justified by the copious abundance of wood in the site region, fact that obviously facilitates their acquisition. Furthermore, we also highlight the ease in turning woody plants and non-timber objects of everyday use, and the speed with which traces are formed on the edges that worked this category of material.

Even with the identification of some edged tools with signs of use on skin, nothing was found in the excavations that indicate the existence of some kind of utensil in this matter. Natural indeed in most cases due to the difficulty of preserving organic matter that environment. Added to all this the fact that the temperature in the periods in which there was human occupation at Lapa do Boquete has been practically the same as nowadays, i.e., warm for most of the year, which does not justify, for example, the use of fur to protect themselves from the cold.

In regards to the bone, if we base ourselves only on the artifacts found in this area in Boquete, it is possible to suggest that it would be associated only to the

manufacture of knives (name given by archaeologists), objects of still doubtful utility.

The consequences predicted from the results obtained from this research, are analyzes of pieces with natural edges of over 90°. Another consequence is the identification of parts with possible traces of use resulting from cutting, scraping, or drilling of calcite. This effort is justified by the fact that we have found in the excavations fragments of stalactite probably brought from another cave in the same region, as in Boquete there are no such fragments, and also because polished necklace beads with incisions were found (probably caused by the attempt to cut them) made on stalactites found in the Archaeological site Lapa dos Bichos, which is also in Peruaçu river valley, in the Januária county.

These results indicate the importance of functional analysis when it may be applied to archaeological sites. The development of this form of analysis should allow the further deepening of the knowledge about the daily life of prehistoric human groups.

## References

ALONSO, M. 1991. Indústria Lítica de Santana do Riacho: Tecnologia, Tipologia e Traceologia – Análise Funcional de Microtraceologia. Arquivos do Museu de História Natural/UFMG, Belo Horizonte, v. 12, p. 275-284.

ALONSO, M. 2008. Estudo de Indústrias Líticas do Brasil Central. Dissertação de Mestrado, FAFICH/UFMG, Belo Horizonte.

ALONSO, M & MANSUR M.E. 1986/1990. Estudo Traceológico de Instrumentos em Quartzo e Quartzito de Santana do Riacho (MG). Arquivos do Museu de História Natural/UFMG, Belo Horizonte, v. 11, p. 173-190.

ANDERSON-GERFAUD, P.C. 1981. Contribution méthodologique à l'analysedes micro traces d'utilisation sur les outils préhistoriques. 1981. 161f. Thèse de Doutorado, Universidade de Bordeaux I, Bordeaux.

ARQUIVOS DO MUSEU DE HISTÓRIA NATURAL/UFMG 1991. Santana do Riacho, v.XII.

FOGAÇA, E. 2001. Mãos para o pensamento. A variabilidade tecnológica de indústrias líticas de caçadores-coletores holocênicos a partir de um estudo de caso: as camadas VIII e VII da Lapa do Boquete (Minas Gerais), Brasil – 12.000/10.500 BP, Tese de Doutorado, Porto Alegre.

KEELEY, L.H. 1980. Experimental Determination of Stone Tool Uses: A Microwear Analysis. Chicago: Universityof Chicago Press.

MALTA, I.; KOHLER, H. 1991. O cenário geográfico e geológico do planalto de Lagoa Santa. Revista do Museu de História Natural da UFMG, Belo Horizonte, v. 12, p. 3-12.

MANSUR, M.E. 1986/1990. Instrumentos líticos: Aspectos da análise funcional. Arquivos do Museu de História Natural/UFMG, Belo Horizonte, v. 11, p. 115-169.

MANSUR, M.E. 1999. Análisis Funcional de instrumental lítico: problemas de formación y deformación de rastros de uso. Actas XII Congreso Nacional de Arqueología Argentina, La Plata, v. I, p. 355-366.

MANSUR-FRANCHOMME, M.E. 1981. Las estrias como microrrastros de utilización: clasificación y mecanismos de formación. Antropologia y Paleoecologia Humana, Granada, v. 2, p. 21-47.

MANSUR-FRANCHOMME, M.E. 1986. Microscopie du Matériel Lithique: traces d'utilisation, altérations naturelles, accidentelles et technologiques. Cahiers du Quaternaire, n. 9, CNRS, Bordeaux.

MANSUR-FRANCHOMME, M.E. 1987. Outils ethnographiques de Patagonie emmanchement et traces d'utilisation. La Main et l'Outil: manches e emmanchements préhistoriques, Lyon, v. 15, p. 297-307.

MOURA, M.T.T. 1996/1997. O vale dos rios Cochá e Carinhanha: Caracterização da paisagem regional. Arquivos do Museu de História Natural/UFMG, Belo Horizonte, v. 17/18, p. 71-74.

PLISSON, H. 1985. Étude fonctionnelle d'outillages lithiques préhistoriques par l'analyse dês micro-usures: recherche méthodologique et archéologique. Thése de 3e. cycle, Université de Paris I.

PROUS, A.; JUNQUEIRA, P.A.; MALTA, I.M. 1984. Arqueologia do Alto Médio São Francisco – Região de Januária e Montalvânia. Revista de Arqueologia, Belém, 2:59-72.

POIRIER, A.P.P. 2004. Apuntes para análisis de Industrias Líticas. Ortegália, Fundación Federico Maciñeira, Ortigueira.

SEMENOV, S.A. 1964. Prehistoric Technology. Trad. M. Thompson-Bath. London: Adams and Dart.

STAHL, P.W.; BRINKER, U.H. 1991. Removal of Calcareous Incrustation from Bone and Teeth with Acid and Ultrasound. Journal of Field Archaeology, Boston, v. 18, p. 138-140.

VIEIRA, L.S. 1975. Manual da Ciência do Solo. São Paulo: Ed. Agronômica Ceres.

# EXPERIMENTS IN BONE TECHNOLOGY: A METHODOLOGICAL APPROACH TO FUNCTIONAL ANALYSIS ON BONE TOOLS

Myrian ALVAREZ, María Estela MANSUR and Nélida PAL

Centro Austral de Investigaciones Científicas – CADIC CONICET; Laboratorio de Antropología;
B. Houssay 200, 9410 Ushuaia, Tierra del Fuego, Argentina
myrianalvarez@gmail.com;     estelamansur@gmail.com;     nelidapal@yahoo.com.ar

**Abstract**: *The study of bone tools represents a key-element for the investigation of many hunter-gatherer-fisher societies. In the case of those that inhabited the extreme south of America, bone technology had a particular importance considering both the frequency and the diversity of tools design. Consequently, the identification of the uses to which bone artifacts were devoted constitutes a fundamental problem in order to understand their socio-economical dynamics.*

*On this goal, we started a research project oriented towards functional analysis of bone instruments. The experimental program aimed at characterization of microscopic traces produced by three different processes: manufacturing of various types of bone artifacts, their utilization, and the alterations resulting from taphonomical processes. Microwear analysis was developed by means of different optical devices and magnifications (stereomicroscope, reflected light microscope and scanning electron microscope).*

*In this paper we present the methodology and results obtained and discuss their implications for microwear analysis of bone tools.*

**Key words**: *bone tools, use-wear, experimental program*

**Résumé**: *L'étude des outillages en os constitue un élément clé pour les recherches sur beaucoup de sociétés de chasseurs-cueilleurs-pécheurs. Dans le cas de celles qui habitaient l'extrême sud d'Amérique, la technologie osseuse avait une importance particulière en même temps par la fréquence et la diversité des types d'outils. Par conséquent, l'identification de l'usage auquel ces outils étaient destinés constitue un problème fondamental pour comprendre leur dynamique socio économique.*

*Dans ce but, nous avons commencé un projet de recherche orienté vers l'analyse fonctionnelle d'outillages en os. Le programme expérimental a été orienté vers la caractérisation des traces microscopiques produites par trois processus: la fabrication de différents types d'outils, leur utilisation et les altérations produites par divers processus taphonomiques. L'analyse des traces microscopiques a été développée au moyen de différents équipements et grossissements (stereo-microscope ou loupe binoculaire, microscope de réflexion et microscope électronique à balayage).*

*Dans ce travail, nous présentons la méthodologie et les résultats obtenus et nous discutons leurs implications pour l'analyse fonctionnelle des outils en os.*

**Mots Clé**: *tracéologie, technologie osseuse, programme expérimental*

## 1. INTRODUCTION

Many hunther-gatherer-fisher societies around the World have used bone as raw material in order to manufacture a wide range of instruments having different roles in their economic system. In the case of those societies that inhabited the extreme south of America, bone technology had a particular importance considering both the frequency and the diversity of tools design. Within the canoe people from the Magellan-fuegian channels, manufacturing and utilization of bone tools and weapons (wedges, harpoons, spatulae, etc) are important parts of an adaptive system to littoral environment which lasted in the region about 6000 years (Scheinsohn and Ferreti 1995; Scheinsohn 1997; Orquera and Piana 1999). Consequently, the identification of the uses to which bone artifacts were devoted constitutes a fundamental problem in order to understand their socio-economical dynamics.

For this reason, we have started a research project oriented towards functional analysis of bone tools. In that project, we developed an experimental program aiming to characterize and distinguish the microscopic traces produced by three different processes: manufacturing of various types of bone artifacts, their utilization, and the alterations resulting from taphonomical processes. With these objectives in mind, different experimental bone tools were manufactured, and then used to work different materials. Afterwards, microwear analysis was carried out, by means of different devices and magnifications (stereomicroscope, reflected light microscope and scanning electron microscope). The first results of that program were presented in a conference in 2008 (Alvarez *et al.* 2008). Afterwards, new scanning electron microscope investigation was developed, which gave new information about the aspect of natural structure of bone surface and that of use-wear modifications on used bone surfaces.

This paper has two main goals: a) To discuss the formation of use-wear traces on bone tools, and b) to present the preliminary results obtained by the analysis of the experimental sample and to assess their general implications for use-wear analysis of bone tools.

## 2. METHODOLOGICAL BACKGROUND: USE-WEAR METHOD FROM STONES TO BONES

From seminal works of Sergei Semenov onwards, use-wear analysis on lithic tools has experienced continuous growth and strengthening, due to the contributions of several researchers worldwide who deal with the paramount problems behind the method. These are for example the mechanisms of wear formation on different raw materials (among others, Anderson-Gerfaud 1981; Castro 1994; Hurcombe 1986; Keeley 1980; Lerner 2007; Mansur-Franchomme 1983; Mansur 1999; Ollé and Vergés 2008; Semenov 1964), the preservation of traces under diverse depositional contexts (*i.e.* Plisson and Mauger 1988), the improvement of new techniques in order to achieve a more accurate interpretation of wear patterns (Alvarez *et al.* 2012; Evans and Donahue 2008; Stemp and Stemp 2003).

Nowadays use-wear analysis has become an important approach to identify the context of use of lithic tools since it allows discriminating working materials, kinematics and length of work, on the basis of observation of use-wear and technological traces as well as taphonomical alterations.

Most authors recognize four types of diagnostic features, or microtopographic modifications, produced on lithic surfaces as a consequence of utilization, that are observable under a reflected light microscope. These are: a) edge damage or scarring, formed by secondary flake scars lined up along the edge; b) edge-rounding; c) striations or linear features; and d) micropolish, as smoothed portions of the lithic surface reflecting the incident light in a distinctive way (*sensu* Keeley 1980; Keeley and Newcomer 1977; Knutsson 1986; Mansur-Franchomme 1983; Plisson 1986; Semenov 1964; Vaughan 1985). This last feature is generally described according to the first definition given by Keeley (1980), this is in terms of its optical appearance, brightness, smoothness and the presence of particular microtopographic features. Notwithstanding the micropolish formation involves a structural modification of the superficial silica of the tool, which takes place in the interface between worked material and tool edge. It includes a mechanical process that produces superficial cracking disorganizing the crystalline structures and chemical agents attack on the already disorganized weakened structures (Anderson-Gerfaud 1981, Mansur 1997, 1999). Researchers who have observed micropolishes in SEM describe them as a layer developing from the tool edge surface; then micropolishes consist of material from both contacting surfaces and frequently form a strip along the tool edge.

Despite the fact that S. Semenov included the analysis of bone tools in his pioneering research, the study of microwear traces on bone tools has been undertaken more recently than studies on lithics and it still remains in a developing phase. The main problems in use-wear studies on bone tool surfaces are related at the same time to bone preservation, and to manufacturing techniques, that render difficult the identification of use-wear traces. Nevertheless, during the last decades, this situation has considerably started to change, as the study of use-wear traces on bone tools has received an increasing attention (among others, Peltier et Plisson 1986; Buc 2005, 2011; Clemente *et al.* 2002; Le Moine 1997; Maigrot 2003a, 2003b, 2005; Sidera & Legrand 2006; Van Gijn 2006).

In order to identify the use of bone tools, these scholars generally take into account the same diagnostic features usually considered on lithic analysis; but there is not a general agreement on which are the more relevant traces to determine use actions.

From our perspective, bone tools have very special characteristics that make them differ from lithics, because of the nature of bone as raw material. Therefore, functional analysis of bone artifacts requires taking into account three different criteria: raw material properties, manufacturing techniques and taphonomical alterations.

### 2. 1. Raw material properties

Raw material used for tool manufacture is an important variable to be considered in the analysis of the formation processes and characteristics of wear traces produced by manufacture, use or taphonomical alterations. Consequently, the first step before experimental manufacture and use, and microscopic analysis, is the study of bone basic structure.

Bone is formed by bone cells and an interstitial substance composed by an organic phase including collagen (90%), other proteins and polysaccharides complexes, and a mineral phase which is a carbonated form of hydroxya-patite, called bio-apatite (Currey 1984). Hardness and resistance of bone are determined by the connection existing between collagen fibers and bio-apatite. Although proportions of organic matrix and inorganic components in bone vary, the average is about 70% mineral phase and 30% organic phase (Currey 1984).

Analysis of the composition and organization of the bone structure is essential in order to identify its different elements when surfaces are observed in light reflected microscopy and SEM analysis. It also allows understanding how these structural elements become modified by action of different processes: manufacture, use, taphonomical alterations.

We have taken into account two main characteristics of bone structure that we considered as relevant when analyzing tool manufacture and use. These are: anisotropy and mechanical properties. Anisotropic materials are those showing different properties accor-

*Figure 1 – Experimental tools*

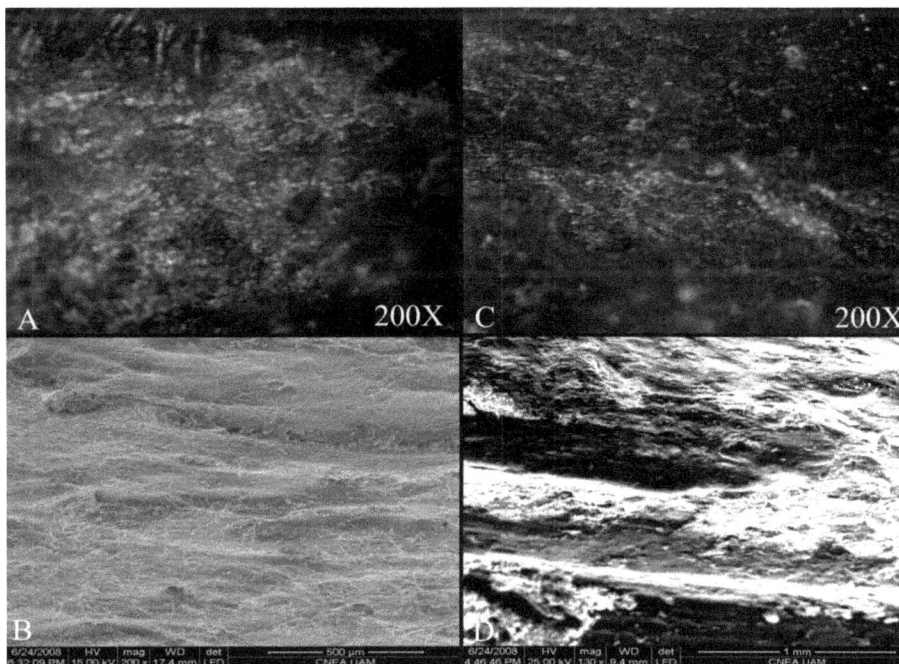

*Figure 2 – Natural bone surfaces: A) External bone surface through LM and B) through ESEM;*
*C) Fracture surface along diaphysis through LM and D) through ESEM*

ding to the direction of the charge. In the case of bone, anisotropy is due to the spatial distribution of elements that constitute the bone tissue. As to mechanical properties, they depend on composition where the mineral phase is more resistant to compression and more rigid than the organic phase, which in turn is more resistant to traction (Bonfield y Li 1967 in Scheinsohn 1997).

These properties influence the mechanisms of wear formation and therefore, the distribution and degree of development of use wear traces. For example, as aspect and properties of the internal and external faces of the bone differ, we expect the aspect of wear -traces also to

be different between surfaces of the internal and external faces of the bone (Figs. 1 and 2). In the same way, we expect differences between spongious or compact bone sectors, which differ in bone structure, hardness and characteristics of microtopography.

## 2.2. Manufacturing techniques

Technological traces resulting from bone tools manufacture are closely related to the techniques employed to shape the artifact. To recognize their visual appearance is crucial to distinguish them from those formed by tool usage. According to raw material

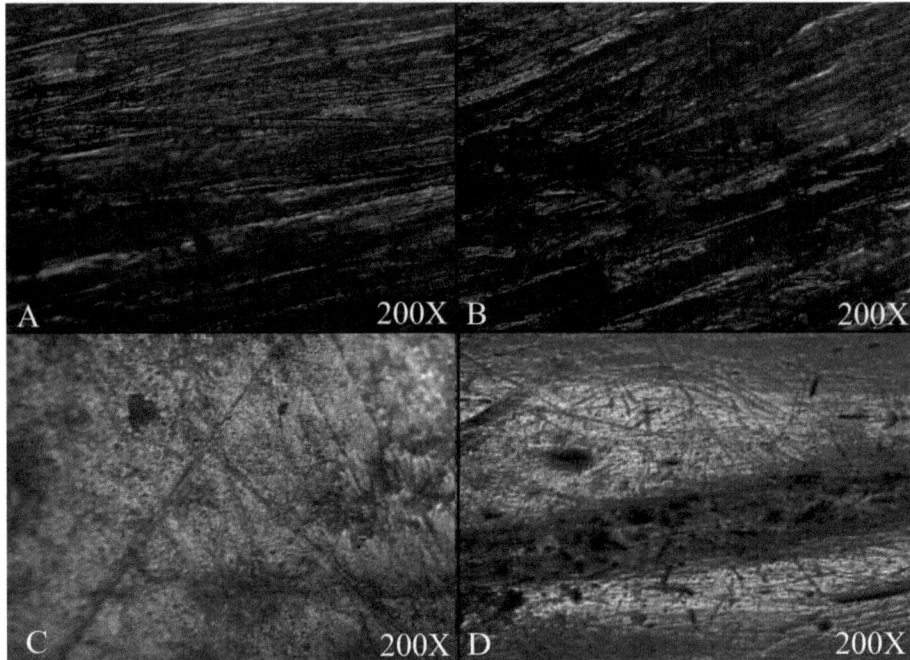

*Figure 3 – Experimental tool during polishing process: A) Polished external surface of fresh bone; B) polished inner surface of fresh bone. Technological polishing traces; C) Experimental polished surface without use; D) Archaeological polished tool, away from edge, showing technological polishing traces*

properties, bone tool production usually starts with percussion in order to break the initial blank. This process provokes crushing on impact zones; flakes and negatives with technological traces are also formed. However, these traces are difficult to identify on fracture surfaces of the bone; they are very similar to osteon structures. Cutting is another kind of action which produces linear traces; this operation involves pressure with bidirectional displacement, causing compression and crushing of the material on the bottom and the sides of the grooves which progressively show a smoothed aspect.

But undoubtedly, the most common technique to manufacture bone tools is polishing. This process produces removal and displacement of matter which is re-organized in an interface between the contact area of the working tool and worked material surface. Variables such as heat build-up for friction and humidity of fresh bone enhance this process favoring superficial dissolution; in some cases water can be added. The result is a bright, smooth and even surface of manufacturing polish (Mansur-Franchomme *et al.* 1987-88; Mansur 1997). The mechanisms of polish formation follow the same pattern as the mechanisms of microwear polish produced by utilization on lithic tools; polish is formed by material from both contacting surfaces (the tool and the worked material). In the case of bone polished surfaces, polish is bright and smooth, but it may exhibit technological striations that have to be distinguished from linear features of the Haversian system (Fig. 3).

### 2.3. Post-depositional phenomena

Finally, taphonomical alterations also play a crucial role in the preservation of both technological and use-wear traces. However, due to the strong development of zooarchaeological research, the processes, as well as the agents that affect archaeological bone record, are relative well-known. During the last decades, a solid theoretical and methodological *corpus* has been constructed; bone modifications related to their taphonomic histories have been deeply studied (Klein and Cruz Uribe 1984; Lyman 1994, Gutierrez 2004). Consequently, in this work we will principally focus on technological and use-wear traces.

### 3. THE EXPERIMENTAL PROGRAM

In order to observe and to characterize technological and use-wear traces, we carried out an experimental program that included different steps and techniques:

1) Percussion flaking in order to make blanks of fresh bones;

2) Polishing of some of the blanks, to make tools such as awls and spatulas;

3) Utilization of these polished tools to work on wood, bark and hide;

4) Utilization of non polished edges produced by simple fracturing of the bone (unmodified fracture surfaces), also to work on wood, bark and hide.

All the experimental bone tools were made on cow fresh long-bones; the techniques employed to make the bone blank and tools involved percussion, cutting and polishing.

Then, bone tools were used in processing activities that involved longitudinal, transverse and rotation

The motions. materials were worked in fresh state and the duration of use ranged between 10 and 20 minutes.

The experimental sample includes 3 spatulas, 3 awls and two soft hammers (Fig. 1). The spatulas were used to scrape sheep hide *(Ovis aries)*, beech (*Nothofagus pumilio*) bark and wood. Awls were used to pierce hide *(Ovis aries)*. Natural fracture edges were also used on hide *(Ovis aries)* and on beech (*Nothofagus pumilio*) bark and wood.

Before and after their manufacturing and usage, the experimental tools were observed under a reflected light microscope (LM), with magnification ranges comprised between 50x to 500x, and with an environmental scanning electron microscope (ESEM) with magnification ranges between 10x to 200x. The aim of this analysis was twofold:

a) to identify to what extent is modified the bone structure, first by technological traces and afterwards by use-wear traces;

b) to distinguish the traces left by polishing technique, from microwear polishes formed by different working process.

Figure 2 shows a comparison between the external bone surface and a fracture surface along diaphysis, through metallographic microscope and ESEM. Figure 3 shows aspect of experimental tools during polishing process, both external and inner surface, with technological polishing traces (A and B). These traces can also be seen as polishing process continues, as well as on archaeological tools (C and D).

## 4. RESULTS

The analysis of this experimental sample let us see the progress in manufacturing polish and microwear polish formation processes. As for manufacturing, during the polishing process, polish formed progressively on bone tools surfaces. The study of these surfaces at different time-lengths allowed distinguishing two different stages in polish formation:

a) First, wide and deep striations of dark appearance formed on the bone surface (Fig. 3 A);

b) Then, the ridges became progressively smother and regular; striations and micro-topographical traits of the bone structure started to fill-in, and surfaces turned to be brighter and smoother (Fig. 3 C).

When the external and the internal faces of bone artifacts were compared, both surfaces showed practically the same pattern: dark and wide striations cover the polished area (Fig. 3 A and B).

Regarding use-wear traces, it could be observed that micropolishes developed on natural surfaces of bone tools (fractures or natural edges) are clear and diagnostic, and that they show features similar to those observed on lithic tool surfaces (Fig. 4 B; Fig. 5 C and D; Fig. 6 C and D).

In contrast, on bone polished surfaces, it is more difficult to differentiate use-wear from technological traces (Fig. 4 A; Fig. 5 A and B; Fig. 6 A and B). Despite these difficulties, diagnostic traits could be identified in relation to both kinematics and worked material. Wood-working micropolish exhibits a bright and smooth appearance, it extends from the elevations to the

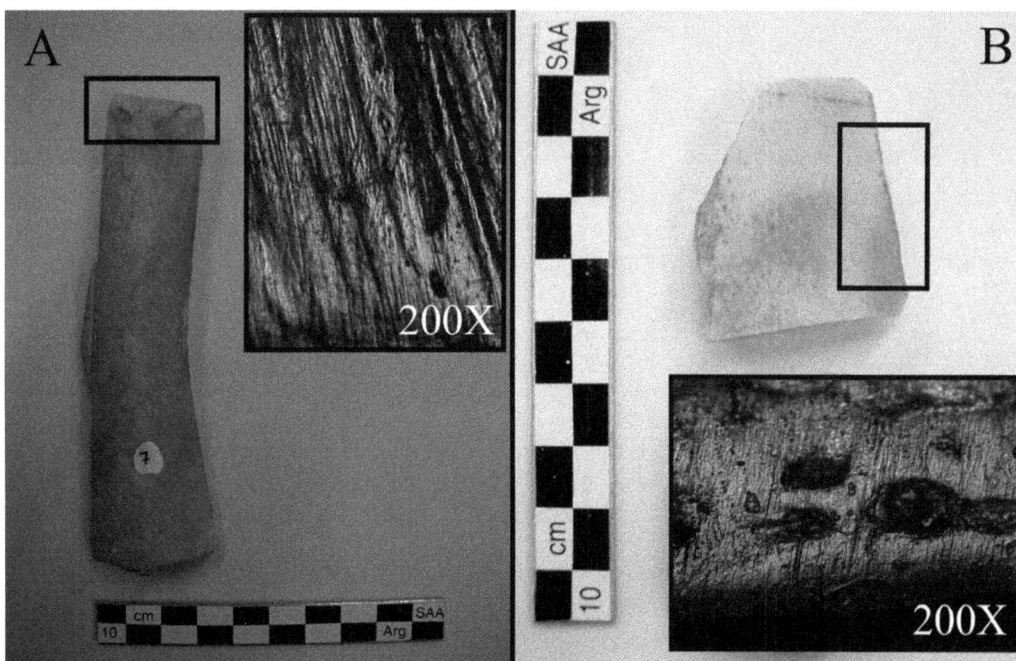

*Figure 4 – Use-wear traces: A) wood scraping B) Hide scraping*

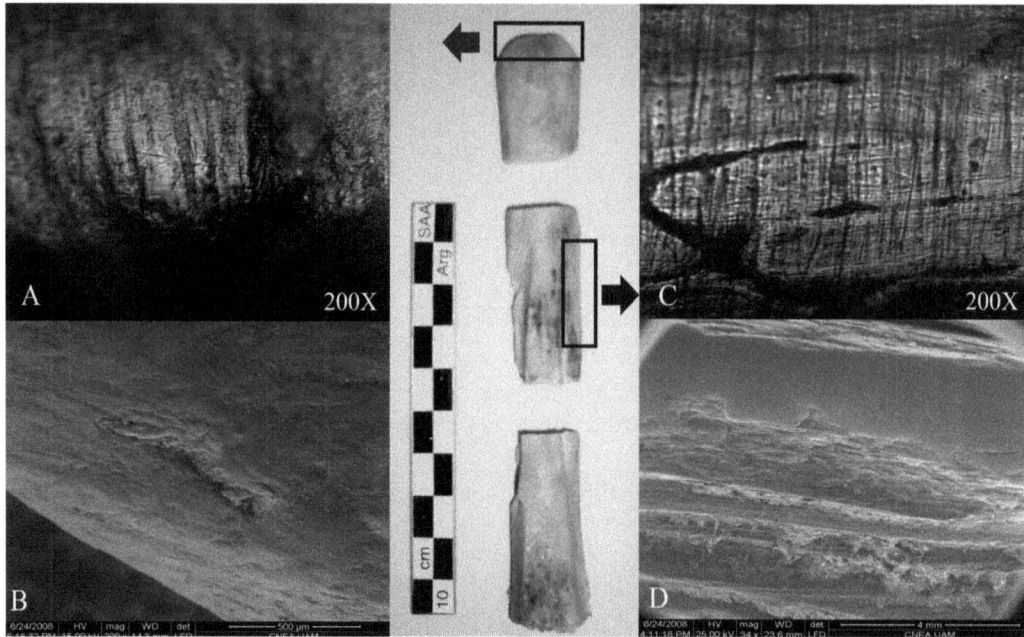

*Figure 5 – Wood scraping traces on natural and polished edges of an experimental tool (cut into 3 parts for microscopic analysis): A) Microwear traces on polished edge through LM; B) Idem through ESEM; C) Microwear traces on natural fracture edge (unpolished) through LM; D) Idem through ESEM*

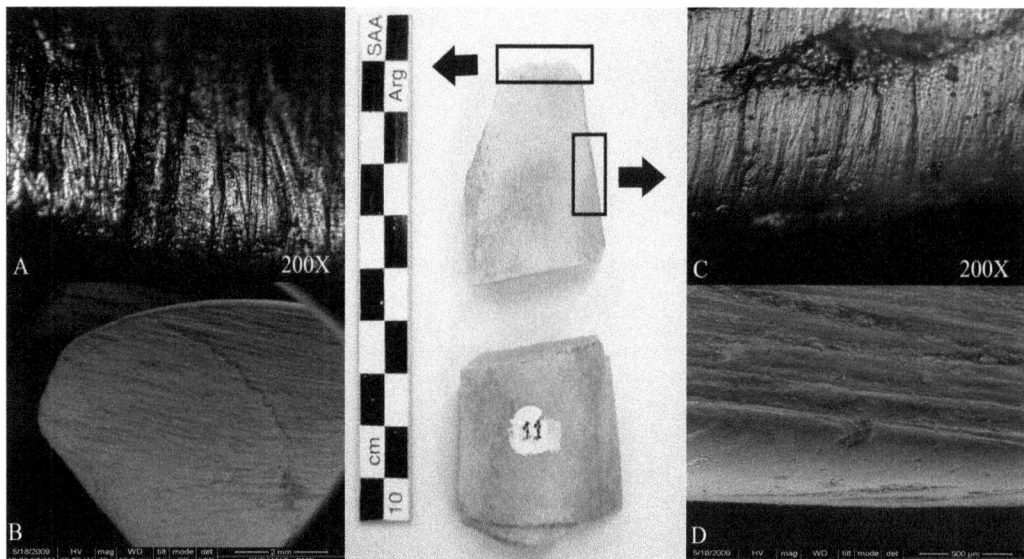

*Figure 6 – Hide scraping traces on natural and polished edges of an experimental tool (cut into 2 parts after use, for microscopic analysis): A) Microwear traces on polished edge through LM; B) Idem through ESEM; C) Microwear traces on natural fracture edge (unpolished) through LM; D) Idem through ESEM*

depressions of the micro-topography of the tool forming waves; striations are also formed due to the removal and sliding of particles during the action. In polished bone tool surfaces, striations related to artifact manufacture are still visible in LM; but the structural traits of bone are completely hidden in LM as well as in ESEM images. On the other hand, on natural fracture surfaces, bone structures, such us osteons, can be observed under the striations and micropolish produced by wood-working. The ESEM images also show a notable difference between use-wear micropolish and unused surfaces. Use-wear micropolish forms a strip along the edge. Hide-

working micropolish looks dark and dull and wide grooves perpendicular to the direction of the motion, as well as semi-spherical holes can be observed on the micropolish layer; the entire edge is remarkably rounded (Figs. 4, 5 and 6).

## 5. CONCLUDING REMARKS

The aim of this work was to present the preliminary results of an experimental program oriented to the identification of the formation processes of technological and use-wear traces on bone tools. As a consequence of this program, the following outcomes have been obtained:

1. Technological traces produced on bone surfaces, by percussion flaking and by polishing processes could be identified;

2. Use-wear traces and, particularly, micropolishes formed on non polished bone surfaces could be identified, as well as on lithic tools;

3. On the contrary, on polished surfaces, use-wear traces were observed but they are more difficult to distinguish from technological traces;

4. Structural properties of bone raw material notably influence use-wear development.

The results presented here highlight the potential of microwear analysis of bone tools to provide useful information to make inferences about socio-economic dynamics of past societies. This method can become an alternative heuristic tool to acknowledge of multiple aspects of past technologies as well as the processes of resource exploitation. For that reason, we aim to continue this research in order to gain a deeper comprehension of the mechanisms embedded in structural modifications of bone surfaces.

## References

ÁLVAREZ, M.; MANSUR, M. and PAL, N. 2008. Tecnología ósea en el Canal Beagle: aportes metodológicos al análisis de los rastros de uso. *Primer Congreso de Zooarqueología Argentina*. Museo de Historia Natural de San Rafael, Mendoza.

ÁLVAREZ, M.; FUENTES N.; FAVRET, E.; DOLCE, M.V and FORLANO, A. 2012. Quantifying use-wear traces through RIMAPS and Variogram Analyses. *Archaeological and Anthropological Sciences* 4: 91-101.

ANDERSON-GERFAUD, P. 1981. *Contribution méthodologique à l'analyse des microtraces d'utilisation sur les outils préhistoriques*. Thèse de Doctorat, Université de Bordeaux I. Impr. Bât Géologie, Bordeaux.

BUC, N. 2005. *Análisis de microdesgaste en tecnología ósea. El caso de punzones y alisadores en el noreste de la provincia de Buenos Aires (humedal del Paraná inferior)*. Tesis de Licenciatura. Facultad de Filosofía y Letras, Universidad de Buenos Aires.

BUC, N. 2011. Experimental series and use-wear in bone tools. *Journal of Archaeological Science* (38): 346-557.

CASTRO, A. 1994. *El análisis funcional por medio del estudio microscópico de huellas de usos: aportes para un modelo de clasificación tipológica*. Tesis de Doctorado, Universidad Nacional de La Plata.

CLEMENTE, I.; GYRIA, E.Y.; LOZOVSKAYA, O.V. and LOZOVSKI, V.M. 2002. Análisis de instrumentos en costilla de alce, mandíbulas de castor y caparazón de tortuga de Zamostje 2 (Rusia). *In*: Clemente, I.; Risch, R.; Gibaja, J.F. éd., *Análisis Funcional: su aplicación al estudio de sociedades prehistóricas*. Oxford: Brithish Archaeological Reports, International Series 1073, p. 187-196.

CURREY, J.D. 1984. The mechanical properties of materials and the structure of bone. In: *The mechanical adaptation of bone*, pp. 3-37. University Press. Princeton.

EVANS, A. and DONAHUE, R. 2008. Laser scanning confocal microscopy: a potential technique for the study of lithic microwear. *Jounal of Archaeological Science* 35:2223-2230.

GUTIERREZ, M.A. 2004. *Análisis tafonómicos en el Área Interserrana (Provincia de Buenos Aires)*. Tesis Doctoral. Facultad de Ciencias Naturales y Museo, Universidad Nacional de La Plata. Argentina.

HURCOMBE, L. 1986. *Microwear analysis of obsidian chipped stone tools in the Western Mediterranean*. PhD Thesis. University of Sheffield.

KEELEY, L.H. 1980. *Experimental Determination of Stone Tool Uses: a Microwear Analysis*. University of Chicago Press. Chicago.

KEELEY, L. and NEWCOMER, M. 1977. Microwear analysis of experimental flint tools: A test case. *Journal of Archaeological Science* 4 (1): 29-62.

KLEIN, R. and CRUZ-URIBE, K. 1984. *The Analysis of Animal Bones from Archaeological Sites*. Chicago University Press, Chicago.

KNUTSSON, K. 1986. Sem-analysis of wear features on experimental quartz tools. *Early Man News* 9/10/11:35-46. Newsletter for Human Paleoecology. D. Clark, H. Laville, H. Müller-Beck & A. Ranov (Eds.) Tübingen.

LE MOINE, G. 1997. *Use wear analysis on bone and antler tools of the Mackenzie Inuit. British Archaeological Reports International Series* 679, Oxford.

LERNER, H. 2007. Digital image analysis and use-wear accrual as a function of raw material: an example from Northwestern New Mexico. *Lithic Technology* 32 (1):51-67.

LYMAN, R.L. 1994. *Vertebrate Taphonomy*. Cambridge Manuals in Archaeology, Cambride University Press, Cambridge.

MAIGROT, Y. 2003a. Cycles d´utilisation et reutilizations: Le cas des outlis en matières dures animals de Chalain 4 (Néolithique final, Fontenu, Jura, France). *Préhistoire Anthropologie Méditerranéennes* 12:197-2007.

MAIGROT, Y. 2003b. *Etude technologique et fonctionnelle de l'outillage en matières dures animales, la station 4 de Chalain (Néolithique final, Jura, France)*, Thèse de Doctorat, Paris, Université de Paris 1, 284 p.

MAIGROT, Y. 2005. Ivory, bone and antler tools production systems at Chalain 4 (Jura, France), late

Neolithic site, 3rd millennium. *In*: Luik, H.; Choyke, M.A.; Batey, C.E.; Lougas, L. dir., *From hooves to horns, from Mollusc to Mammoth, manufacture and use of bone artefacts from prehistoric times to the present, 4th Meeting of the Worked Bone Research Group, Tallinn, 26-31 August 2003*. Tallinn: Muinasaja teadus, 15, p. 113-126.

MANSUR-FRANCHOMME, M.E. 1983. *Traces d'utilisation et technologie lithique: Exemples de la Patagonie*. Thèse de Doctorat, Université de Bordeaux I. Impr. Bât Géologie, Bordeaux.

MANSUR, M. 1997. Functional Analysis of Polished Stone-Tools: Some Considerations about the Nature of Polishing. *In: Siliceous Rocks and Culture. Ramos Millán A., Bustillo M.A., eds. Pp. 465-496. Granada: Editorial Universidad de Granada.*

MANSUR, M.E. 1999. Análisis funcional de instrumental lítico: Problemas de formación y deformación de rastros de uso. *Actas del XII Congreso Nacional de Arqueología Argentina*, pp. 355-366. La Plata.

MANSUR-FRANCHOMME, M.; ORQUERA, L. and PIANA, E. 1987-1988. El alisamiento de la piedra entre cazadores-recolectores: el caso de Tierra del Fuego. *Runa*. 17-18: 111-205.

OLLÈ, A. and VERGÈS. J. 2008. Sem functional analysis and the mechanism of microwear formation. En: *Prehistoric Technology 40 years later: Functional studies and the Russian legacy*, L. Longo y N. Skakun (Eds), pp. 39-49. BAR International Series 1783. BAR Publishing, Oxford.

ORQUERA, L. and PIANA, E. 1999. *Arqueología de la región del canal Beagle (Tierra del Fuego, República Argentina)*. Buenos Aires: Sociedad Argentina de Antropología.

PELTIER, A. and PLISSON, H. 1986. Micro tracéologie fonctionnelle sur l'os: quelques résultats expérimentaux. En: *Outillage peu élaboré en os et en bois de cervidés II. Artefacts 3,* Editions du C.E.D.A. pp. 69-80.

PLISSON, H. 1986. Analyse des polis d'utilisation sur le quarzite. *Early Man News* 9/10/11:47-49. Newsletter for Human Paleoecology. Editado por D. Clark, H. Laville, H. Müller-Beck y A. Ranov. Tübingen.

PLISSON, H. y MAUGER, M. 1988. Chemical and mechanical alteration of microwear polishes: an experimental approach. *Helinium* XXVII, 1:3-16.

SCHEINSOHN, V. 1997. *Explotación de materias primas óseas en la Isla grande de Tierra del Fuego.* Tesis Doctoral, Facultad de Filosofía y Letras, Universidad de Buenos Aires.

SCHEINSOHN, V. & FERRETI, J.L. 1995. Mechanical Properties of Bone Materials as Related to Design and Function of Prehistoric Tools from Tierra del Fuego (Argentina). *Journal of Archaeological Science* 22: 711-717.

SEMENOV, S.A. 1964. *Prehistoric technology*. Adams y Dart. Inglaterra.

SIDERA, I. & LEGRAND, A. 2006. Tracéologie fonctionnelle des matières osseuses: une méthode. *Bulletin de la Société Préhistorique Française* 103(2):291-304.

STEMP, W. & STEMP, M. 2003. Documenting Stages of Polish Development on Experimental Stone Tools: Surface Characterization by Fractal Geometry Using UBM Laser Profilometry. *Journal of Archaeological Science* 30 (3):287-296.

VAN GIJN, A.L. 2006. Implements of bone and antler: a Mesolithic tradition continued. In: Louwe Kooijmans, L.P.; Jongste, P.F.B. (Ed)., *Schipluiden – Harnaschpolder. A Middle Neolithic Site on the Dutch Coast (3800-3500 BC)*, p. 207-224. (Analecta Praehistorica Leidensia 37/38).

VAUGHAN, P. 1985. *Use-wear analysis of flaked stone tools*. University of Arizona Press. Tucson.

# MICRO-WEAR FORMATION ON GLASS: AN ARCHAEOLOGICAL AND EXPERIMENTAL STUDY

Hernán DE ANGELIS

Centro Austral de Investigaciones Científicas – CADIC CONICET, Laboratorio de Antropología,
B. Houssay 200, 9410 Ushuaia, Tierra del Fuego, Argentina
hernandeangelis@yahoo.com.ar

**Abstract**: *Glass has been extensively exploited as a lithic raw material by the hunter-gatherer populations of Tierra del Fuego. This material started being utilized even before the concrete settlement of European estancias in the island, due to the fact that fragments of glass proceeding from shipwrecks were arriving to the shores since the seventeenth century.*

*From the functional point of view, glass has always been seen as a very fragile raw material, in which traces of use could hardly be preserved. Nevertheless, experimental and archaeological studies on glass tools let us demonstrate that this is not always the case.*

*In this work, we present the experimental program, which includes the techno-morphologic and the microscopic-functional analysis of two series of tools made of glass. The program followed the general guidelines applied in other studies of this kind, including manufacturing of one series of glass scrapers and another of arrowheads, collection and techno-morphological analysis of all the retouch fragments and microflakes. Then, the experimental scrapers were used to work on three basic types of materials: wood (Nothofagus and Berberis sp.), with and without its bark; fresh bone and hides (with and without additives), and considering different kinematics and working angles.*

*The results obtained from the experimentation were used as criterion for the study of glass artifacts from two sites belonging to Ewan archaeological locality: Ewan I and Ewan II, which were used in 1905 AC. On the basis of retouch flakes discovered in the excavations, it was possible to infer which had been the types of instruments made in both sites. It was also possible to determine the specific use given to the scrapers.*

**Key words**: *glass, lithic technology, experimental program, functional analysis*

**Résumé**: *Le verre a été largement utilisé en tant que matière première lithique par les populations de chasseurs-cueilleurs de la Terre de Feu. Ce matériau a commencé à être utilisé avant même l'installation des Estancias européennes sur l'île, car des fragments de verre provenant de naufrages arrivaient sur les côtes depuis le XVII siècle.*

*Du point de vue fonctionnel, le verre a toujours été considéré comme un matériau très fragile, qui ne pouvait guère conserver des traces d'utilisation. Cependant, des études expérimentales et archéologiques sur des outils en verre montrent que ce n'est pas toujours le cas.*

*Dans cet article nous présentons le programme expérimental, qui comprend l'analyse techno-morphologique et l'analyse fonctionnelle microscopique de deux séries d'outils en verre. Ce programme a suivi les normes générales utilisées dans d'autres études de ce type, notamment pour la préparation d'une série de grattoirs et une de pointes de flèche en verre, ainsi que pour la récupération et l'analyse techno-morphologique de tous les fragments et micro-éclats liés à la retouche. Enfin, les grattoirs expérimentaux ont été utilisés pour travailler trois types de matériaux: bois (Nothofagus et Berberis sp.) avec et sans écorce, de l'os frais et des peaux (avec ou sans additifs), avec différentes cinématiques et angles de travail.*

*Les résultats obtenus dans l'étude expérimentale ont été utilisés comme critères d'analyse pour l'étude des matériaux en verre de deux sites de la localité archéologique Ewan: Ewan I et Ewan II, qui ont été utilisés en 1905 A.C. L'analyse des micro-éclats liés à la retouche découverts dans les fouilles, a permis de déduire quels ont été les types d'instruments fabriqués sur les deux sites. Il a été possible aussi de déterminer l'utilisation spécifique des grattoirs.*

**Mots-clés**: *verre, technologie lithique, programme expérimental, l'analyse fonctionnelle*

## 1. INTRODUCTION

The use of glass as a raw material for the manufacture of lithic tools was an extended practice among the hunter-gatherer societies that inhabited the Isla Grande de Tierra del Fuego. It started around the XVIIth century, even before the permanent settlement of the european estancias in the island -which took place as late as the last decade of XIXth century-. Before that, glass was obtained as fragments from shipwrecks that arrived to the coasts of Tierra del Fuego.

The use of glass, as mentioned in different chronicles (Gallardo 1910, Gusinde 1982 [1937], Chapman 1986, Outes 1906, cf. De Angelis *et al.* 2010) is confirmed by the discovery of glass materials in several archaeological sites in Tierra del Fuego and Patagonia, in which glass has replaced stone for the manufacture of all or part of the artifacts.

These series of artifacts were found in archaeological sites from different contexts. The examples included here come not only from the continental Patagonia, from

*Figure 1 – Example of stone tools made of glass (Site Ewan)*

Campo Indio site (Carballo *et al.* 2011), but also from Tierra del Fuego. In Isla Grande, glass materials were discovered in the Beagle Channel region, especially in the Acatushún site (a burial in an older shell midden) dated 650 ± 100 AP (Piana *et al.* 2006), in the recent component of Lancha Packewaia site, dated in 280 ± 84 AP (Orquera *et al.* 1978) and also in the central region of the island, in Ewan I and Ewan II sites, belonging to the Ewan archaeological locality, which was dated by dendrochronology in 1905 (Mansur *et al.* 2006 a and b, Mansur *et al.* 2005, Bogdanovic *et al.* 2008, Mansur and Piquè 2008) (Fig. 1).

Due to the importance of glass among the lithic assemblages of sites dating from the last centuries, and considering the scarce methodological developments done up to date in order to carry out techno-morphological and functional analysis on this raw material, we decided to undertake an experimental program that could establish the methodological basis for such studies.

From the functional perspective, glass has always been considered as a very fragile raw material, on which traces of use would be hard to preserve. Nevertheless, based on these experimental and archaeological studies, it could be noticed that this is not always the case.

## 2. MATERIALS AND METHODS

### 2.1. The experimentation

The experimental program followed the general guidelines of microscopic functional analysis established by S. Semenov (1964, cf. Mansur 1999, Clemente Conte and Gómez Romero 2006, De Angelis *et al.* 2007) and it was centered in four main aspects:

- Manufacture of a series of 13 glass scrapers out of a bottle fragment, comparable to those documented in the sites. They were shaped by pressure-flaking using retouching tools made of antler and bone. We aimed to replicate the edge characteristics of archaeological scrapers, which are regular and straight to slightly convex.

- Use of the scrapers on different materials: Wood, hide and bone.

- Microscopic functional analysis of the edges carried out at different intervals during work (from fresh edges up until 30 minutes of use).

- Image capture of these edges at the different intervals of analysis.

### 2.1.1 Functional Experimentation

Materials on which the scrapers were used:

– 5 scrapers worked on fresh wood (genus *Nothofagus* and *Berberis*), with and without the bark,

– 5 scrapers worked on fresh bone (bovine),

– 3 scrapers worked on hide (sheep and lamb) dry and with additives of fat and mineral pigments.

In all the cases, transversal kinematics were utilized (the axis of the edge transversal to the movement performed); ventral face of the flake was used as contact surface. Each tool was utilized during two 30-minute intervals (Fig. 2).

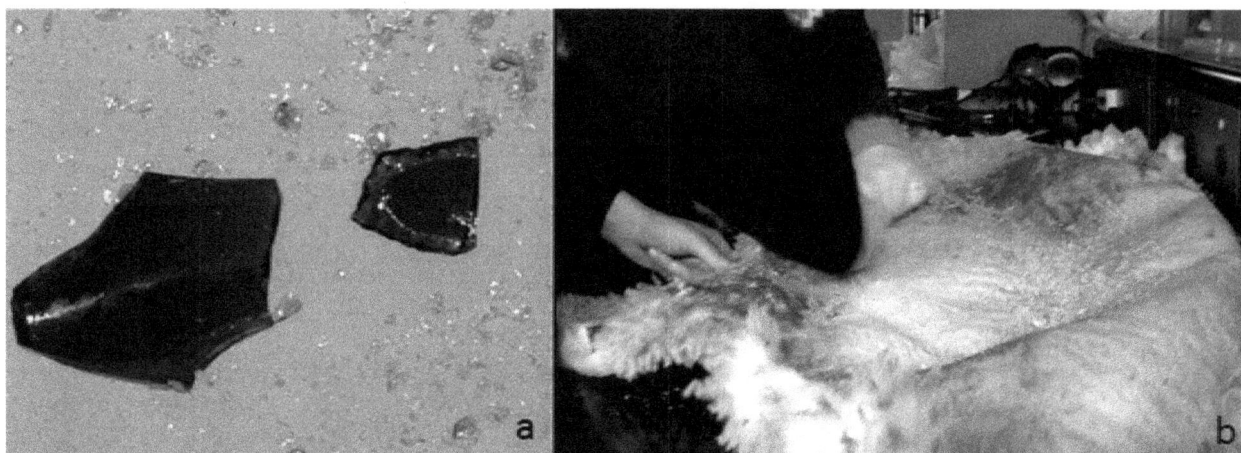

*Figure 2 – a, experimental manufacture of glass scraper, b, scraping on fresh hide*

*Figure 3 – a, glass scrapers Campo Indio site, b, glass scrapers Acatushún-burial sites (top) and Ewan II. (below)*

## 2.2. The archaeological series

The scrapers analyzed up till now belong to three different (sets). The first one is formed by three scrapers belonging to the Ewan II site; the second one includes two scrapers from Acatushun site, and finally the third series is formed of 25 scrapers from Campo Indio site (Fig. 3).

## 2.3. Functional analysis

The analysis was carried out following the methodology formerly started by S. Semenov (1964). Specially, we considered the model of "Microwear formation in Homogeneous materials" *(sensu* Mansur 1999), and taking into account different variables referred to edge scarring, edge rounding, striations and microwear characteristics. Regarding the equipment, we used a stereomicroscope (10 to 60x) and an Olympus reflected light metallographic microscope, with direct system to capture and digitalize images and magnifications from 50 to 500x.

Systematic analysis were made on all the fresh edges (before the use in the case of the experimental scrapers) in order to characterize the technological traces produced during the manufacturing process. We preset a series of reference points for observation, and then carried out microscopic analysis every 10, 15 and 30-minute

intervals of use. These analysis included capture and digitalization of images at the already mentioned reference points, in order to document any modification produced during the process of use. For this purpose, a digital camera was utilized (Paxcam Digital Microscope Camera) incorporated to the microscope, with a resolution of 3.1 Mega Pixels.

After each use, the instruments were washed with water and soap; cleaning with alcohol was also performed before and during the analysis. Several angles of observation were utilized, although the most effectives (due to the raw materials) were: Ventral side, perpendicular to the beam of light, with angles comprised between 70° and 90° or with angles higher than 90°.

## 3. RESULTS

## 3.1. Experimental scrapers

The results from the experimental program do not differ from those presented in preliminary communications (D Angelis *et al.* 2007, De Angelis and Mansur 2010). The functional analysis of the glass scrapers allowed confirming a series of particular processes regarding the formation of traces of use. The most notorious feature is that, at the beginning of this work, the edges fracture releasing small microflakes, not only on the front but also

**Work on fresh hide**

**Work on bone**

**Work on wood**

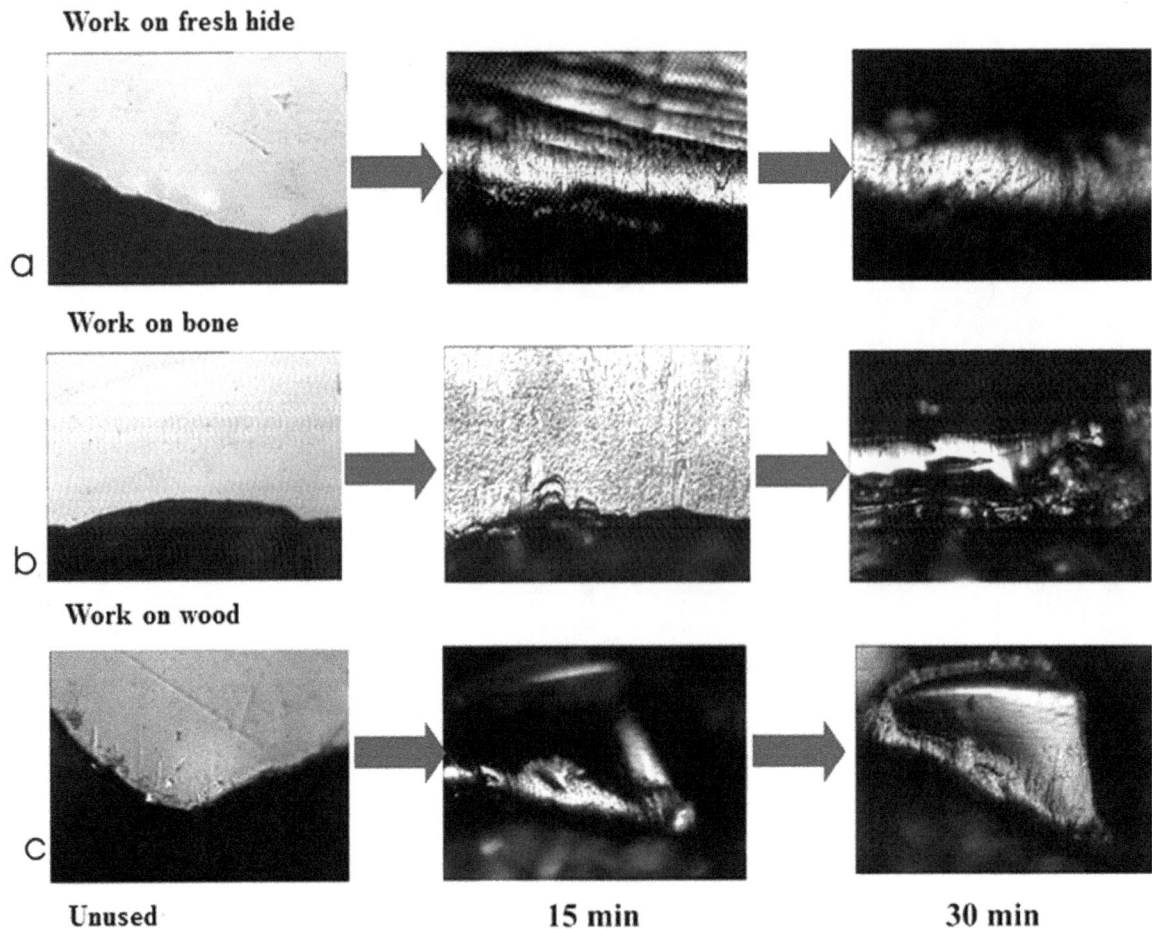

| Unused | 15 min | 30 min |

*Figure 4 – Microwear polish development on experimental endscrapers. Photomicrograph at 200x.*
*(From De Angelis et al. 2009 pp. 138)*

on the contact face, until they become regular reaching their stability profile. This process takes place in the first minutes of work with the scraper.

Before use, the scrapers reveal relatively smooth faces and fresh edges with some technological traces of retouch. After the initial 15 minutes of use, there are many negatives of microflaking, showing their characteristic technological traces; percussion waves, percussion striae, comets, etc. Well developed, micro-polishes could not be seen; on the contrary, practically all the edges show micro-polishes that correspond to the first stages of development, manifested by smoothing, until almost complete erasing of technological traces. In hides working, the edge shows an intense rounding along with striations oriented following the direction of use. Unlike with the work on hard materials (vegetal and animal), the edge scarring is much more pronounced; micro-polishes are shiny, they are more developed in the high areas of micro-topography and show smooth surfaces and a slightly wavy appearance. The release of splinters causes a backward movement of the scraper's fronts, removing the cutting edge in which the micro-wear are developed, and avoids reaching the stage of well-developed micro-wear. This process becomes evident comparing the degree of development of the traces of wear in the reference points selected for that purpose (Fig. 4).

The analysis of the tools after the second work phase (30 minutes) allowed to detect fully developed micro-wear, characteristic of the materials utilized on. In the work on wood and bone, these are for the most part scarcely extended along the scraper's edge, appearing only in some parts. The micro-wear produced by bone working presents the characteristic "craquélée" analog to that observed on lithic raw materials. It is deep, but it shows less volume than micro-polish produced in the work on woods. In this last case, on the contrary, micro-polish is slightly thicker and it shows characteristic striations. In the tools used on hides, we can observe an intense rounding, manifested along most of the edge involved in the work process. The micro-wear is well developed and is accompanied by a great number of short and dark striations; both the edge rounding and the striation formation are much more abundant in the works on hides with the addition of natural pigment.

### 3.2. Archaeological scrapers

The lithic series analyzed show several alterations, such as iridescent patinas, different degrees of abrasion in the surfaces, splintering, and polishes. Such post-depositional alterations could be related to the context where the tools were (Fig. 5).

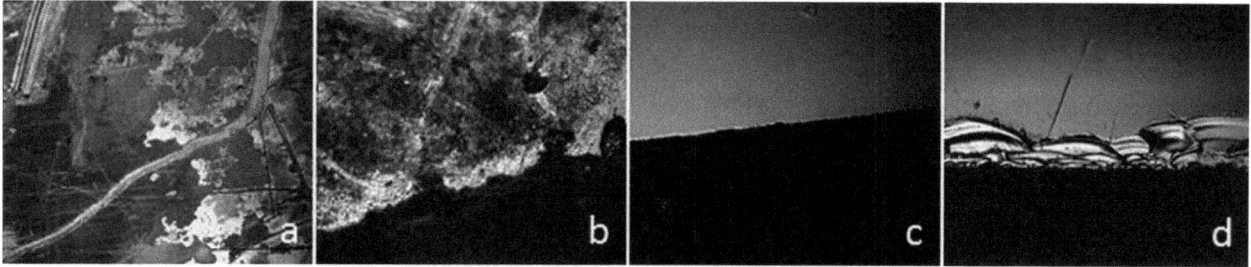

*Figure 5 – Alterations on glass surfaces. a, patina; b, abrasion; c, fresh edges; d, micro fractures on the edge. Photomicrograph at 200x*

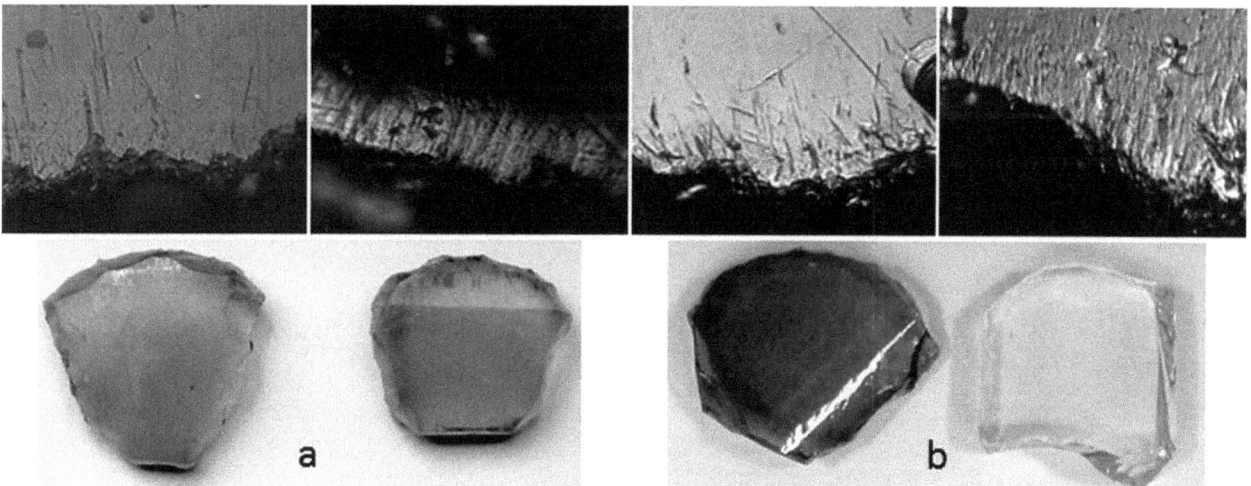

*Figure 6 – Microwear polish produced by hide working. a, scrapers from Campo Indio; b, scrapers from Ewan II. Photomicrograph at 200x*

Thus, the superficial set (Campo Indio) shows an iridescent patina in the majority of the tools, that could be related to the contact with water and sun, and the worn surfaces could be the result of the almost constant collision with sediments carried by the wind (Fig. 5 a-b). Nevertheless, since the gradient of alterations in this series goes from almost unaltered to totally altered, it was possible to determine micro-wear polish in different degrees of development, work kinematics, and whenever possible, the material on which tools were utilized.

Besides, scrapers belonging to stratigraphic excavations present surfaces with better levels of preservation, with very small patina development (Fig. 5 c). It was possible to determine, on the three scrapers from the Ewan site, the kinematics and material that they had worked (hide, in all three cases) (Fig. 6). While the scrapers coming from the Beagle channel area, even though they showed unaltered surfaces, it was not possible to determine if they had been used at all.

## 4. DISCUSSION

The introduction of glass in Tierra del Fuego represented an interesting possibility for the native hunter-gatherer societies, since glass is a material that offers excellent knapping and retouching potential. Generally, glass could be obtained from diverse objects, such as bottles, windows or dishes and with it, scrapers, arrowheads and some other long-edged retouched tools.

In the case of glass, since it is a very fragile raw material, a high degree of post-depositional alteration would be expected once the tool is abandoned. In spite of this, recent studies on glass tools (surface and stratigraphic studies) demonstrated that even though they suffered alterations, it is possible to apply functional studies with some positive results.

## 5. CONCLUSION

The experimentation on glass tools allowed widening the scope of functional analysis. These analyses, although initial, showed that this raw material, despite its fragility, could preserve valuable information for the researches like the one exposed here.

As it was mentioned, there is still a lot to do, like further studies on the many alterations that affect the archaeological assemblages, widen the spectrum of materials to be analyzed, kinematics, thermo-alteration studies, etc. Nevertheless, the results obtained were extremely positive and served to confirm the potential for microscopic studies in such materials.

## References

BOGDANOVIC, I.; CAMAROS, E.; DE ANGELIS, H.; LASA, A.; MANSUR, M.; MAXIMIANO, A.; PARMIGIANI, V.; PIQUE HUERTA, R. and VICENTE, O. 2009. El paraje de Ewan, un lugar de reunión Selknam en el centro de la isla. In: Arqueología de la Patagonia: una mirada desde el último confín. Tomo 2, p. 941-956. Edit. Utopías.

CARBALLO MARINA, F.; BELARDI, J.B.; SÁENZ, J.L. 2011. Distribución espacial del registro arqueológico en la unidad de paisaje terrazas, cuenca media del río Coyle (provincia de Santa Cruz, Argentina). Punta Arenas. Magallania 39 (2). p. 207-222.

CLEMENTE CONTE, I. and GÓMEZ ROMERO, F. 2006. "Análisis de vidrios 'retocados' del Fortín Miñana (Azul, Provincia de Buenos Aires)". Estudios de Arqueología Histórica. Tapia, A.; Ramos, M. y Baldasarre, C. (Eds.): p. 109-124. Museo de Río Grande (Tierra del Fuego).

CHAPMAN, A. 1986. Los Selk'nam. La vida de los Onas. Buenos Aires: Emecé editores.

DE ANGELIS, H.; LASA, A, MANSUR, M.E.; SOSA, L. and VALDEZ, G. 2009. Análisis tecnológico y funcional de artefactos de vidrio: resultados de un programa experimental. In: Arqueometria Latinoamericana. 2do. Congreso Argentino, 1ro. Latinoamericano. Buenos Aires. Palacios, O.; Vázquez, C.; Palacios, T. Cabanillas, E. (Eds.): p. 134-141. Comisión Nacional de Energía Atómica.

DE ANGELIS, H. and MANSUR, M.E. 2010. Artefactos de vidrio en contextos cazadores recolectores. Revista Atlántica-Mediterránea de Prehistoria y Arqueología Social. 12: p. 59-73.

GALLARDO, C. 1910. Los Onas. Cabaut & Cia., Buenos Aires. (Ed. facsimilar, Zagier & Urruty, Ushuaia 1998).

GUSINDE, M. 1982. [1937] Los indios de Tierra del Fuego. Tomo 1: Los Selk'nam. 2 vols. Buenos Aires: Centro Argentino de Etnología Americana.

MANSUR, M.E. 1999. "Análisis funcional de instrumental lítico: problemas de formación y deformación de rastros de uso". La Plata, p. 355-366.

Actas del XII Congreso Nacional de Arqueología Argentina.

MANSUR, M.E. and LASA, A. 2005. Diversidad artefactual vs. especialización funcional. Análisis del IV componente de Túnel I (Tierra del Fuego, Argentina). Magallania 33 (2): p. 69-91. Universidad de Magallanes, Punta Arenas, Chile.

MANSUR, M.E. and PIQUÉ, R. 2009. Between the forest and the sea: hunter-gatherer occupations in the subantarctic forests in Tierra del Fuego (Argentina). Arctic Anthropology 46 (1-2): p. 144-157.

MANSUR, M.E.; DE ANGELIS, H. and PARMIGIANI, V. 2010. Explotación de materias primas y circuitos de movilidad en la zona central de Tierra del Fuego. In: Arqueología Argentina en el Bicentenario de la Revolución de Mayo. Tomo V: p. 1935-1940. Mendoza. Actas del XVII Congreso Nacional de Arqueología Argentina.

MANSUR, M.E.; MAXIMIANO, A.; PIQUÉ, R. and VICENTE, O. 2007. Arqueología de Rituales en Sociedades Cazadoras-Recolectoras. Una aproximación desde el Análisis del Espacio Socialmente Producido. In: Arqueología de Fuego-Patagonia. Levantando piedras, desenterrando huesos...y develando arcanos. Editado por F. Morello, M. Martinic, A. Prieto y G. Bahamonde, p. 741-754. Ediciones CEQUA, Punta Arenas, Chile.

MANSUR, M.E.; PIQUE, R. and VILA MITJA, A. 2007. Etude du rituel chez les chasseurs-cueilleurs. Apport de l'ethnoarchéologie des sociétés de la Terre de Feu. In: "Chasseurs-cueilleurs. Comment vivaient nos ancêtres du Paléolithique supérieur", S. de Beaune (Ed.), Editions du CNRS. Paris. p. 143-150.

ORQUERA, L.A.; SALA, A.E.; PIANA, E.L. and TAPIA, A.H. 1978. Lancha Packewaia: arqueología de los canales fueguinos. Buenos Aires: Editorial Huemul, p. 266.

OUTES, F. 1906. Instrumentos modernos de los Onas (Tierra del Fuego). Anales del Museo Nacional de Buenos Aires, 3ª ser, t. VI, p. 287-296.

PIANA, E.L.; TESSONE, A. and ZANGRANDO, A.F. 2006. Contextos mortuorios en la región del canal Beagle... del hallazgo fortuito a la búsqueda sistemática. Punta Arenas. Magallania 34 (1): p. 87-101.

# USE-WEAR AND RESIDUES ON OBSIDIAN ARTEFACTS FROM MELANESIA

Nina KONONENKO

The University of Sydney, Australia
kononenkonina@hotmail.com

**Abstract**: *An integrated use-wear/residue study of middle and late Holocene obsidian artefacts from 18 sites in Melanesia has significantly extended the range of tool functions particularly in relation to tropical resources. The study proposes diagnostic sets of wear attributes resulting from working eight categories of tropical plant and non-plant materials. The duration of use of prehistoric artefacts was also estimated through comparisons with experimental data providing important insights into the expedient pattern of use of flakes as single purpose tools in prehistoric peoples' daily activities.*

**Keywords**: *Melanesia, the Pacific, use-wear, residues, obsidian*

**Résumé**: *Une étude intégrale comprenant analyse des traces d'utilisation et des résidus sur des outils en obsidienne de l'Holocène moyen et supérieur de 18 sites de Mélanésie, a permis d'étendre le rang d'activités des outils, en particulier par rapport aux ressources tropicales.*

*L'étude propose des séries de traces diagnostiques produites par l'utilisation sur huit catégories de matières végétales et not végétales tropicales. La durée de l'utilisation des outils préhistoriques a été aussi estimée en fonction de comparaisons avec les données expérimentales, ce qui a donné une aperçue importante sur l'utilisation expéditive d'éclats en tant qu'outils à une seule fonction dans les activités quotidiennes des gens préhistoriques.*

**Mots-clés**: *Mélanésie, Pacifique, traces d'utilisation, résidus, obsidienne*

## 1. INTRODUCTION

Following S.A. Semenov's (1964) pioneering research in the 1930s to 1960s, new approaches adopted for functional analysis of stone tools have been developed by a number of scholars. The most significant area of investigation employs both low and high magnification to study distinctive polishes and other use-wear features observed on tools (Anderson-Gerfaud 1990, Fullagar 1991, Hurcombe 1992, Keeley 1980, Vaughan 1985). A second important aspect of functional studies involves the microscopic investigation of a range of plant (e.g. phytoliths, starch), animal (e.g. blood) and inorganic (e.g. ochre) residues preserved on tool surfaces (e.g. Anderson 1980, Briuer 1976, Fullagar 2006b, Kealhofer *et al.* 1999, Lombard and Wadley 2007, Loy 1983, 2006, Petraglia *et al.* 1996, Shafer and Holloway 1979). Scholars have realised that the reliability of identification of prehistoric tool functions is markedly increased when use-wear examination and residue analysis are integrated into a single study (e.g. Fullagar 2006a, Högberg, Puseman and Yost 2009, Kealhofer *et al.* 1999, Robertson *et al.* 2009, Rots and Williamson 2004).

In the Pacific region, the study of stone tool function involving the microscopic examination of wear patterns, residues and experimental replication was initiated by Kamminga (1982), Fullagar (1998) and Loy (Loy, *et al.*, 1992). Fullagar (1998) introduced the integrated approach to the study of tool function combining replication experiments with low and high powered microscopic analysis of both wear traces and residues. This approach provided more reliable data for the reconstruction of human behaviour than simpler, traditional techniques. Further integrated studies of stone tools made significant contributions into interpretations of tool functions and their association with a range of prehistoric people's activities (e.g. Barton *et al.* 1998, Fullagar *et al.* 1998, Haslam and Liston 2008, Kealhofer *et al.* 1999, Robertson *et al.* 2009). However, current interpretations of lithic assemblages, subsistence and settlement history still leave many questions under-resolved and more complete functional information about prehistoric tool use strategies is required. This is an especially important subject for the Pacific region because much of the archaeological record of consists of simple flakes with few recognisable types of retouched tools and only microscopic examination allows the determination of the function of both types. This paper contributes to that field of functional analysis of obsidian artefacts based primarily on the observation of macroscopic and microscopic traces of wear, residual materials and the replication experiments involving tropical resources.

## 2. MATERIAL AND METHODS

The lithic assemblage analysed in this study comprises 1653 middle and late Holocene obsidian artefacts from 18 sites including 1395 flakes found within seven test pits at FAO site on Garua Island excavated by R. Torrence (2002) and 232 artefacts from a wider geographical area deliberately selected by R. Torrence, J.C. Galipaud, C. Reepmeyer, S. Bedford, J. Specht and P. White for use-wear-residue examination.

Functional analysis of the sampled stone artefacts took into consideration the properties of the raw material used, manufacture, and design characteristics of the artefacts, use-wear features and residues. The examination of use-wear and residues has been conducted in four basic stages. The first step involves the observation of the whole surface of each artefact using magnification in the range of 20-100x provided by a Dino-LiteTM (AM413ZT) digital microscope mounted on a rack (Dino-LiteTMMS35B) with multiple brackets that enable wide scale movement and easy access. The low magnifications with a reflected light permit the examination of surface alteration (e.g. abrasion, smoothing), edge scarring, striations and some residues. The next step of the initial use-wear analysis was to photographically record the residues assumed to be use-related. These residues may be visible directly on artefact surfaces under a high power microscope with reflected light. However, the identification of extracted residues required their transfer to glass slides for examination under a transmitted light microscope. The third step involved the detailed examination of use-wear characteristics such as scarring, rounding, striations, polish and residues using a metallographic microscope (Olympus BX60M) with vertical incident and transmitted light, bright and dark field illuminations and cross polarizing filters using 100x to 1000x magnifications. Wear patterns and residues were recorded with a ColorView II camera and by a Soft Imaging System GmbH attached to the metallographic microscope. This digital camera system produces images of good quality and is easy to record all forms of surface modification and residues on the artefacts, peels and glass slides. The pattern of wear features in combination with observable residues enabled the mode of use and the processed material to be determined. In the final stage, the functional interpretation of tools was made on the basis of the comparison of observed characteristics of use-wear/residues on artefacts and experimental tools. In addition, all available experimental data on residues and wear patterns (Fullagar 19984, Kamminga 1982, Kononenko 2011, Robertson *et al.* 2009) were also used for comparative identification of tool function.

The experimental study involved 292 separate experiments each using a different tool to perform a specific activity for a predetermined period of time in as realistic a situation as it was possible to achieve. The tools were mostly employed to carry out single tasks, although the multifunctional use of particular tools was the subject of some experiments. Most of the experiments were conducted near archaeological sites in West New Britain, Papua New Guinea. Many experiments were performed by local people from Kimbe (Figure 1: A-B), a small town located on the mainland of West New Britain. The materials used in replication experiments were determined by prior examination of use-wear patterns observed on obsidian artefacts, ethnographic data about native plant species used by indigenous people and by

current local environmental conditions. All materials used in the field experiments were available locally. The range of green, fresh plants included 7 species of highly siliceous palms, 17 species of soft and hard wood which vary in silica content and nine species of herbs, grasses and tubers which were combined in a group of "non-woody plants". The soft elastic materials are represented by three species of fish, chicken skin, as a suitable substitute for human tissue (David, Castle and Mossi 2006), pig skin and monitor lizard (*Varanus* sp.) skin. Additional use-material such as human skin (shaving) was also included in the experimental program. Hard dense materials included half-dry clay and two species of shells: cowrie (*Cypraeidae spp.*) and cockle (*Katylesia spp.*).

## 3. RESULTS

Use-wear/residue analysis of a total 1653 obsidian artefacts identified 247 tools. The comparison of identified tools with experimental tools indicated that the wear patterns on the prehistoric artefacts were caused by processing of eight groups of worked materials: (1) siliceous soft wood, palms and bamboo, (2) non-siliceous soft wood, (3) siliceous hard wood and hard palms, (4) non-siliceous hard wood, (5) non-woody plants (tubers), (6) non-woody plants (greens which include leaves, stems and grasses), (7) soft elastic materials (skin and fish) and (8) dense, hard materials (shell and clay). This range of materials was worked using various modes of use, including scraping, sawing, whittling, carving, drilling, cutting, slicing, peeling and piercing.

### 3.1. Processing siliceous soft wood, palms and bamboo

Wear patterns on artefacts used for processing siliceous soft wood, palms and bamboo are characterised by moderate to intensive edge scarring with smoothed and rounded scar ridges, and both developed and well-developed flattened polish. Well defined shallow and short striations are densely packed and are often observed within scars. Similar wear patterns were formed on experimental tools used for the same tasks during the first 5 to 10 minutes and, after 15 minutes of use, the efficiency of tools usually decreases significantly.

This short use-life of the tool leads to a high rate of discard and must be taken into account in assessing prehistoric artefacts. The working edges of artefacts used for processing siliceous soft wood, palms and bamboo often preserved plant tissue and starch grains (Figure 1: C-E).

### 3.2. Processing non-siliceous soft wood

Wear patterns on artefacts used for working non-siliceous soft wood are also characterised by moderate to intensive edge scarring, medium to intensive edge rounding, developed and well-developed but less smooth and flattened polish. The most distinctive wear attributes on these tools are long and deep striations which are well

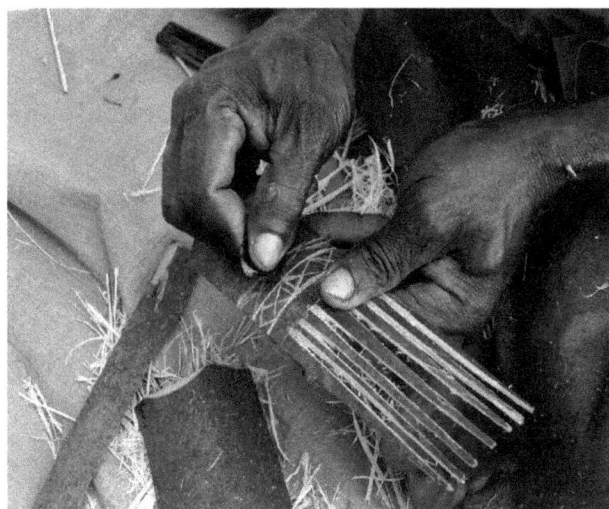

A

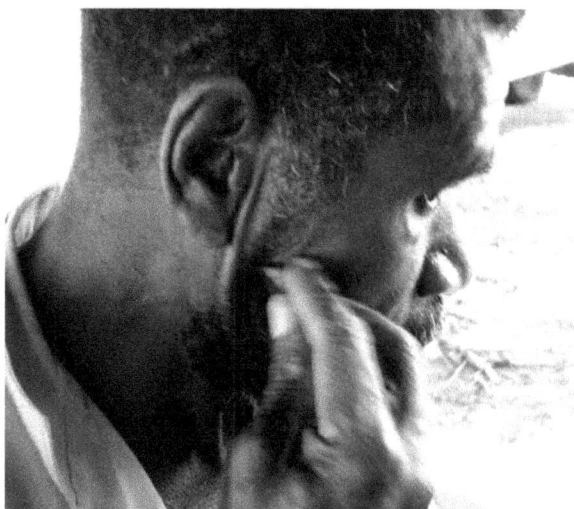

B

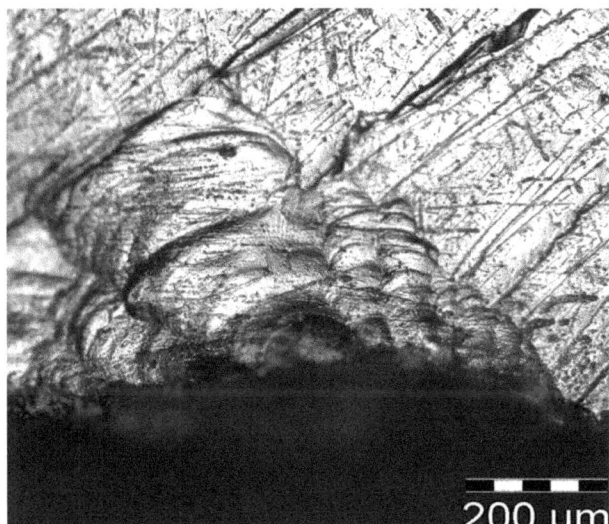

C

D

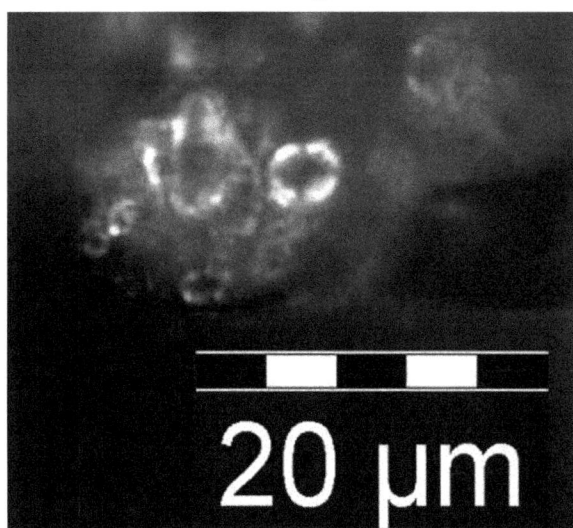

E

F

*Figure 1 – Experiments (A-B) and wear patterns (C-E) on artefacts used for processing siliceous soft wood, palms and bamboo (C-E) and non-siliceous soft wood (F). Experiments: A – making a comb from bamboo, B – shaving the face. Wear patterns and residues: C – sawing siliceous soft wood, palms and bamboo (100x), D – sawing siliceous soft wood, palms and bamboo (200x), E – starch residues on the working edge of the artefact D (1000x), F – sawing non-siliceous soft wood (100x)*

separated from each other despite their relatively high frequency of occurrence (Figure 1: F). The experiments demonstrate that diagnostic wear on the tools forms after 15 to 20 minutes and the tools can be used further with less efficiency for between 30 and 60 minutes. This suggests that the formation of identifiable wear attributes on artefacts used for the working of non-siliceous soft wood would probably require slightly longer periods of use: more than 15 to 20 minutes. Used edges often preserved plant tissue, sometimes starch and black or coloured residues which are probably associated with processing resinous woods.

### 3.3. Processing siliceous hard wood and hard palms

The most recognisable and frequent wear features on tools used for processing siliceous hard wood and hard palms are the heavily scarred working edges, patches of intensive edge rounding, patches of well-developed, smooth and flattened polish, densely packed and shallow and short striations. The formation of diagnostic wear on experimental tools involved in processing similar plant materials occurred very quickly. Tools can be most effective during the first 5 to 15 minutes of use, and after 15 minutes of work, the efficiency of tools usually dropped significantly, although some were relatively efficient for up to 30 minutes. The comparison between wear patterns on artefacts and experimental tools indicates that the prehistoric tools used to process siliceous hard wood and palm were only used for a short period of time. Plant tissue and starch residues are common on these tools.

### 3.4. Processing non-siliceous hard wood

Tools used for working non-siliceous hard wood are characterised by intensive scarring which is continuously distributed along their edges, and by patches of pronounced edge rounding and light to developed polish. Isolated, long and deep striations are seen, in contrast to densely packed and shallow striations observed on tools used for processing siliceous hard plant. Residues are common on woodworking implements. They are represented by plant tissue and in some cases starch grains. Reliable diagnostic wear in the form of intense edge scarring and patches of rounding, light and developed polish and isolated striations appear on experimental tools after 15 to 20 minutes of use in working non-siliceous hard wood. Further use of the tool is inefficient although the wear pattern on the edge may be more pronounced after 30 minutes of use. This indicates that prehistoric artefacts were usually used for a short duration of time when involved in processing hard and non-siliceous woody plants.

### 3.5. Processing non-woody plants (tubers)

The set of wear variables observed on tools used for processing non-woody plants such as tubers includes: (1) less intensive edge fracturing by small and very small bending and feathered scars, (2) low and moderate density of long, deep, shallow, and well separated striations, (3) medium and intensive edge rounding, and, (4) developed and well-developed slightly merging polish distributed relatively continuously along the edge (Figure 2: A). These attributes of wear are comparable with experimental data which also demonstrate that a diagnostic combination of wear variables can form on tools after more than 30 minutes of use for processing tubers. It is reasonable to propose that tools for processing tubers were used for much longer time periods than the woodworking implements because most of the tools examined have identifiable wear variables. Prehistoric tools often preserved plant tissue, starch grains and raphides (Figure 2: B).

### 3.6. Processing non-woody plants (greens): leaves, stems and grasses

Wear patterns on tools used for working greens by cutting, scraping and slicing have some peculiarities in comparison with those involved in processing tubers. Firstly, there is slight edge damage usually in the form of small scars and microscars on tools used on working greens. Scars are often distributed in a discontinuous manner. Secondly, a few to a low number of shallow, slightly diagonal, parallel or crossed striations can be seen. Finally, the used edges are usually very slightly or slightly rounded. The surface alteration by light polish on tools is less extensive and the polish does not have a merging appearance. The comparison between wear attributes on experimental tools which were used for processing greens and the artefacts from the sites indicates similarities in wear patterns. These similarities make it possible to suggest that some prehistoric tools could have been involved in the performance of tasks similar to those for which experimental tools were used in processing greens. Experiments with working greens by obsidian flakes demonstrate that, only after 30 minutes, a combined set of scars, striations, rounding and polish is formed that is distinctive of the mode of use and, to a lesser extent, the material worked. Similarities in wear patterns, however, do not exclude some specific differences in polish development and the type and appearance of striations on tools used: for instance, in the extraction coconut meat or the processing of croton or ginger (Kononenko 2011:30-32). However, in the archaeological context, such peculiarities of wear patterns on the tools are difficult to correlate precisely to the particular species of plant processed unless diagnostic residues are present. Therefore, artefacts with wear patterns similar to experimental tools, were considered as a group of implements used for working non-woody plants and named "greens" and which included leaves, green stems and grasses.

### 3.7. Processing soft elastic material (fish and skin)

Tools used for *gutting/cutting fish* are characterized by small or very small scars and microscars which are distributed continuously along the edge. Medium rounded edges preserved patches of smooth, light and developed polish which is visible as a thin line on both faces of the edge profile. The polish extended from the higher peaks

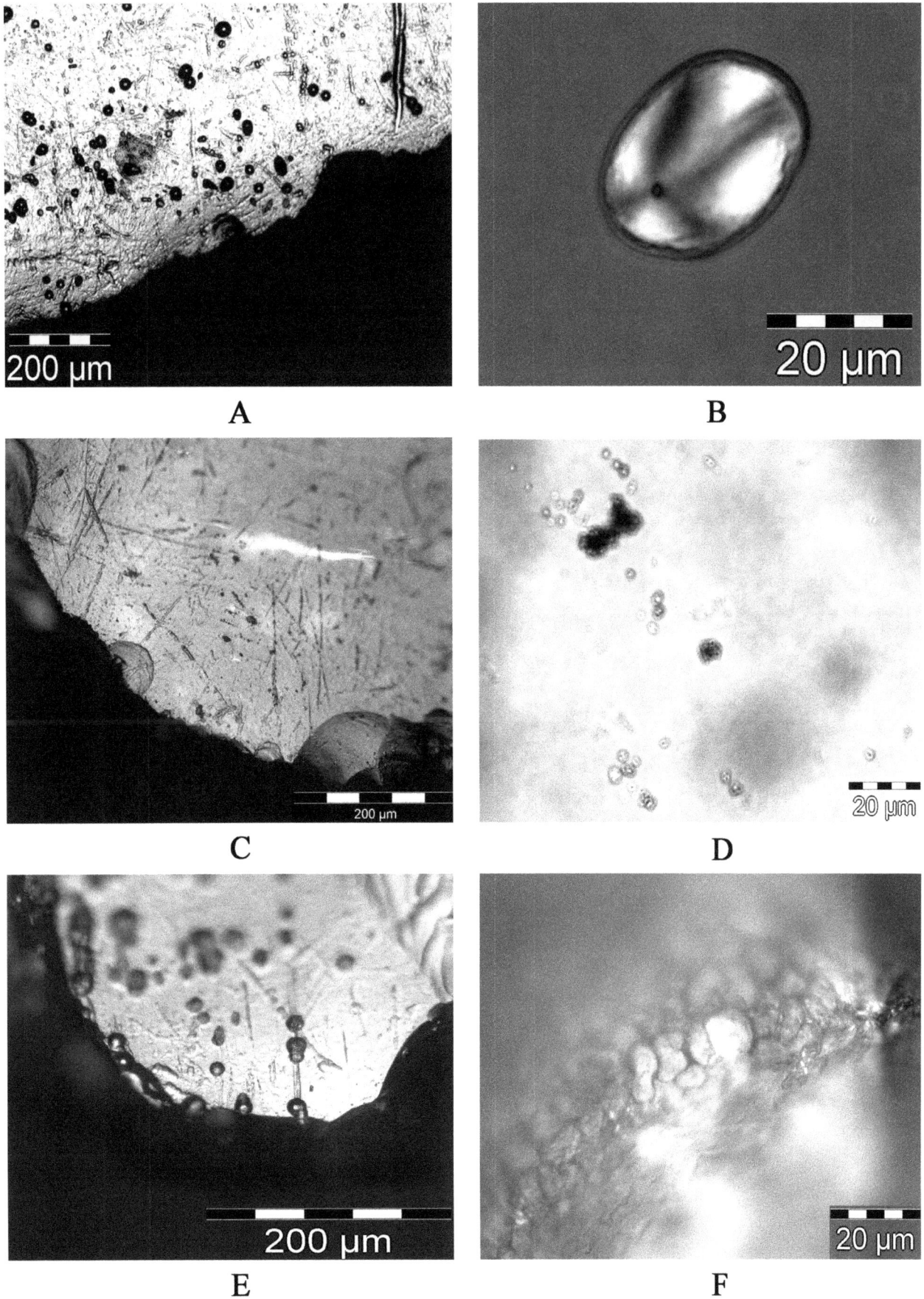

Figure 2 – Wear patterns and residues on artefacts used for processing tubers (A-B), fish (C-D) and skin (E-F): A – cutting/slicing tubers (100x), B – starch grain extracted from the working edge of the artefacts used for cutting/slicing tubers (1000x), C – gutting/cutting fish (200x), D – blood cells with nuclei extracted from the tool used for processing fish (1000x), E – piercing soft skin (200x), F – blood residues on the surface of the skin-working tool (1000x)

of the microtopography into surface depressions. Smoothed and polished areas are associated with isolated, parallel or slightly diagonal and intersecting long striations which reflect a relatively wide range of motions (Figure 2: C). Distinctive residues on fish working tools include blood from which blood cells with nuclei were extracted (Figure 2: D), animal tissue and white, black and rainbow coloured residues. These distinctive wear patterns and residues on the archaeological flakes are comparable with those produced on experimental tools used for processing fish. More than 30 minutes of use is required to produce identifiable wear patterns, although surface alteration by scars and sometimes striations becomes visible after 10-15 minutes.

The working edges of tools used for *piercing skin* usually exhibit irregular and discontinuous microscars on the tip and along adjacent edges. A thin line of slight to medium edge rounding and patches of light to developed smoothed polish can be observed under more than 200x magnification. Striations are much less common and are mostly represented by isolated, long and shallow sleeks which are orientated slightly diagonally or are perpendicular to the tip (Figure 2: E), indicating penetrating motions. Blood-like residues are often embedded into the working edge and observed as thinly smeared, highly reflective films, or as a thicker film with polygonal cracking (Figure 2: F). These residues gave a weak positive reaction for blood to the presumptive test, Hemastix[TM]. Red cells extracted from blood residues on the tools have a circular outline and contain no nuclei and, therefore, indicate that the blood residue is of mammalian origin. Experiments involving piercing chicken skin, as a suitable substitute for human tissue, produce wear patterns similar to piercing artefacts. It is possible to suggest that obsidian artefacts identified as having been used for piercing and cutting soft skin which also preserved mammal blood residue could have been utilized in the performance of some special tasks related to the human body, such as tattooing and scarification. From ethnographic records, it is known that sharp obsidian pieces were used for blood-letting by skin cutting, trephination, hair cutting, circumcision, tattooing, scarification and shaving (*cf. ref in* Kononenko 2012). These activities are an integral aspect of social behaviour among peoples in the Pacific region and were probably established at least 5,000 years ago. According to experimental data, the formation of identifiable wear patterns on tools used for piercing and cutting soft skin requires at least 30 minutes of use. This means that examined prehistoric artefacts with similar wear must have been used for a similar task for a relatively long period and so they should be assessed as having had moderate to long-term use-life.

Wear pattern on artefacts used *for shaving* the human face is characterised by few micro- and small scars which are distributed in a discontinuous fashion on one side of the edge. A thin line of light edge rounding and very rare spots of smoothed, merging, light polish are visible under high magnifications. A few perpendicular and slightly diagonal long, isolated striations can be seen under 200x

and higher magnifications. Residues similar to skin tissue, as well as red, white and black residues are often observed on some spots on the edge. The shaving experiments demonstrate the limited ability of use-wear analysis to identify artefacts used to shave human skin. However, in conjunction with residue studies, it may be possible to make a tentative identification of the most intensively used artefacts. The men who performed the experiments (Figure 1: B) noted that flakes with thin and sharp edges are efficient for this task for only a very short time (2 to 5 minutes) before the edges became blunted.

### 3.8. Processing dense, hard materials (shell and clay)

Tools used for sawing and *scraping shell* exhibit the thick working edges which are intensively damaged by continuous, bending and step scars with poor defined boundaries because of the crushing effect. The edge profile of these tools is rough and intensively rounded. The working surfaces are covered with dense and mainly shallow and short striations having been flattened by well-developed polish, but this polish does not extend into the surface depressions. Some white coloured residues are embedded into the edge surface. This pattern of wear and residues is similar to that observed on experimental tools used for sawing and scraping shell.

As with shell-working implements, the edge of the tools used for *scraping clay* is extensively damaged by small, step and bending scars with poorly defined boundaries. The intensively rounded edge profile contains patches of well-developed polish which, in contrast to the polish on the shell-working tool, has a more smooth and flattened appearance. There are also some differences in the types of striations. They are mostly long and shallow sleeks indicating the working of more abrasive material than shell. White and yellow coloured residues are embedded into the working surfaces. The comparison of wear variables observed on these artefacts with experimental tools used for scraping of half-dry white clay shows close similarities in wear patterns and residues. Experimental tools used for working shell and clay produce similar wear patterns during first five to 10 minutes. After 15 minutes of use, the efficiency of the tools dramatically decreases and they are discarded. This suggests a short-term use of the late and middle Holocene artefacts which were involved in processing shells and clay.

## 4. DISCUSSION

It is apparent from the comparative analysis of functional data obtained from prehistoric artefacts and experimental tools that the set of activities undertaken and resources utilised in Melanesia were generally similar for both middle and late Holocene periods. Functional identification of obsidian tool assemblages demonstrates a wide range of economic and social activities which were performed by the inhabitants. Tools were involved in subsistence practices, particularly, food processing (fish and tubers), domestic activities (manufacturing items from woody plants and shells), and social activities, such as human body modification by tattooing, scarification and shaving.

Since the experimental data substantiate an obvious relationship between wear formation and duration of use, they provide a valuable basis for a general assessment of the use-life history of prehistoric obsidian artefacts and, by inference, past discard behaviour. The approximate estimation for the length of time prehistoric artefacts were used can be defined as: (1) short term and intensive use for less than 15 minutes generating identifiable wear patterns resulting from working hard siliceous palms, wood and hard dense materials, (2) moderate use which suggests a use-time of between 15 and 30 minutes during which well-developed wear variables are formed on palm and woodworking tools and identifiable wear occurs on tools involved in processing non-woody plants and soft elastic materials, and (3) long-term use which can be determined by the presence of relatively developed wear patterns in association with sharp and still useable working edges, as observed on the tools used for 30 and more minutes for processing soft elastic materials (Kononenko 2011:38-40). These results made it possible to come to the conclusion that with rare exceptions, obsidian artefacts in Melanesia were expediently used for short periods of time as single purpose tools in both the middle and late Holocene periods.

There are some methodological issues with use-wear and residue analysis of obsidian artefacts which have to be addressed. The efficiency of identification of wear patterns on obsidian artefacts depends strongly on the extent of surface preservation. Obsidian is a fragile raw material and can be altered easily by both physical and chemical processes which can greatly reduce the opportunity for an accurate functional definition of used tools (Hurcomber 1992:24). However, by combining data on types of wear attributes and residues, the mode of use and, to a lesser extent, the material worked can generally be determined even on tools with altered surfaces.

One of the distinct features of post-depositional edge damage visible on archaeological obsidian flakes is the irregular nature of the distribution of scars with very fresh flaked surfaces that clearly contrast with other parts of the artefact. Scars can be easily observed under low magnification and therefore cannot be confused with use-wear attributes. Chemical damage of obsidian surfaces, in the form of numerous, roughly hemi-spherical pits which are unequally distributed on the surface, was observed on all obsidian artefacts but to differing degrees. Sometimes the surface may be so greatly altered that any use-wear definition is impossible. Many used artefacts, however, preserve patterned edge scarring and striations (Figure 1: D). These striations may change from sleek to intermittent forms and can become oval depressions and pits (Hurcomber 1992:81). Pits that are arranged in lines may indicate the direction of etched striations and may assist in the definition of the mode of use.

Some artefacts with heavily altered surfaces have spots on the edge with well preserved and distinctive use-wear

characteristics and residues. The residues are attached and embedded into the surface and act as protective cover against chemical etching (Kononenko 2011:38).

These residues are often observed on artefacts and have good potential for further identification of the material worked (Figure 1: E).

Although the degree of chemical damage may vary on each artefact, there is often a relationship between the degree of surface alteration and age. The surfaces of most late Holocene tools in Melanesia are medium or low pitted (Figures 1C and 1F). In contrast, tools with heavy and medium pitted surfaces dominate in the middle Holocene (Figures 1D and 2A). This observation suggests that the surface alteration may act as an additional chronological indicator for stone assemblages found in similar environmental conditions.

## 5. CONCLUSION

Microscopic analysis of wear attributes, including scarring, rounding, striations, abrasion, polish, and residues, determined the mode of use, materials processed and the duration of the use-life of tools used by prehistoric inhabitants in Melanesia. The results of the study demonstrate, firstly, that obsidian tools were used by middle and late Holocene population for working a variety of tropical plant and non-plant resources. A range of materials (palms, soft and hard wood, bamboo, leaves, stems, grasses, tubers, fish, shell and clay) was worked using various modes of use, including scraping, sawing, whittling, carving, drilling, cutting, slicing, peeling and piercing. Secondly, non-modified obsidian flakes were single purpose tools mainly for short-term use and, to a lesser extent, used for moderate periods of time. This demonstrates obvious expedient tool use strategies adopted by both the middle and late Holocene inhabitants of Melanesia. Finally, the mode of use and the material worked can generally be determined even on tools with altered surfaces by combining data on types of wear attributes and preserved residues. In some cases, preserved residues on the working edges are the only signs of tool use and, in association with morphological features of the tool, allow the identification its function. This indicates the importance of microscopic analysis of both residues and wear patterns present on prehistoric stone artefacts in the investigation of lithic assemblages.

### Acknowledgements

I offer thanks to the Australian Museum for providing laboratory equipment and assistance, Australian National University Scholarship for funding my PhD project and Mahonia na Dari Research centre, Kimbe, West New Britain for assistance with my experimental research. My thanks are extended to R. Torrence, J. Specht, P. White, S. Bedford, J.C. Galipaud, C. Reepmeyer and R. Fullagar who provided access to collections of artefacts, assistance and valuable advice in this research. I am especially grateful to R. Torrence, P. White and J. Rannard for their comments and editing of earlier drafts. Support was received from the Australian Research council Discovery-Project Grant (DP0986004) and the University of Sydney.

## References

ANDERSON, P.C. 1980. A testimony of prehistoric tasks: diagnostic residues on stone tool working edges. *World Archaeology* 12(2):181-194.

ANDERSON-GERFAUD, P. 1990. Aspects of behaviour in the Middle Paleolithic: functional analysis of stone tools from Southwest France. In *The Emergence of Modern Humans*, ed. P. Mellars, p. 389-419. Edinburgh: Edinburgh University Press.

BARTON, H.; TORRENCE, R. & FULLAGAR, R. 1998. Clues to stone tool function re-examined: comparing starch grain frequencies on used and unused obsidian artefacts. *Journal of Archaeological Science* 25: 1231-1238.

BRIUER, F.L. 1976. New clues to stone tool function: plant and animal residues. *American Antiquity* 41(4): 478-484.

DAVID, J.E.; CASTLE, S.K.B. & MOSSI, K.M. 2006. Localization tattoos: An alternative method using fluorescent inks. *Radiation Therapist* 15(1): 1-5.

FULLAGAR, R. 1991. The role of silica in polish formation. *Journal of Archaeological Science* 18: 1-25.

FULLAGAR, R. 1994. Objectives for use-wear and residue studies: view from an Australian microscope. *Helinium* 34(2): 210-22.

FULLAGAR, R. 1998. Use-wear, residue and lithic technology. In *A Closer Look. Recent Australian Studies of Stone Tools*, ed. R. Fullagar, p. 13-17. Sydney: Archaeological Computing Laboratory, University of Sydney.

FULLAGAR, R. 2006a. Residue and use-wear. In *Archaeology in Practice: a Student Guide to Archaeological Analysis*, ed. J. Balme and A. Paterson, pp. 207-234. Oxford: Blackwell Publishing.

FULLAGAR, R. 2006b. Starch on artefacts. In *Ancient Starch Research*, ed. R. Torrence and H. Barton, pp. 177-203. Walnut Creek: Left Coast Press.

FULLAGAR, R.; LOY, T. & COX, S. 1998. Starch grains, sediments and stone tool function: evidence from Bitokara, Papua New Guinea. In *A Closer Look. Recent Australian Studies of Stone Tools*, ed. R. Fullagar, pp. 50-60. Sydney: Archaeological Computing Laboratory, University of Sydney.

HASLAM, M. & LISTON, J. 2008. The use of flaked stone artifacts in Palau, Western Micronesia. *Asian Perspectives* 47(2): 405-428.

HÖGBERG, A.; PUSEMAN, K. & YOST, C. 2009. Integration of use-wear with protein residue analysis—a study of tool use and function in the south Scandinavian Early Neolithic. *Journal of Archaeological Science* 36: 1725-1737.

HURCOMBE, L.M. 1992. *Use Wear Analysis and Obsidian: Theory, Experiments and Results*. Sheffield Archaeological Monographs 4. Dorset: Dorset Press. 226 p.

KAMMINGA, J. 1982. *Over the Edge. Functional Analysis of Australian Stone Tools*. Occasional Papers in Anthropology 12. St Lucia: Anthropology Museum, University of Queensland. 198 p.

KEALHOFER, L.; TORRENCE, R. & FULLAGAR, R. 1999. Integrating phytoliths within use-wear/residue studies of stone tools. *Journal of Archaeological Science* 26: 527-546.

KEELEY, L.H. 1980. *Experimental Determination of Stone Tool Uses*. Chicago: University of Chicago Press. 212 p.

KONONENKO, N. 2011. Experimental and archaeological studies of use-wear and residues on obsidian artefacts from Papua New Guinea. *Technical Reports of the Australian Museum, Online* 21. 244 p. http://dx.doi.org/10.3853/j.1835-4211.21.2011.1559.

KONONENKO, N. 2012. Middle and late Holocene skin-working tools in Melanesia: Tattooing and scarification? *Archaeology in Oceania* 47:14-28.

LOMBARD, M. & WADLEY, L. 2007. The morphological identification of micro-residues on stone tools using light microscopy: progress and difficulties based on blind test. *Journal of Archaeological Science* 34: 155-165.

LOY, T.H. 1983. Prehistoric blood residue: detection on tool surfaces and identification of species of origin. *Science* 220: 1269-1271.

LOY, T.H. 2006. Raphides. In *Ancient Starch Research*, ed. R. Torrence and H. Barton, p. 136-137. Walnut Creek: Left Coast Press.

LOY, T.H.; SPRIGGS, M. & WICKLER, S. 1992. Direct evidence for human use of plants 28,000 years ago: Starch residues on stone artefacts from the northern Solomon Islands. *Antiquity* 66: 898-912.

PETRAGLIA, M.; KNEPPER, D.; NEWMAN, P. & SUSSMAN, C. 1996. Immunological and microwear analysis of chipped-stone artefacts from Piedmont contexts. *American Antiquity* 61(1): 127-135.

ROBERTSON, G.; ATTENBROW, V. & HISCOCK, P. 2009. Multiple uses for Australian backed artefacts. *Antiquity* 83: 296-308.

ROTS, V. & WILLIAMSON, B.S. 2004. Microwear and Residue Analysis in Perspective: the Contribution of Ethnoarchaeological Evidence. *Journal of Archaeological Science* 31:1287-1299.

SEMENOV, S.A. 1964. *Prehistoric Technology: An Experimental Study of the Oldest Tools and Artefacts from Traces of Manufacture and Wear*. London: Cory Adams & Mackay. 230 p.

SHAFER, H.J.; HOLLOWAY, R.G. 1979. Organic residue analysis in determining stone tool function. In *Lithic Use-Wear Analysis*, ed. B. Hayden, pp. 385-399. New York: Academic Press.

TORRENCE, R. 2002. Cultural landscapes on Garua Island, Papua New Guinea. *Antiquity* 76: 766-776.

VAUGHAN, P. 1985. *Use-wear Analysis of Flaked Stone Tools*. Tucson: University of Arizona Press. 204 p.

# EL ANÁLISIS FUNCIONAL DE MATERIAS PRIMAS HETEROGÉNEAS Y SU APLICACIÓN A DIFERENTES VARIEDADES DE CUARCITAS DE LA REGIÓN PAMPEANA (ARGENTINA): RESULTADOS EXPERIMENTALES Y ARQUEOLÓGICOS

Marcela LEIPUS

Facultad de Ciencias Naturales y Museo, Universidad Nacional de La Plata, 1900 La Plata, Argentina
mleipus@hotmail.com

**Abstract**: *This paper presents the results obtained from application of microscopic functional analysis methodology to quartzitic raw materials from the Pampas region (Argentina), both experimental series and archaeological tools from three sites. The study enabled to characterize qualities of the edges when they are used in different utilization processes. Concerning the archaeological artifacts, microscopic analysis revealed that they were used on diverse materials and with different kinematics. It was concluded that there was not a specific relationship between utilization and raw material or tool type. This variability suggests that quartzites could have been selected to make versatile and durable artifacts, as a part of a conserved technologic strategy.*

**Key words**: *Pampas region, technofunctional analysis, raw materials, quartzite*

**Résumé**: *Dans cet article nous présentons les résultats obtenus à partir de l'application de la méthodologie d'analyse fonctionnelle microscopique aux matières premières quartzitiques de la région de la Pampa (Argentine), tant pièces expérimentales qu'outils archéologiques provenant de trois sites. Cette étude a permis de caractériser les qualités des tranchants lorsqu'ils sont utilisés en divers processus d'utilisation. Concernant les outils archéologiques, l'analyse microscopique révèle qu'ils ont été utilisés sur des matériaux divers et avec différentes cinématiques. Nous avons conclu qu'il n'a pas existé de spécificité fonctionnelle en ce qui concerne la relation entre utilisation et matière première ou catégorie morphotechnique. Cette diversité suggère que les quartzites ont été choisies pour faire des outils versatiles et durables, comme partie d'une stratégie technologique conservée.*

**Mots clés**: *Pampa, analyse technofonctionnelle, matières premières, quarzites*

## 1. INTRODUCCION

La región pampeana es una llanura extensa ubicada al Este de la República Argentina entre los 31° y los 39° de Lat. Sur. Tradicionalmente ha sido dividida en dos subregiones denominadas "Pampa Húmeda" o "Pampa Oriental", y Pampa Seca" o "Pampa Occidental", siguiendo la isohieta de los 600 mm. Tiene su límite oriental en los ríos Paraná y De La Plata y el Océano Atlántico (Fig. 1).

Incluye aproximadamente 600.000 $km^2$ de praderas y planicies herbáceas con pendientes de gradiente muy bajo y dos conjuntos de cordones serranos de baja altitud (hasta 1.200 msnm), Sistemas de Tandilia y Ventania. Hay numerosas lagunas de agua dulce y/o salobre, los ríos son escasos, la gran mayoría de cauce ondulante y lento. Gran parte está cubierta de depósitos potentes de loess de edad pleistocénica y holocénica, a partir de los cuales se desarrollaron suelos en diferentes períodos del Cuaternario.

Se conocen tres áreas de abastecimiento de materias primas líticas: los dos sistemas serranos (Tandilia y Ventania) y la costa atlántica, a las cuales se suman algunos afloramientos menores entre ambos cordones serranos. La base de recursos líticos pampeanos se caracteriza por las diversas variedades de rocas y porque las rocas útiles se localizan en sectores discretos del paisaje (Flegenheimer y Bayón 2001).

Las rocas más utilizadas a escala regional son las ortocuarcitas de la Fm. Sierras Bayas, del sistema de Tandilia. Son rocas de buena calidad para la talla, para las cuales se detectaron grandes áreas de aprovisionamiento con un uso espacial y temporal amplio (Flegenheimer y Bayón 2001; Flegenheimer *et al.* 1996; Bayón *et al.* 1999). Otras rocas utilizadas, pero de manera secundaria, son las metacuarcitas procedentes de los depósitos gravosos del sistema de Ventania, que se presentan en forma de rodados. Otras materias primas, tales como dolomías silicificadas, ftanitas y riolitas, fueron empleadas de forma mayoritariamente local y secundariamente a nivel regional y areal. Las dos primeras afloran en sectores del sistema de Tandilia y la riolita en el sistema de Ventania. Son materias primas que predominan en las zonas de abastecimiento, apareciendo de manera minoritaria en los sitios de la región. Otras materias primas del sistema de Tandilia son los cuarzos del basamento cristalino, los cuales generalmente fueron empleados en forma secundaria. En el área Interserrana, se han localizado afloramientos de metacuarcitas, rocas vinculadas al sistema de Ventania (Flegenheimer y Bayón 2001). Por último, la franja costera de la región, está conformada por depósitos secundarios de rodados volcánicos de diversas rocas, principalmente basaltos,

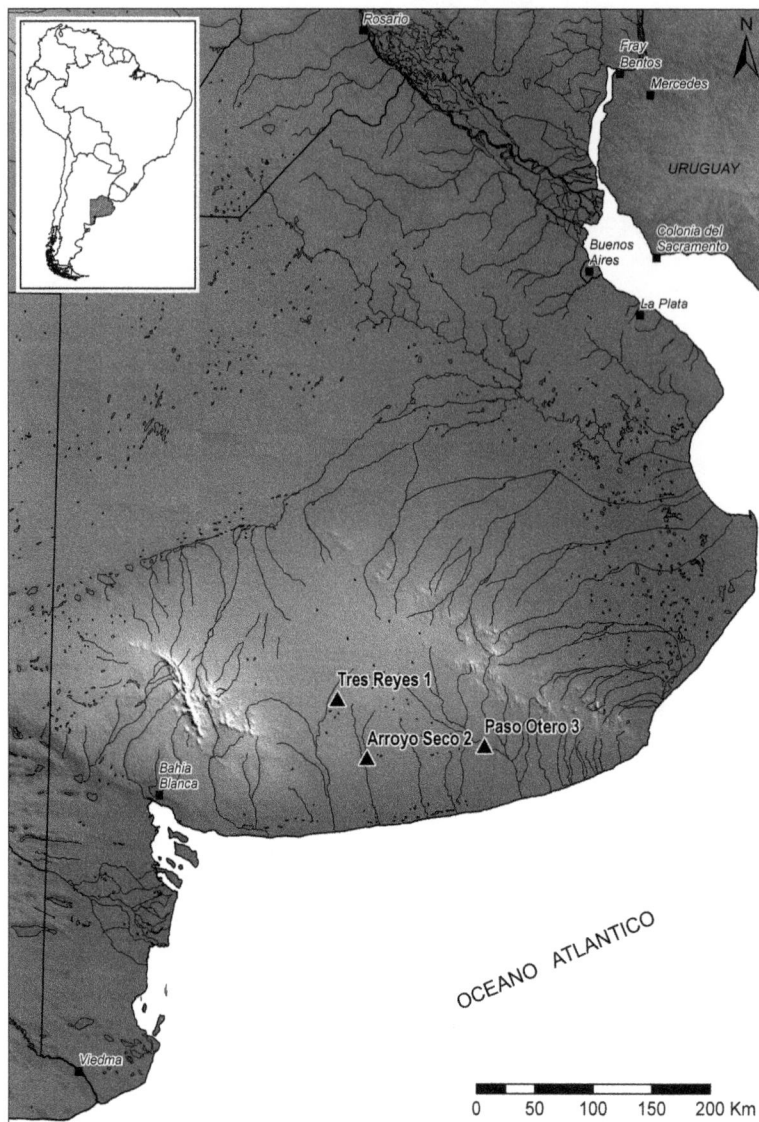

*Figura 1 – Localización de la región Pampeana, zonas de abastecimiento
de materias primas y de los sitios arqueológicos*

riolitas y andesitas. Estos fueron trabajados *in situ* pero también frecuentemente fueron trasladados al interior (Bonomo 2005; Flegenheimer y Bayón 2001).

En general, estas materias primas de origen sedimentario, ígneo y metamórfico, formadas por cristales y matriz de cimentación, son denominadas "heterogéneas" (cf. infra). El estudio de los conjuntos arqueológicos reveló que estas rocas heterogéneas fueron talladas en su gran mayoría por percusión a mano alzada, para confeccionar diversos tipos de instrumentos, entre los cuales predominan los filos largos. Al contrario, las materias primas silíceas criptocristalinas (sedimentitas químicas o ftanitas) tienden a ser empleadas para la confección de instrumentos con filos cortos (principalmente raspadores) (Leipus 2006; Leipus y Mansur 2007). Estas opciones tecnológicas podrían guardar relación con criterios de disponibilidad, ya que las sedimentitas químicas criptocristalinas parecen ser menos abundantes y/o de más difícil localización. Pero también es cierto que la utilización de uno u otro tipo de materia prima podría

guardar relación con criterios tecnológicos y/o funcionales, tales como la implementación de técnicas de talla particulares o la producción de filos destinados a actividades específicas (Leipus 2006, Leipus y Mansur 2007). Por ello, se decidió encarar un primer acercamiento a la organización tecnológica desde el enfoque del análisis tecnofuncional de los materiales.

A fin de determinar los usos particulares de los instrumentos líticos, empleamos el marco teórico-metodológico del análisis funcional de base microscópica (*sensu* Semenov 1964, *cf. ref in* Mansur 1999), que explica las características particulares de los rastros microscópicos resultantes de diferentes procesos de confección, de uso y de alteración en contextos sedimentarios y tafonómicos diversos. Los diferentes tipos de rastros microscópicos generados por estos procesos son descriptos en función de criterios de análisis y variables que nos permiten compararlos con los observados en diferentes materias primas (véase Mansur 1986, 1999 y bibliografía allí citada).

## 2. CARACTERISTICAS GENERALES DE LAS CUARCITAS PAMPEANAS

Las materias primas cuarcíticas son rocas sedimentarias conformadas por cristales de cuarzo de diversos tamaños, cementados por una pasta o matriz silícea, que puede ser microcristalina, criptocristalina o amorfa. Entre las cuarcitas utilizadas en la región pampeana existen distintas variedades, que difieren entre sí en cuanto a la resistencia de los filos naturales y retocados en diferentes procesos de uso, la velocidad de desarrollo de los rastros de uso, las características particulares de los rastros producidos por el trabajo sobre diversos materiales y los procesos de desarrollo de alteraciones postdeposicionales y tecnológicas (Leipus 1999, 2006, Mansur 1991, 1999).

La caracterización de las cuarcitas pampeanas fue efectuada por el equipo de investigación dirigido por las Lics. Bayón y Flegenheimer (Bayón *et al.* 1999; Flegenheimer *et al.* 1996), en trabajos que incluyeron el análisis de sus características litológicas, procedencia, estudios de afloramientos y canteras y formas de abastecimiento y traslado de las rocas, etc. El estudio de diversas variedades de cuarcitas procedentes de afloramientos de Tandilia y Ventania permitió poner en evidencia las diferencias petrográficas entre ambas series, una correspondiente a ortocuarcitas (localizadas en la zona de Tandilia) y la otra a metacuarcitas (zona de Ventania) (Bayón *et al.* 1999).

Las ortocuarcitas están compuestas por más de un 95% de cristales de cuarzo de tamaño arena, cimentados por una matriz generalmente silícea; estas características les confieren dureza y tenacidad. El contacto entre los granos puede ser directo, a través de un crecimiento secundario, o a través de la matriz de cimentación. Las metacuarcitas son rocas de naturaleza primaria ortocuarcítica, pero que sufrieron transformaciones por metamorfismo, de tal forma que sus caracteres originales han variado: los granos de cuarzo se han molido y recristalizado, han cambiado sus tamaños y se han orientado tectónicamente. No presentan cemento y no tienen crecimiento secundario de los cristales de cuarzo; su grado de cohesión se debe a un proceso de recristalización. A partir del análisis petrográfico es posible diferenciarlas debido a que las metacuarcitas presentan bandas de deformación de los cristales originales y mortero de recristalización entre los cristales originales; las ortocuarcitas en cambio tienen cristales con crecimiento secundario y granos originales sin deformación (Bayón *et al.* 1999). Estas diferencias estructurales entre ambas también pueden reconocerse cuando se realizan análisis microscópicos de las superficies de fractura en microscopía de reflexión. Observadas a 200x, las ortocuarcitas presentan cristales de cuarzo grandes y abundantes en una matriz apenas perceptible, en tanto que las metacuarcitas muestran cristales más pequeños y abundante mortero de recristalización (Fig. 2 a y b) (Leipus 2006).

Ambos tipos de cuarcita difieren entre sí en sus cualidades para la talla, que se relacionan principalmente con dos propiedades de los materiales: tipo de fractura y tenacidad. El tipo de fractura concoidea está estrechamente vinculado con el grado de silicificación de la matriz. Cuando la cementación de los granos es completa, la roca se comporta como un cuerpo homogéneo; en tal caso el tamaño de los cristales de cuarzo no es relevante en relación a su calidad para la talla. Al contrario, cuando la roca ha sufrido procesos metamórficos, las anisotropías producidas por tales procesos dificultan su previsibilidad. Así, las metacuarcitas del macizo de Ventania, son menos predecibles y más tenaces; cuando son talladas con percutor duro, se fracturan formando charnelas y presentan un aspecto "escamoso". Las ortocuarcitas de Tandilia, específicamente las del Grupo Sierras Bayas, en cambio, presentan mayor grado de cohesión entre cristales y matriz de cimentación, lo cual les confiere características de fractura concoidea que hace que se tallen bien, mediante percutor duro o blando y también por presión, aunque al ser rocas tenaces, muchas veces puede resultar difícil (Bayón *et al.* 1999).

Se han localizado diferentes fuentes de aprovisionamiento, tanto primarias como secundarias, en los sistemas serranos de Ventania y Tandilia. En el primero fuentes primarias de abastecimiento de metacuarcitas, así como de fuentes secundarias en los valles fluviales y en la costa atlántica. En Tandilia, se detectaron varias canteras de ortocuarcitas correspondientes a las Cuarcitas Superiores de la Fm. Sierras Bayas (canteras del Arroyo Diamante y La Numancia) (Flegenheimer *et al.* 1996). También se ha detectado un caso de aprovisionamiento en un afloramiento de ortocuarcitas de la Fm. Balcarce en Cueva Tixi (Mazzanti 1993).

En base a los resultados de tales investigaciones, se ha postulado que las cuarcitas de buena calidad son abundantes pero que su disponibilidad se encuentra restringida a un área específica. Ello podría generar un patrón de selección de la cuarcita por calidad, con un desperdicio importante de material en la cantera y una maximización de la materia prima en regiones más distantes (Flegenheimer *et al.* 1996).

## 3. EL ANÁLISIS FUNCIONAL DE MATERIALES CUARCÍTICOS. LOS RASTROS MICROSCÓPICOS EN ROCAS CUARCÍTICAS PAMPEANAS

El análisis funcional de base microscópica aplicado a materiales experimentales confeccionados en materias primas cuarcíticas permitió generar un modelo sobre las modificaciones superficiales de los materiales y proponer modos de análisis particulares para diferentes materias primas líticas, teniendo en cuenta su variabilidad estructural y composicional así como la forma en que reaccionan al ser sometidas a experimentos de utilización, alteración o tecnológicos (Mansur 1991, 1999). En ese marco, se denomina "materias primas heterogéneas" a las formadas por una matriz generalmente micro o criptocristalina de composición variable y cristales

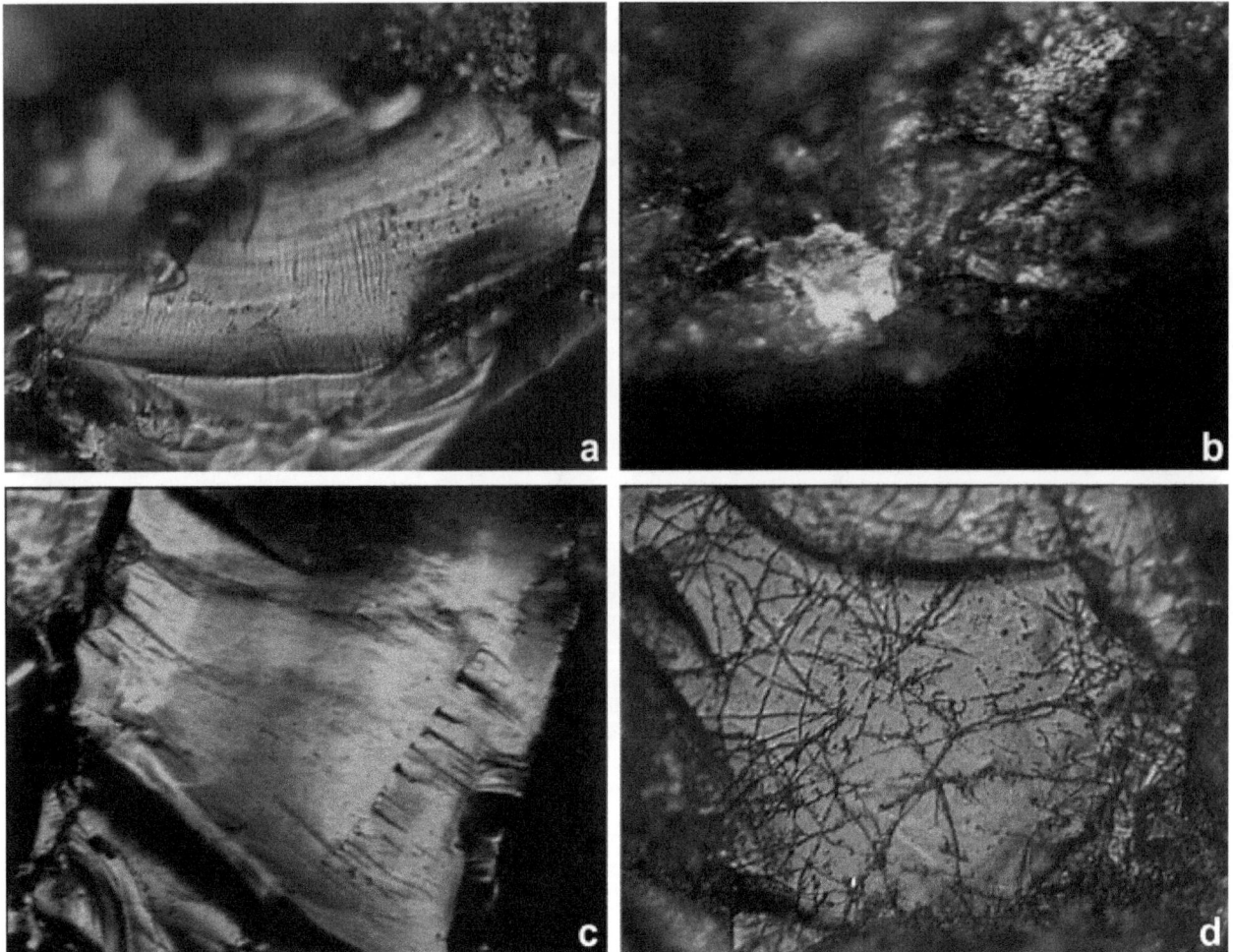

*Figura 2 – Superficies de Piezas sin uso, 200x: a) Ortocuarcita; b) Metacuarcita;*
*c) Rastros tecnológicos; d) Alteración postdepositacional*

incluidos en esa matriz. Entre las llamadas "homogéneas", se destacan dos tipos básicos, el de los materiales amorfos, como la obsidiana, y los cristalinos, como el cuarzo hialino. En los materiales heterogéneos, matriz y cristales reaccionan de modo diferente y en consecuencia el enfoque del análisis microscópico de rastros de uso debe considerar criterios diferentes a los que se utilizan para analizar materias primas "homogéneas". En este trabajo se ha empleado el enfoque que implica un análisis mixto analizando de modo complementario las alteraciones producidas sobre la matriz y sobre la superficie de fractura de los cristales de cuarzo (Alonso Lima y Mansur 1986/90, Mansur 1999, Clemente 1995).

Para el análisis de las cuarcitas se tomó como referencia el marco teórico-metodológico del análisis funcional de base microscópica y los resultados del estudio de series experimentales confeccionadas en materiales locales (cf. Mansur 1999; Leipus 2006). Los criterios y variables se refieren a diferentes clases de rastros: esquirlamiento y microesquirlamiento de los filos, alisamiento o redondeamiento, estrías microscópicas y micropulidos. Las diferentes posibilidades y combinaciones de estos rastros permiten diferenciar a los producidos por factores tecnológicos, funcionales o post-depositacionales.

Los rastros tecnológicos son aquellos generados durante el proceso de manufactura de los artefactos. La percusión produce rompimientos y estrías oscuras perpendiculares u oblicuas al filo, ubicadas sobre la cara opuesta al retoque. Se caracterizan por su fondo rugoso, aspecto oscuro y por ser más grandes (en ancho y en largo) que las estrías de uso. Los filos pueden a veces presentar fracturas involuntarias y esquirlamiento, así como microesquirla- miento detectable a escala microscópica.

Sobre las superficies de fractura de los cristales se observan los rasgos tecnológicos característicos: ondas concéntricas y estrías tecnológicas que convergen hacia el punto de percusión y/o presión, y rasgos en forma de cometa con una o dos prolongaciones en el sentido del desplazamiento de la fuerza (Mansur 1999) (Fig. 2 c).

Durante el uso, la modificación de las superficies y biseles del filo afecta tanto a las caras de fractura de los cristales como a la matriz. En los cristales, la modificación comienza por un desdibujado gradual de los rasgos tecnológicos, hasta su casi total desaparición, y un alisamiento general de las superficies, acompañado por la modificación de los bordes del cristal. En un estadio más avanzado, estas modificaciones se acentúan y las caras de fractura adoptan aspectos característicos según

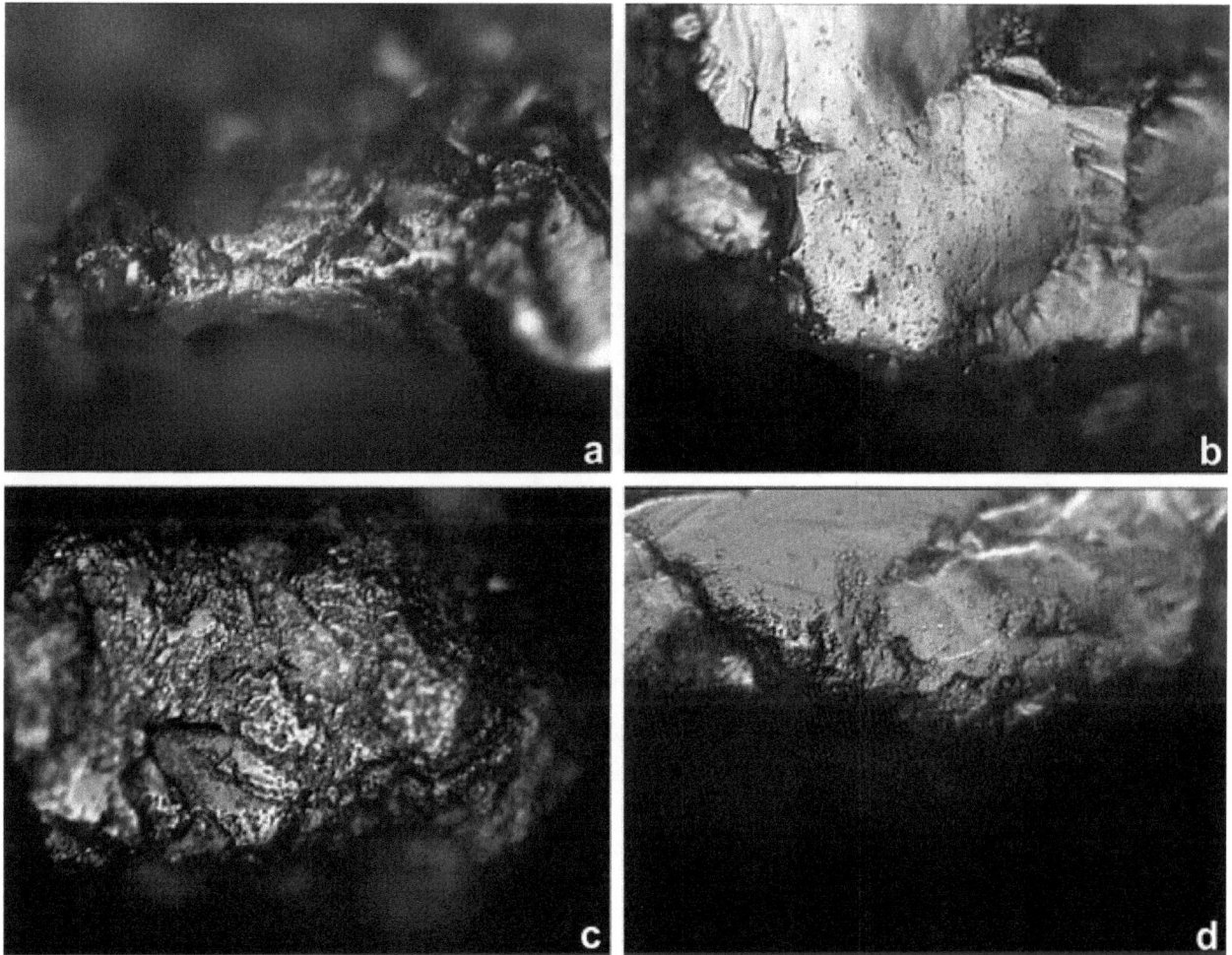

*Figura 3 – Trabajo sobre madera, 200x: a) Experimental, micropulido sobre matriz; b) Experimental, micropulido sobre cristal; c) Arqueológica, micropulido sobre matriz; d) Arqueológica, micropulido sobre cristal*

el tipo de material trabajado (cf. infra). En la matriz, el alto grado de silicificación y la cohesión entre cristales hacen que las superficies sean resistentes a la deformación, produciéndose micropulidos de modo muy lento. En ambos tipos de cuarcitas, ortocuarcitas y metacuarcitas, pudo observarse que es necesario un tiempo de uso más o menos prolongado (entre 30' y 60') para que se presenten atributos diagnósticos, característicos del tipo de material trabajado (Leipus 1999, 2006; Mansur 1991, 1999).

El microesquirlamiento de los filos que se produce por el uso es muy poco frecuente y casi siempre de pequeñas dimensiones. El grado de cohesión entre granos en los materiales y su tenacidad hacen que los filos tengan más tendencia al redondeamiento por desprendimiento de granos que a la fractura. El redondeamiento es mínimo en las ortocuarcitas y algo más pronunciado en las metacuarcitas, aún cuando vaya acompañado por micropulido bien desarrollado. En las acciones transversales, tal como en el modelo del sílex, el grado de redondeamiento varía entre una y otra cara del filo: es más pronunciado sobre la cara en contacto con el material trabajado, criterio que puede ser tomado en cuenta para reconstruir el movimiento efectuado durante el uso.

La mayoría de las piezas experimentales de cuarcita carecen de estrías. Sobre la matriz son siempre superficiales, difícilmente observables. En los cristales son más frecuentes las estrías colmatadas, que acompañan a la modificación general de la superficie. En los instrumentos usados en acciones transversales, (i. e. raspado con materiales abrasivos), el redondeamiento del filo es más pronunciado y acompañado por estrías superficiales orientadas en ángulos de 30° a 90°.

Los micropulidos, cuando están bien desarrollados, presentan características distintivas según el tipo de material trabajado y la cinemática de utilización. Los primeros rastros de uso se manifiestan por la desaparición gradual de los rasgos tecnológicos, acompañada por un suavizado general de las superficies, en las que aparecen depresiones similares a las de corrosión. En un estadio más avanzado, los micropulidos bien desarrollados son característicos del material trabajado. A modo de ejemplo, ilustramos el aspecto de los rastros de uso producidos por el trabajo de la madera y de pieles, sobre piezas experimentales y arqueológicas de ortocuarcita. En el caso de la madera (Fig. 3), el micropulido es brillante, espeso, tiene superficie lisa y regular, haciéndose progresivamente más plano y rugoso a medida que se aleja del filo. Los bordes de los cristales se redondean,

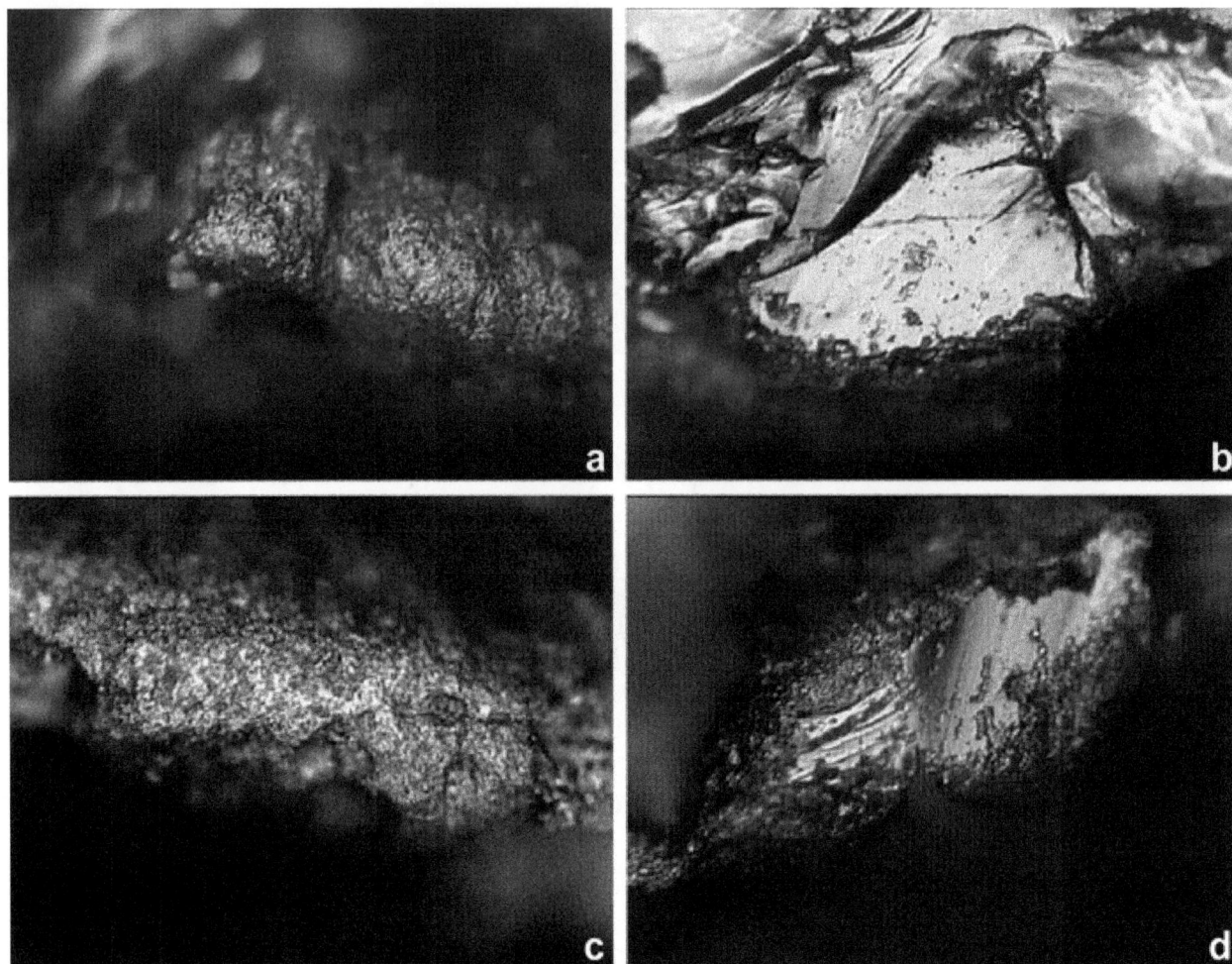

*Figura 4 – Trabajo sobre pieles, 200x: a) Experimental, micropulido sobre matriz; b) Experimental, micropulido sobre cristal; c) Arqueológica, micropulido sobre matriz; d) Arqueológica, micropulido sobre cristal*

presentando un aspecto disuelto característico del micropulido. Es más fácilmente reconocible cuando se presentan estrías asociadas (colmatadas y no colmatadas), micropoceado o surcos lineales sobre los cristales. Se observan estriaciones de depresiones intermitentes alineadas y microagujeros de morfología irregular. En el caso del trabajo de piel seca o cuero (Fig. 4), el micropulido es poco brillante (prácticamente mate), plano y su extensión sobre el filo es amplia, dependiendo del ángulo de trabajo. Se produce también un picoteo pequeño, muy abundante, generalmente formado por huecos de contorno circular, que confiere a los cristales un aspecto rugoso, similar al de la matriz de cimentación. El contacto de los cristales con ésta se produce de manera brusca, por fractura de los bordes de los cristales. Si bien los filos utilizados para trabajar pieles se redondean fuertemente, así como las aristas de los negativos de los microlascados, mantienen el aspecto oscuro de las superficies irregulares de rotura (Fig. 4).

El estado de conservación está directamente relacionado con las propiedades de las materias primas, con las características sedimentológicas de las unidades litoestratigráficas y con los diversos procesos tafonómicos a los que han estado sometidos. En los materiales cuarcíticos contenidos en niveles eólicos de sitios al aire libre de la región pampeana, como los incluidos aquí se registraron alteraciones leves producidas por el contacto bajo presión con las partículas abrasivas de las distintas unidades eólicas. Estas son identificables a escala microscópica, en forma de lustres de suelo, playas de abrasión localizadas o abrasión generalizada de las superficies, acompañadas por estrías entrecruzadas en los casos más intensos y por un ligero redondeamiento de aristas (Fig. 2 d). Estos rastros son mucho menos frecuentes en los materiales cuarcíticos que en otras materias primas, como las sílices criptocristalinas; cuando están presentes, también son mucho menos intensos. Los porcentajes de instrumentos arqueológicos donde se han observado rastros de uso superan ampliamente a los de piezas con evidencias de alteraciones postdepositacionales (Leipus 2006).

## 4. EL ANÁLISIS FUNCIONAL DE CONJUNTOS ARQUEOLÓGICOS

El análisis funcional de base microscópica aplicado a los conjuntos arqueológicos seleccionados permitió caracterizar los usos de una gran variedad de instrumentos. Presentamos una síntesis de los resultados obtenidos (tratados *in extenso* en Leipus, 2006), a fin de

*Tabla 1 – Cantidades de artefactos analizados*

| Sitio/Ocupación | Total de artefactos analizados | Artefactos con rastros de uso | Artefactos no determin. | Artefactos con alteraciones |
|---|---|---|---|---|
| Arroyo Seco 2 PSup Y | 113 | 92 | 10 | 11 |
| Arroyo Seco 2 PInf Y | 43 | 29 | 7 | 7 |
| Arroyo Seco 2 S/Z | 32 | 22 | 4 | 6 |
| Tres Reyes 1 CS | 92 | 76 | 3 | 13 |
| Paso Otero 3 | 35 | 32 | 1 | 2 |

*Tabla 2 – Cantidades de filos utilizados*

| Sitio/Ocupación | Total de filos analizados | Filos con rastros de uso |
|---|---|---|
| Arroyo Seco 2 PSup Y | 136 | 108 |
| Arroyo Seco 2 PInf Y | 51 | 32 |
| Arroyo Seco 2 S/Z | 34 | 23 |
| Tres Reyes 1 CS | 111 | 95 |
| Paso Otero 3 | 45 | 40 |

discutir la pertinencia de las hipótesis tecno-funcionales propuestas al comienzo (*cf. infra* "Discusión y perspectivas"). Tales conjuntos corresponden a los sitios Arroyo Seco (AS2) (Politis 1984; 1986; Politis *et al.* 1992), Laguna Tres Reyes 1 (TR1) (Madrid y Salemme 1991; Madrid y Barrientos 2001) y Paso Otero (PO3) (Martínez 1999; Martínez *et al.* 1997-98) ubicados en la denominada llanura Interserrana (Fig. 1). Los totales de artefactos analizados y resultados han sido resumidos en las Tablas 1 a 5.

Los materiales procesados con los filos de instrumentos de cuarcitas comprenden el trabajo de materiales de los cuales no han quedado evidencias directas en el registro arqueológico, como madera, que es el más representado en todos los conjuntos líticos analizados (Leipus 2004), no sólo en ocupaciones caracterizadas como de actividades múltiples (*i. e.* AS2, TR1) sino también en ocupaciones de actividades específicas, como el procesamiento de presas de caza (i. e. Paso Otero 3). Secundariamente aparece el trabajo de pieles y, en menores frecuencias, el trabajo sobre hueso y materiales duros y medios (Leipus 2006). En la mayoría de los conjuntos estudiados, independientemente de los atributos morfológicos o métricos de los filos, tales como su morfología o el ángulo, los trabajos transversales predominan ampliamente sobre los longitudinales.

En las los instrumentos de ortocuarcita pudieron observarse los estadios máximos de desarrollo, sobre todo en los casos del trabajo sobre madera y pieles, deduciéndose que los filos fueron utilizados durante lapsos prolongados (Leipus 2004; 2006). En algunos casos, debido al escaso desarrollo de los rastros de uso, no fue posible identificar el material trabajado ni la cinemática. Es probable que estos filos hayan sido usados durante lapsos breves o para procesar materiales que

producen rastros de uso con bajo grado de desarrollo (i. e. trabajo de materiales blandos de origen animal) incluso con tiempos de uso prolongados.

No se registraron evidencias macro ni microscópicas definidas producidas por procesos de reactivación así como tampoco de re-utilización de filos, ya sea en cuanto al procesamiento de más de un material o con dos cinemáticas diferentes. Sin embargo no puede descartarse que usos que producen rastros de menor intensidad, tales como el trabajo depieles, en procesos de corta duración, hayan quedado enmascaradas por rastros de uso mejor desarrollados, tales como los de material medio a duro de origen vegetal. En algunos casos se registraron evidencias del uso de intermediarios o mangos de madera (i. e. raederas del sitio AS2 y de un raspador de TR1 (Leipus 2004; 2006).

No existe una clara relación entre los grupos definidos tecnomorfológicamente y los usos a los cuales han estado destinados los instrumentos, ya que piezas correspondientes a un mismo tipo morfológico fueron utilizadas para trabajar diferentes materiales y con diferentes modos de uso. Uno de los casos en los cuales podríamos postular una cierta relación es el de los raspadores, que fueron usados en su totalidad con cinemática transversal pero si bien fueron mayoritariamente empleados para el procesamiento de pieles, algunos presentaron rastros de uso desarrollados por el trabajo sobre madera.

Las categorías morfológicas las raederas y los filos en bisel asimétrico, presentaron la mayor variabilidad de materiales trabajados y modos de uso. Fueron utilizados para procesar madera y pieles y secundariamente hueso. Muchas de las lascas con filos naturales de más de 2 cm de largo presentaron rastros de uso, confirmándose su condición de instrumento y no simplemente de un producto de talla descartado.

Los resultados del análisis funcional confirman la caracterización de las ocupaciones arqueológicas de los sitios AS2 y TR1 como de actividades múltiples. Se desarrollaron actividades tales como el trabajo de la madera y el procesamiento de pieles y secundariamente el de hueso, además de la manufactura de instrumentos líticos y del procesamiento y consumo de presas de caza. Durante la ocupación de PO3, además de las tareas relacionadas con la caza y el desposte de presas, en

*Tabla 3 – Grupos tecnomorfológicos y modos de uso en AS2 por cantidades de filos*

| Grupos tecnomorfológicos | Transversal | | | | | | Longitudinal | | | | | | Indeterminado | | Enmangues | Total |
|---|---|---|---|---|---|---|---|---|---|---|---|---|---|---|---|---|
| | M | P | H | MDM | MD | I | M | H | HC | MDM | MD | I | M | I | EM | |
| **Arroyo Seco 2 PSY** | | | | | | | | | | | | | | | | |
| Raederas | 9 | 6 | 1 | 1 | 4 | 6 | 3 | - | - | 1 | - | 1 | 1 | 1 | 2 | 36 |
| Raspadores | 2 | 11 | - | - | - | 4 | - | - | - | - | - | - | - | - | - | 17 |
| Cepillos | 2 | 2 | - | 1 | - | - | - | - | - | - | - | - | - | - | - | 5 |
| Muescas | 5 | - | - | - | - | 1 | - | - | - | - | - | - | - | - | - | 6 |
| AM/P RBO | - | - | - | - | - | 1 | - | - | - | - | - | 1 | - | 1 | - | 3 |
| Cuchillos | - | - | - | - | - | 1 | - | - | - | - | - | 1 | - | - | - | 2 |
| Filos bisel asimétrico | 1 | - | 1 | - | - | 2 | 2 | 3 | 1 | 1 | 1 | 5 | - | 2 | 1 | 20 |
| Filos naturales | - | - | - | - | - | 1 | - | - | - | 1 | - | 3 | - | 2 | - | 7 |
| Artef. Form. Sumaria | - | - | - | - | - | 3 | - | - | - | - | - | - | - | - | - | 3 |
| Artef.Retoque/Microretoque | - | - | - | 2 | - | - | - | - | 1 | - | - | 1 | - | 1 | - | 5 |
| Frag. De filos de Artef. Form. | - | - | - | - | - | 1 | - | - | - | - | - | - | - | 2 | - | 3 |
| Lasca Nucleiforme | - | - | - | - | - | 1 | - | - | - | - | - | - | - | - | - | 1 |
| **Subtotales** | **19** | **19** | **2** | **4** | **4** | **21** | **5** | **3** | **2** | **3** | **1** | **12** | **1** | **9** | **3** | **108** |
| **Arroyo Seco 2 PIY** | | | | | | | | | | | | | | | | |
| Raederas | 1 | 3 | - | 1 | - | - | 1 | - | - | - | - | - | - | - | 1 | 7 |
| Raspadores | 1 | 1 | - | - | - | 1 | - | - | - | - | - | - | - | - | - | 3 |
| Cepillos | - | 1 | - | - | - | - | - | - | - | - | - | - | - | - | - | 1 |
| Muescas | 1 | - | - | - | - | - | - | - | - | - | - | - | - | - | - | 1 |
| AM/P RBO | - | - | - | 1 | - | - | - | 1 | - | - | - | - | - | - | - | 2 |
| Filos bisel asimétrico | - | 2 | - | - | - | 1 | - | 1 | - | - | 1 | 1 | - | 1 | - | 7 |
| Filos naturales | 1 | - | - | - | - | - | - | - | - | 1 | 1 | 1 | - | 1 | - | 5 |
| Artef. Form. Sumaria | - | 1 | - | - | - | 1 | - | - | - | - | - | - | - | - | - | 2 |
| Artef. Retoque/microretoque | - | - | - | - | - | - | - | - | - | 1 | 1 | 1 | - | - | - | 3 |
| Frag. de filos de Inst. Form. | - | - | - | - | - | - | - | - | - | - | - | 1 | - | - | - | 1 |
| **Subtotales** | **4** | **8** | **-** | **2** | **-** | **3** | **1** | **2** | **-** | **2** | **3** | **4** | | **2** | **1** | **32** |
| **Arroyo Seco 2 S/Z** | | | | | | | | | | | | | | | | |
| Raederas | - | - | - | - | 1 | 2 | 3 | - | - | - | 1 | 1 | - | - | - | 8 |
| Raspadores | - | 2 | - | - | - | - | - | - | - | - | - | - | - | - | - | 2 |
| Cepillos | - | 1 | - | - | - | - | - | - | - | - | - | - | - | - | - | 1 |
| AM/P RBO | - | - | - | - | - | 1 | 1 | - | - | - | - | - | - | - | - | 2 |
| Filos bisel asimétrico | - | - | - | - | - | - | 1 | 1 | - | - | - | 3 | - | 2 | - | 7 |
| Filos naturales | - | - | - | - | - | - | - | - | - | - | - | 1 | - | 1 | - | 2 |
| Frag. De filos de Artef. Form | - | - | - | - | - | - | - | - | - | - | - | 1 | - | - | - | 1 |
| **Subtotales** | **-** | **3** | **-** | **-** | **1** | **3** | **5** | **1** | **-** | **-** | **1** | **6** | **-** | **3** | **-** | **23** |
| **Totales** | **23** | **30** | **2** | **6** | **5** | **27** | **11** | **6** | **2** | **5** | **5** | **22** | **1** | **14** | **4** | **163** |

Ref: M: madera; P: pieles; H: hueso; HC: hueso/carne; MDM: material de dureza media; MD: materiales duros; I: indeterminados

particular guanaco, se desarrollaron otras relacionadas con el procesamiento de madera y pieles (Leipus 2006).

## 5. DISCUSIÓN Y PERSPECTIVAS

La identificación de los usos dados a los instrumentos confeccionados en cuarcita resulta vital para la interpretación de los conjuntos arqueológicos pampeanos, ya que la selección de esta materia prima es predominante en la mayoría de los sitios de la región. Tal identificación, como se ha demostrado, es posible y brinda información relevante cuando se la realiza en conjunción con el análisis tecnomorfológico.

En el caso de los conjuntos estudiados, el análisis tecnomorfológico revela que la opción tecnológica predominante fue la utilización de ortocuarcita para

*Tabla 4 – Grupos tecnomorfológicos y modos de uso en Tres Reyes 1 – CS por cantidades de filos*

| Grupo Tecnomorfológico | Transversal | | | | | Longitudinal | | | Rotación | | Indeterminado | | | Total |
|---|---|---|---|---|---|---|---|---|---|---|---|---|---|---|
| | M | H | P | MD | I | M | H/C | I | M | I | M | P | I | |
| Raederas | 15 | 1 | 7 | 1 | 6 | 2 | - | - | - | - | - | 1 | 8 | 41 |
| Raspadores | 1 | - | 3 | - | - | - | - | - | - | - | - | - | 2 | 6 |
| Muescas | 2 | - | 1 | - | 1 | - | - | - | - | - | - | - | 1 | 5 |
| AM/P RBO | - | - | 2 | - | - | - | - | - | - | - | - | - | - | 2 |
| Filos Bisel Asimétrico | 2 | - | 1 | - | - | 3 | 2 | 1 | - | - | 1 | - | 9 | 19 |
| Filos naturales | - | - | 1 | - | - | 1 | - | - | - | - | - | - | - | 2 |
| Artef.Form.Sumaria | 2 | 1 | - | - | - | - | - | - | - | - | - | - | 1 | 4 |
| Frag. Filo Art. For. | 1 | 1 | - | - | 2 | - | - | - | - | - | - | - | - | 4 |
| Frag.No Dif. Art.For. | - | - | - | 1 | 1 | - | - | 1 | - | - | - | - | 4 | 7 |
| AM/P RBO Complem. * | - | - | - | - | - | - | - | - | - | - | - | - | - | 2 |
| Puntas Destacadas ** | - | - | - | - | - | - | - | - | 2 | 1 | - | - | - | 3 |
| **Totales** | **23** | **3** | **15** | **2** | **10** | **6** | **2** | **2** | **2** | **1** | **1** | **1** | **25** | **95** |

Ref: M: madera; P: pieles; H: hueso; HC: hueso/carne; MD: materiales duros; I: indeterminados

*Tabla 5 – Grupos tecnomorfológicos y modos de uso en Paso Otero 3 por cantidades de filos*

| Grupo Tecnomorfológico | Transversal | | | | Longitudinal | | | | Indeterminado | | | Totales |
|---|---|---|---|---|---|---|---|---|---|---|---|---|
| | M | P | MD | I | M | P | H | I | H | MD | I | |
| Raederas | 3 | - | 3 | 1 | 4 | - | - | - | - | - | - | 11 |
| Raspadores | - | 1 | 1 | - | - | - | - | - | - | - | 1 | 3 |
| Muescas | - | - | - | 1 | - | - | - | - | - | - | 1 | 2 |
| Filos Bisel Asimétrico | 2 | - | 2 | - | 2 | 1 | 1 | 2 | 1 | - | 9 | 20 |
| Unifaz | - | - | - | - | - | - | - | - | - | 1 | - | 1 |
| Frag.No Dif. Artef Form | - | 1 | - | - | - | - | - | - | - | - | 2 | 3 |
| **Totales** | **5** | **2** | **6** | **2** | **6** | **1** | **1** | **2** | **1** | **1** | **13** | **40** |

Ref: M: madera; P: pieles; H: hueso; MD: materiales duros; I: indeterminados

producir principalmente lascas por percusión directa a mano alzada, que fueron sobre todo seleccionadas para la confección de raederas. El segundo tipo representado es el de las lascas con filos retocados, seguido por los raspadores, pero también fueron utilizadas las lascas con filos naturales. Sin embargo, no se ha observado que exista correlación directa entre el tipo de instrumento y su uso específico, ni tampoco a lo referido a cada uno de los subtipos de las categorías tecnomorfológicas mencionadas.

Como fue postulado por otros autores, es probable que el aprovisionamiento de materias primas líticas tales como las ortocuarcitas entre las sociedades cazadoras-recolectoras pampeanas, se realizara mediante viajes específicos, cuyo objetivo principal haya sido el abastecimiento de materia prima y no una actividad secundaria (Flegenheimer *et al.* 1996). En consecuencia la provisión de cuarcitas de buena calidad implicó un esfuerzo importante que debe ser medido en planificación y duración de los desplazamientos, selección, manufactura primaria y transporte, etc. (Bayón y Flegenheimer 2004; Flegenheimer y Bayón 2001).

El esfuerzo realizado para la provisión de la materia prima generalmente es explicado en función de sus cualidades para la talla. Sin embargo, otro aspecto importante que se debe considerar es el de las cualidades de los filos cuando son empleados en diversos procesos de uso. El estudio funcional de diferentes variedades de cuarcitas permitió caracterizar algunas cualidades de los filos, en particular en cuanto a los criterios de efectividad, estabilidad y durabilidad.

Nuestros trabajos experimentales muestran diferencias estructurales entre ortocuarcitas y metacuarcitas. Estas condicionan sus cualidades para la talla y también se reflejan en el aspecto funcional, tanto en cuanto a la velocidad de formación de los rastros de uso como a la resistencia y durabilidad de los filos. En las metacuarcitas de Ventania, los filos naturales son efectivos cuando se los emplea sin formatización, pero los filos retocados tienden a ser menos efectivos. En las ortocuarcitas de Tandilia, al contrario, las lascas presentan buenos filos naturales y los instrumentos retocados son efectivos para ser utilizados, así como duraderos.

Desde este punto de vista, si los instrumentos confeccionados en ortocuarcitas no estuvieron destinados a actividades específicas, cabría preguntarse por qué hubo tal énfasis en la selección de este material cuya provisión, en el caso de los sitios alejados de las canteras, implicaba un esfuerzo considerable, cuando filos igualmente o más efectivos podrían haber sido obtenidos en rocas silíceas criptocristalinas.

Los resultados obtenidos en este trabajo nos permiten proponer una hipótesis que deriva del análisis combinado de criterios morfométricos y funcionales. En los conjuntos analizados, las lascas seleccionadas son de tamaños medianos y grandes y en ellas se formatizaron filos largos, rectos o convexos medios, con ángulos intermedios a altos. Esta relación es interesante porque sugiere que la preferencia por las cuarcitas, que puede tener una aparente causa tecnológica, podría en realidad responder a requerimientos funcionales. La causa tecnológica aparente podría ser que las cuarcitas, que están disponibles en abundancia y en buena calidad, permiten obtener lascas medianas y grandes, para formatizar filos largos, al contrario de los nódulos de ftanitas o los guijarros costeros, que tienden a ser más pequeños.

La causa funcional ha sido puesta en evidencia por la experimentación, y tiene que ver con la resistencia y estabilidad de los filos retocados y los no retocados confeccionados ortocuarcitas. Se trata de filos resistentes en los diversos procesos de uso. Por la tenacidad de la roca, no tienden al esquirlamiento; la cohesión de granos y matriz de cimentación hace que tampoco se produzca demasiado desgranamiento, manteniéndose estables a escala micro, a lo largo de usos intensos y/o prolongados. En los materiales arqueológicos, esta observación se ve corroborada por las escasas evidencias de reactivación y por el alto grado de desarrollo de los rastros de uso.

La diversidad de los usos a los que fueron destinados no refleja especificidad funcional en cuanto a la relación entre materia prima y uso (si bien predominan las acciones transversales, también hay longitudinales; y si el trabajo de la madera predomina ligeramente, hay también uso sobre otros materiales, especialmente pieles, pero también hueso). Esta diversidad indicaría que las cuarcitas fueron seleccionadas para confeccionar artefactos versátiles, destinados a cumplir diferentes tareas, con filos muy efectivos a lo largo del tiempo. Para ello se priorizó la búsqueda de soportes (formas base) que permitiesen producir artefactos de mayor tamaño, con filos con características morfométricas particulares (en especial largos de filo) y relativamente estables en el aspecto funcional. Esta situación, al menos, es la registrada en los sitios analizados de la región pampeana incluidos en nuestra investigación, y por ello la proponemos como hipótesis de trabajo a contrastar con información de otros contextos arqueológicos.

Una estrategia de este tipo se adaptaría relativamente bien a las posibilidades de una región donde la materia prima de relativamente buena calidad es abundante pero tiene distribución localizada. Así, el criterio de maximización no pasaría sólo por la modificación y reutilización de instrumentos fracturados, etc., sino también por la confección de artefactos versátiles y duraderos, que perdurasen en el tiempo como parte de una estrategia tecnológica conservada. Desde este punto de vista, podría postularse que las cuarcitas resultaron ser el mejor material posible entre los disponibles en el área.

## Agradecimientos

Este trabajo ha sido realizado dentro del marco de los proyectos "Arqueología de las poblaciones indígenas del sudeste de la región pampeana desde un abordaje suprarregional" (PIP-CONICET Nro. 5424, dir Dr. G. Politis y P. Madrid) y Proyecto Análisis Tecnofuncional de materiales arqueologicos (CONICET-CADIC, Dir M.E. Mansur). Parte de este trabajo fue realizado en el Centro Austral de Investigaciones Científicas (CADIC-CONICET) de Ushuaia, Tierra del Fuego, Argentina.

Agradezco a la Dra. María Estela Mansur por su constante apoyo y por las correcciones realizadas al manuscrito.

## Bibliografía

ALONSO LIMA, M. y MANSUR, M.E. 1986/1990. Estudio Traceológico de Instrumentos em Quartzo e Quartzito de Santana do Riacho (MG). *Arquivos do Museu de História Natural*, vol. 11: 173-190, Belo Horizonte.

BAYÓN, C. y FLEGENHEIMER, N. 2004. Cambio de planes a través del tiempo para el traslado de roca en pampa bonaerense. *Estudios Atacameños* 28, p. 59-70.

BAYÓN, C.; FLEGENHEIMER, N.; VALENTE, M. y PUPIO, A. 1999. Dime cómo eres y te diré de dónde vienes. La procedencia de rocas cuarcíticas en la región pampeana. *Relaciones* XXIV, p. 187-235.

BONOMO, M. 2005. *Costeando las llanuras. Arqueología del litoral marítimo pampeano.* 334 p. Sociedad Argentina de Antropología, Buenos Aires.

CLEMENTE, I. 1995. *Instrumentos de trabajo líticos de los Yamanas. Una perspectiva desde el análisis funcional.* Tesis de Doctorado, Univ Autónoma de Barcelona.

FLEGENHEIMER, N. y BAYÓN, C. 2001. Cómo, cuándo y dónde?. Estrategias de abastecimiento lítico en Pampa Bonaerense. En: D. Mazzanti, M. Berón y F. Oliva eds. – *Del Mar a los Salitrales. Diez mil años de historia pampeana en el umbral del tercer milenio* p. 231-241. Laboratorio de Arqueología, Facultad de Humanidades, Universidad Nacional de Mar del Plata.

FLEGENHEIMER, N.; KAIN, S.; ZÁRATE, M. y VALENTE, M. 1996. Aprovisionamiento de cuarcitas en Tandilia, las canteras del Arroyo Diamante. *Arqueología* 6, p. 117-141. Buenos Aires.

LEIPUS, M. 1999. Análisis funcional: caracterización de los microrrastros de uso en materias primas líticas de la región pampeana. *Actas del XII Congreso Nacional de Arqueología Argentina,* Tomo I, p. 345-354, La Plata.

LEIPUS, M. 2004. Tendencias en el uso de los artefactos líticos en la Subregión Pampa Húmeda: relación entre morfología y función a partir del análisis de microrrastros de utilización". En: C. Gradín y F. Oliva Eds. *La Región Pampeana – Su Pasado Arqueológico* p. 123-130. Laborde Editor.

LEIPUS, M. 2006. *Análisis de los modos de uso prehispánicos de las materias primas líticas en el Sudeste de la Región Pampeana: Una aproximación funcional.* Tesis Doctoral Inédita. P. 426. Facultad de Ciencias Naturales y Museo, UNLP.

LEIPUS, M. y MANSUR, M.E. 2007. El análisis funcional de base microscópica aplicado a materiales heterogéneos. Perspectivas metodológicas para el estudio de las cuarcitas de la Región Pampeana. En: *Arqueología de las Pampas,* UNS, Tomo I, Pp. 179-200. Bahía Blanca.

MADRID, P. y SALEMME, M. 1991. La ocupación tardía del sitio 1 de la Laguna de Tres Reyes. Pdo. de Adolfo Gonzáles Chaves, Pcia de Buenos Aires. *Boletín del Centro de Registro del Patrimonio Arqueológico y Paleontológico* 3, p. 165-179. La Plata.

MADRID, P. y BARRIENTOS, G. 2001. Estructura del registro arqueológico del sitio Laguna Tres Reyes 1 (provincia de Buenos Aires): nuevos datos para la interpretación del poblamiento humano del sudeste de la región Pampeana a inicios del Holoceno tardío. *Relaciones* XXV, p. 179-206.

MANSUR, M.E. 1986. *Microscopie du matériel lithique préhistorique: Traces d'utilisation, altérations naturelles, accidentelles et technologiques.* Cahiers du Quaternaire 9, Éditions du C.N.R.S., Bordeaux.

MANSUR, M.E. 1991. Microwear on quartz crystals and obsidian: its contribution to use wear analysis on heterogeneous materials. Comunicación presentada en el *VI International Flint Symposium.* Madrid.

MANSUR, M.E. 1999. Análisis Funcional de instrumentos líticos: problemas de formación y deformación de rastros de uso. *Actas del XII Congreso Nacional de Arqueología Argentina,* Tomo I, p. 355-366. La Plata.

MARTÍNEZ, G. 1999. *Tecnología, subsistencia y asentamiento en el curso Medio del Río Quequén Grande: un enfoque arqueológico.* Tesis Doctoral Inédita. Facultad de Ciencias Naturales y Museo, UNLP.

MARTÍNEZ, G.; LANDINI, C. y BONOMO, M. 1997-98. Análisis de los artefactos líticos del sitio Paso Otero 3: una aproximación al entendimiento de la organización de la tecnología lítica en el Curso Medio del Río Quequén Grande. *Publicaciones de Arqueología,* 49 p. 3-22. CIFFyH, Univ. Nac. Córdoba.

MAZZANTI, D. 1993. Investigaciones arqueológicas en el sitio Cueva Tixi (provincia de Buenos Aires). *Etnía* N° 38-39, p. 125-163.

POLITIS, G. 1984. *Arqueología del Area Interserrana Bonaerense.* Tesis Doctoral Inédita. Facultad de Ciencias Naturales y Museo, UNLP.

POLITIS, G. 1986. Investigaciones arqueológicas en el Area Interserrana Bonaerense. *Etnía* 32, p. 3-52. Olavarría.

POLITIS, G.; MADRID, P. y BARRIENTOS, G. 1992. Informe de la campaña 1992 al sitio Arroyo Seco 2 (Pdo. de Tres Arroyos, Pcia. de Buenos Aires, Argentina). *Palimpsesto* 1, p. 80-85. Buenos Aires.

SEMENOV, S. 1964. *Prehistoric Technology.* London: Adams.

# FROM BONE FISHHOOKS TO FISHING TECHNIQUES: THE EXAMPLE OF ZAMOSTJE 2 (MESOLITHIC AND NEOLITHIC OF THE CENTRAL RUSSIAN PLAIN)

## Yolaine MAIGROT

UMR 8215 du CNRS – Trajectoires De la sédentarisation à l'État,
MAE. 21, allée de l'Université, 92023 Nanterre cedex, France
yolaine.maigrot@mae.cnrs.fr

## Ignacio CLEMENTE CONTE

Departament d'Arqueologia i Antropologia, Institució Milà i Fontanals,
CSIC, Egipcíaques 15, 08001 Barcelona, Espagne
ignacio@imf.csic.es

## Evgeny GYRIA, Olga LOZOVSKAYA

Laboratory for Experimental Traceology, Institute for the History of Material Culture of the Russian Academy
of Science (IHMC RAS), Dvortsovaya nab. 18, 191186 St. Petersbourg, Russie
kostionki@yandex.ru      olozamostje@gmail.com

## Vladimir LOZOVSKI

Department of Archaeology, Sergiev-Possad State History and Art Museum-Preserved,
pr. Krasnoï Armii 144, 141300 Sergiev Possad, Russie
zamostje68@gmail.com

**Abstract**: *Fishing played a fundamental role in the subsistence economy of the Mesolithic and Neolithic inhabitants of Zamostje 2, a site located on the Russian plain (Sergiev Possad, Moscow). The abundant ichtiofaunal remains and the tools found at the site (harpoons, needle nets, weight nets, fishhooks and scaling knives) corroborate this importance. In this article, we focus on the consumption of fishhooks through an analysis of the usewear observed on their surfaces. We compare the usewear observed on the archaeological fishhooks with that seen on experimental fishhooks used to capture fish species. We show how some attributes (disposition, quantity and hardness of the fish teeth) influence the nature of the usewear, especially the striations, formed on the surfaces of the fishhooks.*

**Keywords**: *Bone fishhooks, Experimentation, Usewear analysis, Russian Mesolithic and Neolithic*

**Résumé**: *La pêche semble tenir une place primordiale dans l'économie de subsistance des communautés mésolithiques et néolithiques du site de Zamostje 2 localisé dans la plaine centrale russe (Sergiev Possad, Moscou). C'est en tous les cas, ce que laissent entrevoir les quantités astronomiques des restes ichtyologiques ainsi que les divers équipements associés aux activités halieutiques (nasses, poids de filets, harpons, hameçons, couteaux à écailler, etc.) retrouvés sur le site. Dans ce travail, nous nous concentrerons plus particulièrement sur les hameçons en os et présenterons une grille de lecture, établie sur la base d'un référentiel expérimental, permettant de distinguer et de préciser leur mode de fonctionnement.*

**Mots-clés**: *Hameçons en os, Expérimentation, Tracéologie, Mésolithique et Néolithique russe*

## 1. INTRODUCTION

The site of Zamostje 2 is located in the Dubna Valley, 110 km to the north-east of Moscow (Fig. 1, Lozovski 2003). This river bank site was discovered in 1987 by Siderov and was excavated under the direction of V.M. Losovski from 1989-1991 and 1995-2000, and then by O.V. Lozovskaya from 2010-2011. Its long chronological sequence extends from the 6th to the 5th millennia BC, from the Late Mesolithic to the Early Neolithic. A large quantity of fish remains (scales, vertebrae, teeth, mandibles, etc.) were recovered in the occupation levels. According to some estimations, the ichtiological remains

represent 64% of all the fauna consumed (Chaix 2003). An analysis of the ichtiological remains collected in a sondage at Zamostje 2 resulted in the identification of eleven species (versus the twenty currently present in the Dubna watercourses), five of which were present in both the Mesolithic and Neolithic occupations (*Exos Lucius, Perca fluviatilis, Rutilus rutilus, Carassius carassius,* and *Leuciscus idus*). The other taxa, such as *Silurus glanis* and *Sander lucioperca*, appear more sporadically within the sequence (Radu & Desse-Berset 2012). The ichtiological remains are not the only ones associated with halieutic activities and the consumption of fishing products at Zamostje 2. For example, a functional

*Figure 1 – Location of the site of Zamostje 2*

analysis of long knives made from elk ribs show that they were used to scale and clean fish, as well as to remove filets that could have been consumed immediately after cooking or preserved by drying or smoking (Clemente *et al.* 2002, Clemente Conte and Gyria 2003). A coprolite analysis shows that the fish were ingested when only slightly cooked or raw (Lozovski 1996). Finally, a large number of the tools and instruments found at Zamostje could have been more or less directly associated with halieutic activities and indicate the existence of varied fishing strategies: net (float weights, net needles), wooden fish traps, harpoons and fishhooks. In this paper, we focus on this last category, "fishhooks".

## 2. STUDY COLLECTION AND METHODS

Between 1989 and 2011, forty-seven bone "fishhooks" were identified at Zamostje 2 (fig. 2). Among these "fishhooks", two typological groups can be distinguished. Hook-shaped pieces (fig. 2, n° 1 to 18 and n° 26 to 30) and others with a flat section said to be shaped like a "willow leaf" (fig. 2, n° 19 to 25). The technological and functional analysis that we present here is limited to the first typological category, the hook-shaped pieces. It is composed of twenty-seven specimens, most of which originate from the level attributed to the Early Neolithic (Верхневолжская культура or the Upper Volga culture). Several sub-groups can be distinguished according to the general form and dimensions of the objects (Lozovski and Lozovskaya 2010). These sub-groups are fishhooks with a curved hook (Fig. 2, n° 3 and 4) or a straight hook (fig. 2, n° 5 to 10), and small (Fig. 2, n° 18) or large fishhooks (Fig. 2, n° 26). The attachment system also varies: straight shank (Fig. 2, n° 11), shouldered shank (Fig. 2, n° 27), eyed shank (Fig. 2, n° 12). With the exception of the "fishhooks" with a straight hook, which do not appear until the Early Neolithic, it is difficult to give a typo-chronological attribution to all the other types

since they are present in both the Mesolithic and Neolithic.

The hook-shaped "fishhooks" were carefully made using a *chaîne opératoire* that appears to have remained the same throughout the chronological sequence considered, based on the technical pieces. These are transformed objects whose anatomical origin is most often impossible to determine. The shaping traces made by scraping cover the pieces and mask the debitage stigmata, which could thus be reconstructed based only on analysis of the manufacturing by-products. Two debitage by-products thus appear to indicate that the preforms were extracted by grooving bone plaques. We also find traces associated with this technique on the initial roughouts and the pieces representing "mistakes". The objects discarded in the process of manufacturing show that once the preform was extracted, a perforated eye was realized and the shank was regularized by scraping until the debitage traces were erased. The regularity of their walls and striations indicate that the circular eyes were realized by pressure/rotation, probably using a bow-drill tipped with a lithic point. These eyes were initiated on one or both of the faces. The enlargement of the eye, regularization of the curvature, formation of a barb and the preparation of the attachment system all appear to have been realized during the last stages of the manufacturing process.

While the technical aspects of these objects are relatively well understood, this is far from true for their function. This is because the functional interpretation of these pieces has until now been based only on morphological analogies with modern or sub-modern fishhooks and the specific archaeological context of Zamostje 2. Other uses are possible however, such as hooks for the suspension of various objects. Only a global analysis of their usewear, consisting of all the macroscopic (deformation of volumes) and microscopic (modification of the surfaces) traces resulting from the use of these objects can permit such a functional distinction (Semenov 1964, Christidou 1999, Maigrot 2003 and 2005, Van Gjin 2006, Clemente *et al.* 2002).

## 3. EXPERIMENTAL REFERENCE BASE

We created an experimental reference base specific to bone fishhooks. Several specimens were manufactured and used to line fish of four different fish types: sheatfish, perch, pikeperch and trout (Fig. 3, n° 1). All of the experimental fishhooks were subject to usewear analysis after their first capture. The entire collection was analyzed at different scales: the naked eye, binocular magnifier and with a metallographic microscope at magnifications of 50x, 100x and 200x.

The first macroscopic observations show that the usewear is extremely localized. On all of the experimental fishhooks, it is located on the outer edge of the first third of the shank, where the longitudinal striations associated with their shaping by scraping have been partly replaced by a polished surface (Fig. 3, n° 3). Everywhere else, the

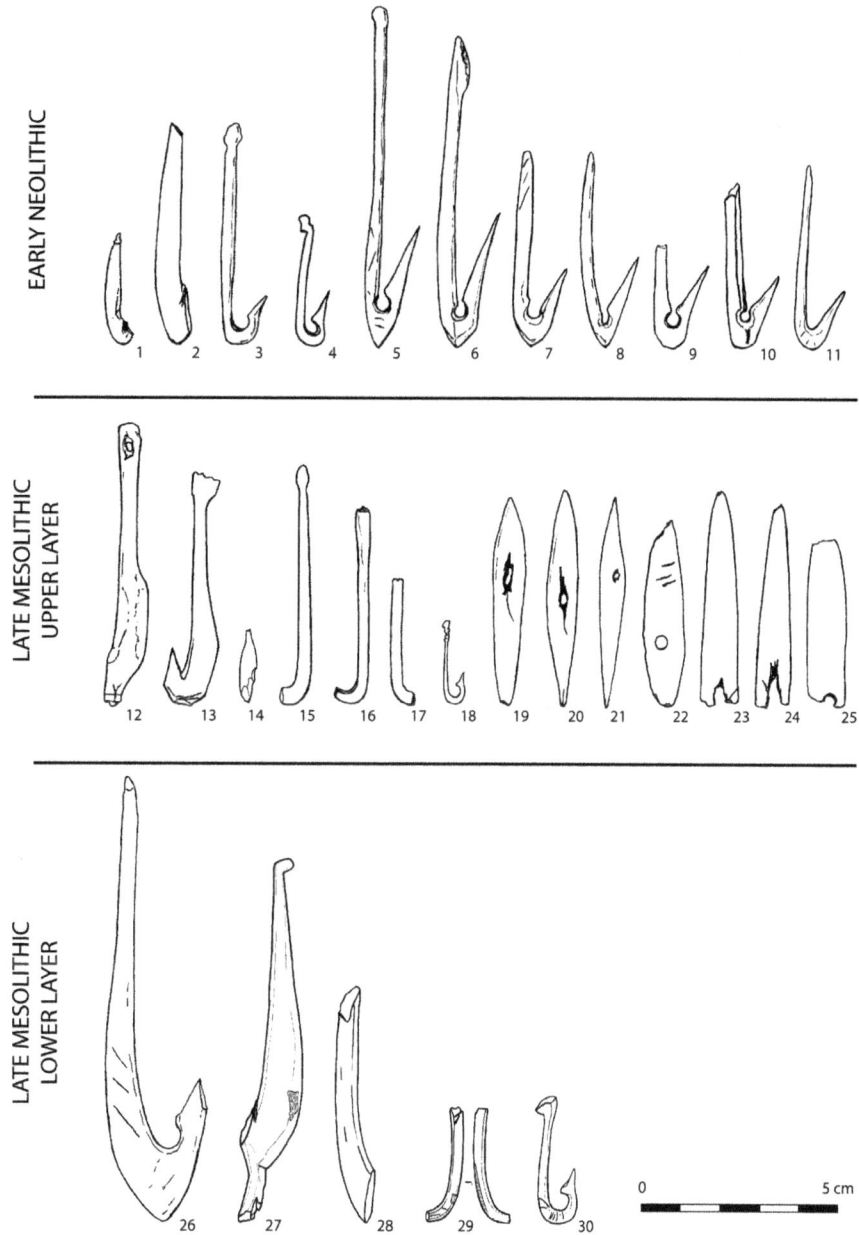

*Figure 2 – Fishhooks found during the excavations at Zamostje (1989 and 1998 seasons).*
*Drawings: Olga Lozovskaya*

traces associated with the manufacturing of the experimental pieces are very clear. The location of the usewear on fishhooks is clearly different from that observed on other types of hooks (for attachment or suspension), which in the latter case mainly concerns the point and the inside of the eye, whose walls are often smoothed. In the case of fishhooks, when there is smoothing, it is visible only with a binocular magnifier and concerns only the angular parts composed by the extremity of the point and the edge of the eye. The distinction between these two types of usewear is thus very clear and can be realized by observation with the naked eye or through low magnification.

When observed at a low magnification (50x), the usewear on the outer edge of the first third of the shank of the fishhooks is characterized by transverse striations, which are more or less numerous, continuous and intertwined. In association with sheatfish or trout fishing, these striations are thin and superficial. The traces associated with pikeperch and perch fishing, on the other hand, are composed of linear depressions that are more numerous, but especially wide, and even macroscopic for pikeperch (Fig. 3, n° 3). When magnified at 200x, the surface appears irregular and displays a more or less intrusive polish. The high points of the micro-relief are slightly eroded, with a rounded profile and sometimes grainy appearance. The transverse striations have slightly eroded edges, a "U" shaped section and a rough bottom, except in association with sheatfish and trout fishing, when the bottom appears to be coalescent (Fig. 3, n° 4 to 7). After the first third of the shank, the shaping traces are fresh and perfectly visible. At 200x, they display a very slight smoothing of the elevations, whose profile is curved.

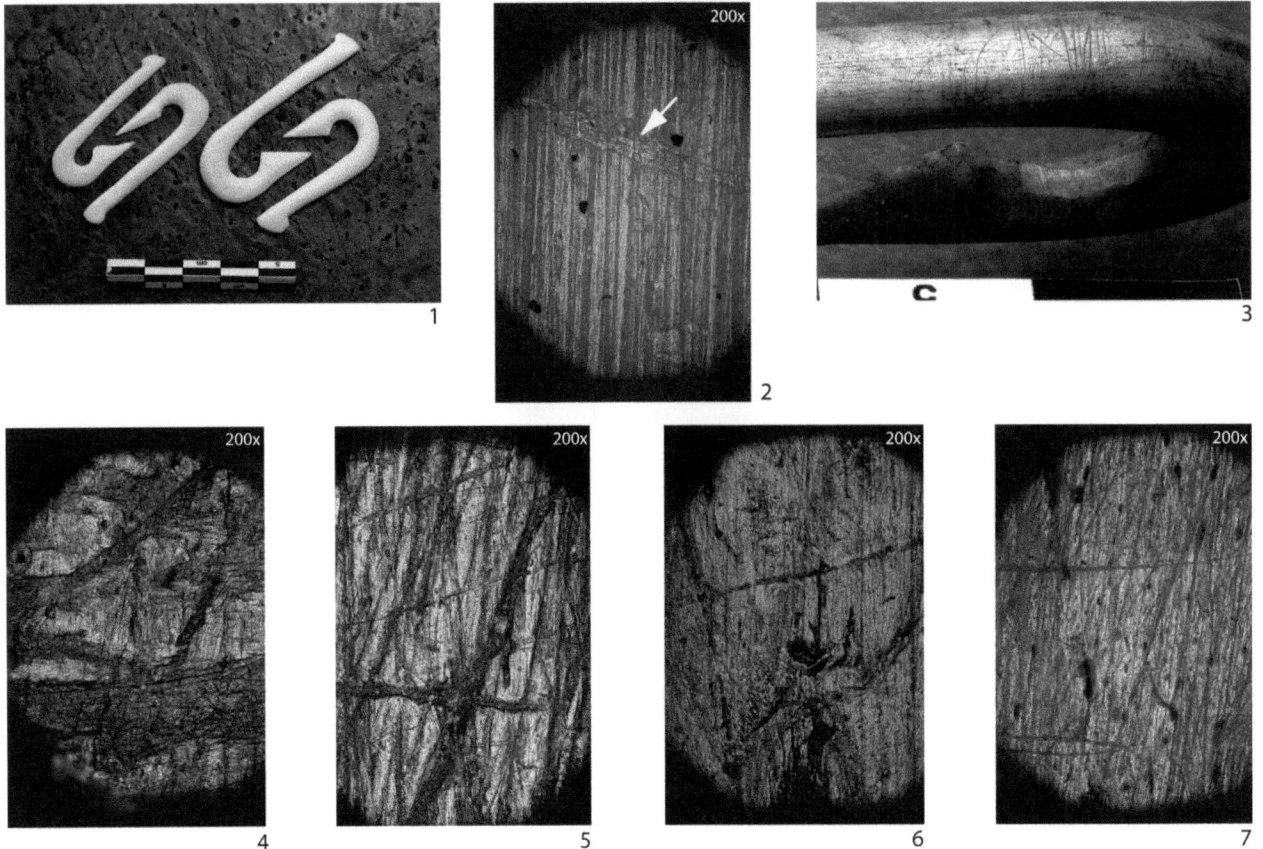

*Figure 3 – Experimental references – 1) examples of experimental fishhooks. 2) Close-up of the microscopic traces observed on the ligature zone. 3) macroscopic traces visible on outer edge of the first third of the shank of an experimental fishhook used to capture a pikeperch. 4) microscopic traces on outer edge of the first third of the shank of an experimental fishhook used to capture a pikeperch. 5) outer edge of the shank of a fishhook used to capture a perch. 6) outer edge of the shank of a fishhook used to capture a sheatfish. 7) outer edge of the shank of a fishhook used to capture a trout. Photo: Evgeny Gyria (1 & 3) and Yolaine Maigrot (2 & 4 to 7)*

Traces associated with the attachment of the fishhooks are rare and often very light. Only two experimental fishhooks display usewear associated with the string used to attach them. These take the form of wide clusters with a coalescent bottom, which follow the original micro-relief, in this case corresponding to the shaping traces (Fig. 3, n° 2).

In summary, the usewear observed on fishhooks is composed of traces that are mostly located on the outer edge of the shank, consisting of a light polish associated with transversal striations. Our first experiments indicate that these striations are produced directly by the teeth of the fish, which would partly explain the morphometric variations observed on different fishhooks.

Pikeperch have four large canines that could have created the macro-striations observed on the experimental fishhooks used to capture them (Fig. 3, n° 4). The mouths of sheatfish are lined with a multitude of minuscule teeth that that produce much more superficial traces on the shanks, which could explain the thin striations (Fig. 3, n° 6).

Following these first experimental tests, it appears that it is possible to distinguish fish types based on the traces

left by their teeth on the fishhooks. While in some cases the distinction is clear (e.g. sheatfish *versus* pikeperch), in others it is less obvious (e.g. sheatfish *versus* trout). Nonetheless, these experiments, currently limited to four taxa, should be multiplied and extended to other species in order to further refine the criteria of distinction.

## 4. USEWEAR ANALYSIS OF THE "FISHHOOKS" OF ZAMOSTJE 2

All of the pieces in the Zamostje 2 assemblage were studied macroscopically, while only some were studied microscopically due to the varied states of their surfaces.

As we have seen, the technological traces are relatively clear on all the pieces in this assemblage, at least those linked to the last manufacturing stages. Only the zone roughly corresponding to the first third or first half of the shank of the fishhooks appears more or less polished and, in some cases short transversal striations are present on the outer edge. The extremity of the barbs and the edge of the eyes are sometimes lightly smoothed. In these terms the distribution of traces observed on the archaeological objects corresponds to that observed on the experimental fishhooks. It is thus probable that the Mesolithic and

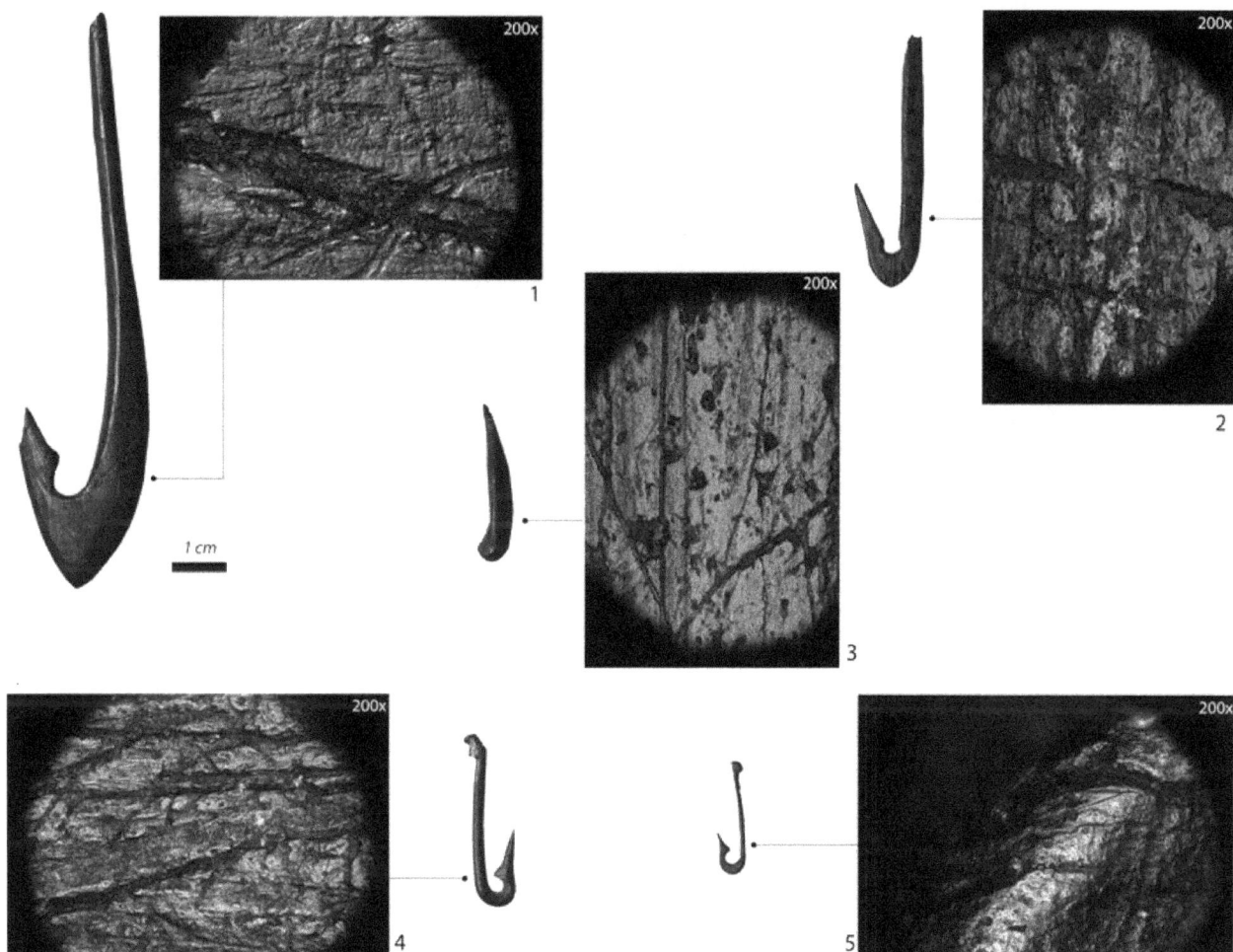

*Figure 4 – Close-up of the microscopic traces observed on the outer edge of the fishhooks of Zamostje 2. Photos: Yolaine Maigrot*

Neolithic hooks were used for fishing. Meanwhile, the Zamostje 2 assemblage includes many fragmented pieces (Fig. 2, n°1 and 2, n° 12 and 17). Most of the fractures, which affect more than half of the fishhooks, are located in the zone of the bend. However, none of our experimental pieces were broken during use; it is possible that our fishhooks, which were subject to the force of only one fish capture each time, may not have resisted the multiple mechanical forces associated with repeated fishing incidents.

Based on the experimental results, the most valid functional indicators are located on the first third of the outer edge of the shank, and we will thus focus on this zone. At low magnifications, groups displaying similar usewear traces appear to be visible among the archaeological objects. Some pieces display short and very thin transversal striations, and others wider striations. These observations are conformed at a high magnification (200x) and permit us to distinguish at least three groups. The first includes only the fishhooks with a straight hook. Their relatively long shank displays very wide striations visible with the naked eye. These are transversal and have a rough bottom (Fig. 4, n° 1 and 2). In comparison to our experimental reference base, these traces are similar to those associated with the fishing of

pikeperch. The second group includes the small curved fishhooks. The usewear on their shank is characterized by more or less numerous transversal striations with a rough bottom, which are similar to the teeth marks produced by perch (Fig. 4, n° 4 and 5). The third group includes fishhooks of diverse sizes, but which have in common a relatively short shank with a rather massive and circular section. The striations present on these pieces are more superficial and have a coalescent bottom, similar to those produced by sheatfish or trout fishing (Fig. 4, n° 3).

## 5. DISCUSSION

This analysis indicates that there is a strong relationship between the morphology of the archaeological fishhooks and their usewear patterns. Is it possible to interpret this correlation in terms of the ways in which the fishhooks were used? We know that for modern fishermen, each type of prey corresponds to a specific type of line and hook. The preliminary results obtained for the Zamostje assemblage appear to follow this pattern and to indicate that the strategies were already known and practiced in the Mesolithic. But in what manner? If we attempt to compare our usewear data with the ichtiological spectrum of Zamostje 2, we are rapidly confronted with the limits of our experiments, in which only four fish species among the identified archaeological taxa were tested. The straight fishhooks in the Neolithic levels were thus associated with usewear patterns similar to those obtained through the experimental fishing of pikeperch. However, all the pikeperch bones found at Zamostje were contained in the levels exclusively attributed to the Mesolithic (Radu and Desse-Berset 2012). The Neolithic levels, on the other hand, contain numerous remains of pike or another predator with formidable teeth that could produce deep traces on the fishhook shanks.

This first usewear analysis of bone fishhooks has permitted us to propose an initial set of criteria for the study of their use traces. The unexpected though promising results incite us to continue in this direction and to conduct more experiments in order to refine the functional interpretations proposed for this type of object. This experimental analysis must integrate new parameters, such as the size and force of the fish. It must also include other species, and should be extended to other typological categories, such as the so-called "willow leaf" fishhooks and harpoons. Through such work, we will be able to shed new light on fishing strategies and evaluate the role of these activities in the economy of the Mesolithic and Neolithic communities of the Russian plain.

## Acknowledgements

This study was carried out as part of a research project entitled *"Recursos olvidados en el estudio de grupos prehistóricos: el caso de la pesca en sociedades meso-neoliticas de la llanura rusa"* (HAR2008-04461/HIST), supported by the Spanish Ministry of Science and Innovation.

## References

CHAIX, L. 2003. A short note on the Mesolithic fauna from Zamostje 2 (Russia). *In*: Larsson, L.; Lindgren, H.; Knutsson, K.; Loeffler, D.; Akerlund, A. éd., *Mesolithic on the move*. Oxford: Oxbow Books, pp. 645-648.

CHRISTIDOU, R. 1999. *Outils en os néolithiques du nord de la Grèce: étude technologique*. Thèse de Doctorat, Nanterre, Université Paris X, 698 p.

CLEMENTE CONTE, I.; GYRIA, E.Y. 2003. Analiz oroudi iz reber lossia so stoïanki Zamostie 2 (7 sloï, raskopki 1996-7gg). *Arkheologitcheskie Vesmi*, 10, p. 47-59. [Клементе Конте, Н.; Гиря, Е.Ю. (2003) - Анализ орудий из ребер лося со стоянки Замостье 2 (7 слой, раскопки 1996-7гг). *Археологические Вести*, 10, p. 47-59.].

CLEMENTE, I.; GYRIA, E.Y.; LOZOVSKAYA, O.V.; LOZOVSKI, V.M. 2002. Análisis de instrumentos en costilla de alce, mandíbulas de castor y caparazón de tortuga de Zamostje 2 (Rusia). *In*: Clemente, I.; Risch, R.; Gibaja, J.F. éd., *Análisis Funcional: su aplicación al estudio de sociedades prehistóricas*. Oxford: Brithish Archaeological Reports, International Series 1073, p. 187-196.

LOZOVSKI, V.M. 1996. *Zamostje 2, Les derniers chasseurs-pêcheurs préhistoriques de la plaine russe*. Treignes: éditions du CEDARC, 96p.

LOZOVSKI, V.M. 2003. *Perekhod ot mezolita k neolitou v Volgo-Okskom mejdouretchie po materialam stoïanki Zamostie 2*. Avtoreferat dissertatsii. Sankt-Peterbourg, Kand.Ist.Naouk, 466p. [Лозовский, В.М. (2003) – *Переход от мезолита к неолиту в Волго-Окском междуречье по материалам стоянки Замостье 2*. Автореферат диссертации , Санкт-Петербург, канд.ист.наук, 466 p.].

LOZOVSKI, V.M.; LOZOVSKAYA, O.V. 2010. Izdelia iz kosti i roga ranneneolititcheskikh sloïev stoïanki Zamostie 2. *In: Tchelovek i drevnosti Pamiati Alexandra Alexandrovitcha Formozova (1928-2009)*. Moskva: A.N. Sorokni, p. 237-252. [Лозовский, В.М.; Лозовская О.В. (2010) – Изделия из кости и рога ранненеолитических слоев стоянки Замостье 2. *In: Человек и древности Памяти Александра Александровича Формозова (1928-2009)*. Москва: А.Н. Сорокни, p. 237-252.].

MAIGROT, Y. 2003. *Etude technologique et fonctionnelle de l'outillage en matières dures animales, la station 4 de Chalain (Néolithique final, Jura, France)*, Thèse de Doctorat, Paris, Université de Paris 1, 284 p.

MAIGROT, Y. 2005. Ivory, bone and antler tools production systems at Chalain 4 (Jura, France), late Neolithic site, 3rd millennium. *In*: Luik, H.; Choyke, M.A.; Batey, C.E.; Lougas, L. dir., *From hooves to horns, from Mollusc to Mammoth, manufacture and use of bone artefacts from prehistoric times to the present, 4th Meeting of the Worked Bone Research Group, Tallinn, 26-31 August 2003*. Tallinn: Muinasaja teadus, 15, p. 113-126.

RADU, V.; DESSE-BERSET, N. 2012. The fish from Zamostje and its importance for the last hunter-gatherers of the Russian Plain (Mesolithic-Neolithic). *In*: Lefèvre, C. ed., *Proceedings of the General Session of the 11th International Council for Archaeozoology Conference*, Oxford: Brithish Archaeological Reports, International Series 2354, p. 147-161.

SEMENOV, S.A. 1964. *Prehistoric technology, An experimental study of the oldest tools and artefacts from traces of manufacture and wear*. London: Cory, Adams & Mackay, 211p.

VAN GIJN, A.L. 2006. Implements of bone and antler: a Mesolithic tradition continued. *In*: Louwe Kooijmans, L.P.; Jongste, P.F.B. ed., *Schipluiden – Harnaschpolder. A Middle Neolithic Site on the Dutch Coast (3800-3500 BC)*, p. 207-224. (Analecta Praehistorica Leidensia 37/38).

# THE PRODUCTION OF BEADS AND LITHIC PENDANTS IN THE SALOBO RIVERBASIN, PARÁ, BRAZIL

Maria Jacqueline RODET

Universidade Federal de Minas Gerais (UFMG), FAFICH end Museu de Historia Natural-UFMG,
Rua Gustavo da Silveira, 1035, Santa Ines, CEP 31080-010, Brasil
jacqueline.rodet@gmail.com

Déborah DUARTE-TALIM

Cooperator Researcher at Museu de Historia Natural – Setor de Arqueologia,
Rua Gustavo da Silveira, 1035, Santa Ines, CEP 31080-010, Brasil
delsduarte@hotmail.com

Maura Imazio da SILVEIRA

Museu Paraense Emilio Goeldi, Departamento de Ciências Humanas,
Avenida Magalhães Barata, 376, São Braz Belém - PA, 66040-170, Brasil
maura@marajoara.com

Elizângela R. de OLIVEIRA

Museu Paraense Emilio Goeldi, Departamento de Ciências Humanas,
Avenida Magalhães Barata, 376, São Braz Belém - PA, 66040-170, Brasil
elisoliveira@yahoo.com.br

Marcondes Lima da COSTA

Universidade Federal do Pará, Museu de Geociencias da Universidade Federal do Pará,
Rua Augusto Correa, 01, Guamá, Belé, CEP 66075-110, Brasil
mlc@ufpa.br

**Abstract**: *Through the project "Archaeological rescue in the area of Salobo Project", developed in the city of Marabá, State of Pará, lithic industries from hunter-gatherer and ceramists groups were studied in archaeological sites of the left bank of the Itacaiúnas Riverbasin. The ceramic material has technological, morphological and stylistic features that refer to Tupiguarani Tradition (Brochado 1981). In this study we present the technological analysis performed in the production of lithic beads produced on silicified kaolinite for each of the sites, and then comparing them with each other. The objects are in varied technical states, what allowed the reconstruction of the different stages of the production.*

**Key-words**: *Technological analysis, Lithic beads, Tupi, Amazon*

**Résumé**: *Dans le projet "Sauvetage archéologique dans la région de Salobo" développé dans la ville de Marabá, état de Pará, nous avons étudié des industries lithiques de groupes des chasseurs-cueilleurs et des potiers de sites archéologiques du bassin de la rivière Itacaiúnas. Le matériel céramique possède des caractéristiques technologiques, morphologiques et stylistiques qui le relie à la tradition Tupiguarani (Brochado 1981). Dans cette étude, nous présentons l'analyse technologique développée dans la production de perles lithiques avec de la kaolinite silicifiée, pour chacun des sites, suivi de leur comparaison. Les objets se trouvaient dans différent stades techniques, ce qui a permis de reconstituer les différents stades de production.*

**Mots-clé**: *Analyse technologique, Perles lithiques, Tupi, Amazone*

## 1. INTRODUCTION

The lithic collection excavated in the city of Marabá, in the southeast of the State of Pará, has, among other things, different types of adornments, including beads and pendants. This work will present only those beads classified by us as disc beads.

The beads are representative of a more general category of objects, the adornments, whose objective is to ornament the body of the individual, embellishing it and personifying it (Barge 1982). These are complex objects, which can often be just one of the component elements of a bigger ornament. They have a *chaîne opératoire* composed by several stages of production and that uses various techniques in each of its phases.

An object is a mental image, which corresponds to the choices, needs and desires of a particular social group (Pelegrin 2005). The objects here presented, because they

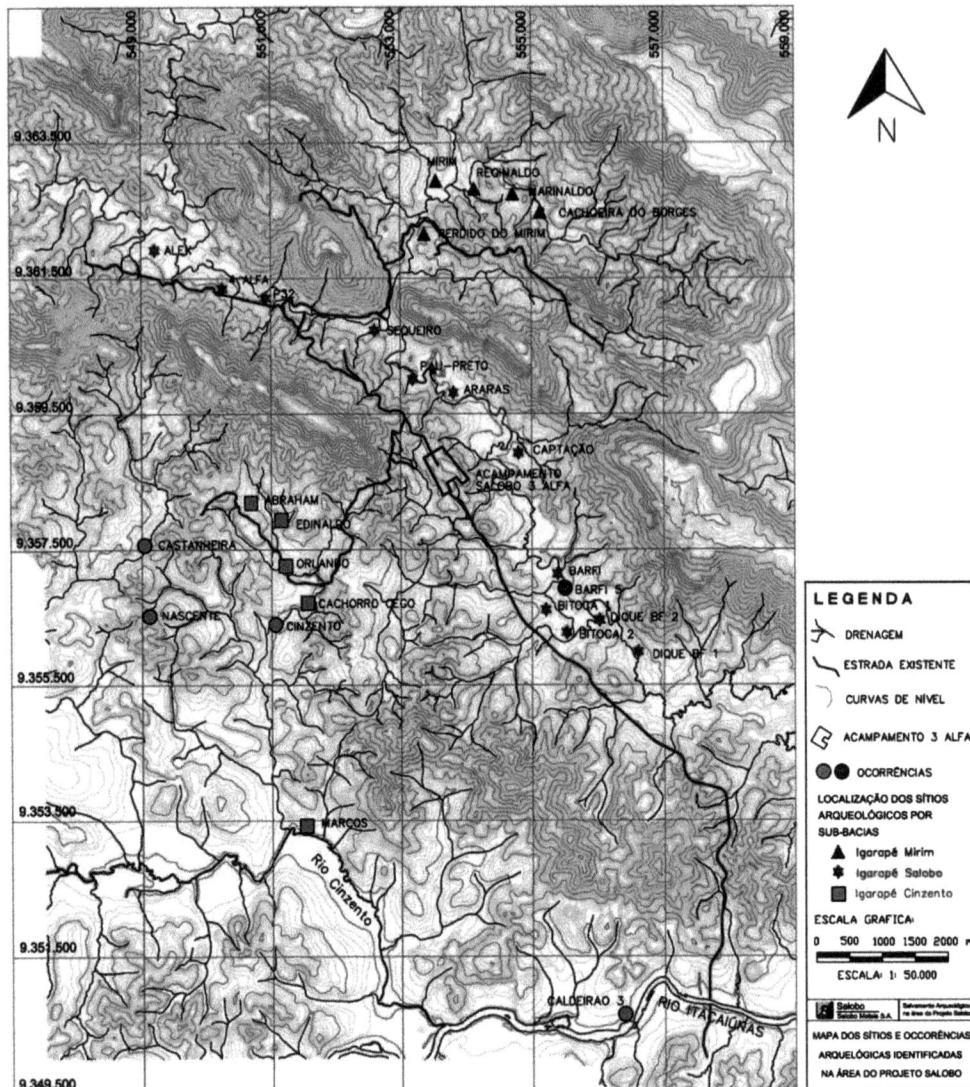

*Figure 1 – Location map of the research area, showing the three sub river basins*
*(Silveira & Rodrigues 2007)*

come from this process of cultural choice, have production rules that may be more or less structured. The technological study (Inizan *et al.* 1995; Pelegrin 2005; etc.) of the beads aims to get us closer to these rules, more or less visible on the traces that they conserve, by revealing them through there construction of the *chaîne opératoire* involved in their production.

This study is the result of the project "Archaeological rescue in the area of Salobo Project – PA", accomplished by researchers of Museu Paraense Emílio Goeldi, in collaboration with researchers from the Federal Universities of Pará and Minas Gerais (Fig. 1).

## 2. CHARACTERIZATION OF THE RESEARCH AREA

The research area is inserted in the eastern part of Tapirapé-Aquiri National Forest (FLONATA), in the city of Marabá, about 600 km south of the city of Belém. In this area there is a copper deposit, which is currently

being commercially exploited, located in a hill called Salobo. This mining deposit is part of the research area so-called "Carajás region" or Carajás Mineral Province.

The ore of the Salobo deposit consists mainly of bornite and chalcocite minerals, besides varying proportions of gold and silver. The soil in the area is characterized as sandy clay with a tendency to sandy, well drained. The main identified soil classes were Latosol (Latosoil) and Podzol (Brandt 1998).

The climate of this region is typically tropical, hot and wet and it fits in Köppen's classification as AW type. The thermal variations range from 24.3° to 28.3°C, while the climate in the plateaus is the mountainous one with annual averages between 21° and 23°C, with two well-defined seasons, a rainy one and a dry one. The driest period occurs from July to September and the one of higher rainfall occurs from December to March. The relative humidity is more than 80% (AB'SABER *apud* Silva 1989: 34).

As regards the forest formation of the FLONA Tapirapé-Aquiri, it is noted a variation of the dense Ombrophilous Forest (Tropical Rainforest). It is a kind of vegetation classified as opened by presenting vegetal species which fit better to the lighting conditions, such as bushes and lianas (long-stemmed, woody vines) (Brandt 1998). In the composition of this forest there are large, medium and small species of secondary forest. There is a diversity of fauna's species, including many zoological grouos – mammals, birds, reptiles, fish and shellfish.

Most of the region is drained by the hydrographic network of the Itacaiúnas river, a tributary of the left bank of the great Tocantins river. Its main tributary is the river Parauapebas (CVRD 1981: 25). This whole network is characterized by steep slopes and the torrential regime because of the rainy season. However, the rivers Parauapebas and Itacaiúnas are navigable by small boats during the rainy season (CVRD 1981: 25).

The Itacaiúnas riverbasin, within the research area, was geographically divided into three sub-basins: Igarapé[1] Salobo, river Cinzento (direct tributaries of the left bank of river Itacaiúnas) and Igarapé Mirim (tributary of the left bank of the Igarapé Salobo).

The iagarapé Salobo sub river basin presents the major area with 11 km$^2$ and 12 archaeological sites registered, then there is the Cinzento sub riverbasin with 7 km$^2$ of area and 5 sites and, at last, the igarapé Mirim with 3 km$^2$ of area and 5 archaeological sites.

The first records about the human occupation on this region were written by Father Manuel Mota, who visited Indian villages located in the lower courses of rivers Itacaiúnasa and Parauapebas, in 1721. Between 1895 and 1896, Henri Coudreau accomplished the geographical survey of the mentioned rivers, referring to the Entradas[2] and occupations of some parts of them (Coudreau 1980).

Only much later, in 1963, the archaeological potential of the area began to be revealed. The first researcher concerned with archaeological questions was Protásio Frikel, anthropologist of the Museu Paraense Emílio Goeldi (MPEG), who studied the Xikrin Indians of the upper course of the Itacaiúnas river, collecting lithic and ceramic vestiges (Frikel 1968). Since the Xikrin had no memory of the production of ceramic among them, P. Frikel related such vestiges to groups from the Tupi linguistic branch (Frikel 1968). The collection of archaeological ceramic was analyzed by the anthropologist Napoleon Figueiredo, who raised the hypothesis that the ceramic remains could be related to

what in Brazil is known as the "Tupiguarani Tradition". Thus, he creates and defines the "Itacaiúnas phase" (Figueiredo 1965).

In the early 1980s, the Companhia Vale do Rio Doce (CVRD) started the Carajas Iron Project, in the southeastern State of Pará and the first systematic archaeological researches also began –"Archaeological Rescue in Carajás" (Silveira *et al.* 1985; Simões *et al.* 1985). Fifty-three archaeological sites belonging to two different cultural contexts were located and researched: **i) pre-ceramic** with two sites in caves entrances and C14 datings around 8,000 years BP and **ii) ceramic** with 51 sites, located on the banks of rivers Itacaiúnas, Parauapebas and its tributaries, whose occupation is between the third and sixteenth centuries of the Christian era according to the radiocarbon dates (Lopes *et al.* in 1988; Silveira *et al.* 1985; Magalhães 1995).

During the 1990s, rescue archaeology researches located other 15 sites related to the pre-ceramic period in several caves in the Carajás region (Magalhães 1995). From the year 2000 onwards, rescue archaeology projects have multiplied in the region (Kipnis *et al.* 2005; Magalhães 1995; Pereira *et al.* 2008; Silveira & Rodrigues 2007; etc.). In these areas, similar vestiges to those recorded in Carajás were found, and related to both periods (Almeida 2008; Kipnis *et al.* 2005; etc.).

Despite the increase in recent studies, the southeast of Pará is still poorly known in terms of its archaeological potential (Kipnis *et al.* 2005). However, researches point out the importance of this area to better understand both the initial process of human occupation in Amazonia (Kipnis *et al.* 2005; Silveira & Rodrigues 2007) and the development and dispersal of groups related to the Tupiguarani Tradition in the region (Almeida 2008; Pereira *et al.* 2008).

More specifically, the project "Archaeological rescue in the area of Salobo project-PA", aimed at understanding the occupations of the pre-historic populations who lived in the region (Silveira & Rodrigues 2007). In this sense, several lithic collections from numerous archaeological sites were studied: the basins of Igarapés Mirim (sites Perdidos do Mirim, Mirim, Reginaldo, Marinaldo and Cachoeira do Borges), Salobo (Alex, 4 Alpha, P-32, Sequeiro, Pau Preto, Araras, Bitoca 1 and Bitoca 2 sites) and from the river Cinzento (Abraham, Edinaldo, Orlando, Cachorro Cego and Marcos sites). Intra-site and sub-basin studies were performed, followed by an inter-basins comparison of the lithic collections in general.

In this paper, we present only the results of the technological analysis of the lithic beads and the preliminary data from the traceological analysis.

## 3. THE ANALYZED ARCHAEOLOGICAL SITES

Lithic vestiges related to the production of ornaments in general were identified in 6 out of the 22 archaeological

---

[1] Igarapé' is an Amazon stream of the first or third order, consisting of a long arm of river or canal. There are only a few of them in the Amazon Basin, characterized for being shallow. They are normally found into the forest.

[2] The term 'Entradas, Bandeiras and Monções' is used to denote, generally, the various types of expeditions undertaken at the time of colonial Brazil, for purposes as diverse as simple exploitation of the land, search of mineral wealth, capture or killing of indigenous or even African slaves.

sites excavated by the project (Mirim, Bitoca 1, Bitoca 2, Pau Preto, Alex and Cachorro Cego).

The archaeological sites are located in flat areas in the lower slopes, approximately 150 m high, on the Banks of Igarapés Salobo or Mirim, and they are naturally bounded by the Igarapés, by ravines and sometimes by hills or outcrops. Bitoca 1, 2 and Alex sites are formed by spots of Archaeological Dark Earth, while the Mirim, Pau Preto and Cachorro Cego sites by spots of dark reddish/yellowish brown soil (acrisol). Dark Earth deposits' depths varying from 30/50 to 100 cm, and comprising large areas (over 60,000 m$^2$), were considered welling sites. The archaeological interventions comprised sectorized surface collection, survey openings of several units in different areas and in trenches.

In the Mirim site, 35 m$^2$ were excavated, with 22,921 exhumed (unearthed) ceramic fragments and 400 lithic vestiges. At the site Bitoca 1 approximately 140 m$^2$ were excavated, with 28,623 ceramic fragments and 2,125 lithic vestiges, as well as burnishers by the river side. At the site Bitoca 2 around 57 m$^2$ were excavated, with 6,180 ceramic fragments, 790 lithic vestiges and burnishers. The excavation at the Alex site was about 18 m$^2$, resulting in 8,631 ceramic fragments and 428 lithic vestiges. The Cachorro Cego site provided 12,859 ceramic fragments and 754 lithic vestiges, excavated from 24 m$^2$. The archaeological site Pau Preto is an exception to this characterization, once it shows reduced dimensions (60 x 50 m) and only a shallow (25 cm) spot of dark brown soil (8 x 4 m). Therefore, it was considered a camping site or temporary dwelling. In this site, 8 m$^2$ were excavated and 1,222 ceramic fragments and 89 lithic vestiges were found (Bueno 2008 apud Silveira et al. 2009). The datings place them in both occupations of hunter-gatherer (Mirim site 5,780 to 3,750 BP) and ceramists (Mirim site, 1,170 BP to 680 AP,[3] Pau Preto, 950 BP to 440AP; Bitoca1, 1,500 to 240 BP; Bitoca 2, 1,300 to 370 BP). In all the sites there was evidence of hearths, sometimes structured with carbonized seeds, and postholes (Silveira & Rodrigues 2007, etc.).

## 4. TECHNOLOGICAL STUDY OF THE BEADS AND PENDANTS

### 4.1. Methodological Procedures

The analyses of the beads in this article are the result of a combination of different methods: X-ray diffraction and fluorescence, for the identification of the raw material, and technological analyse is for the study of the production of lithic collection.

The identification of the raw material was carried out on the type of rock most used in the production of beads and pendants, as this is a hit her to unusual raw material in the archaeological record. The procedures were performed by

the team of Marcondes Costa, Universidade Federal do Pará (UFPA), and consisted of analysis of X-Ray Diffraction (XRD) and X-Ray Fluorescence (XRF), both non-destructive procedures, since the samples of lithic material were taken directly to the devices, without any removal of particles.

The XRD was performed by a diffractometer model X'Perth Pro Mpd (PW3040/60) of PANalytical with goniometer PW3050/60(θ/θ), X-ray ceramic tubes and Cuanode (Kα1 =1.540598 Å), model PW3373/00, with long fine focus (2200 W-60 kV), nickel Kβfilter. The instrumental conditions used were scans from 5° to 75 in 2 θ; voltage of 40 kV and 30 m A current, step size: 0.02° and 2θ and 10s the time/step. For the XRF, a chemical analysis was performed using aspectrometer Axios-Minerals of PANalytical.

The technological study was conducted through the use of concepts developed by the French school (Tixier, 1982; Inizan et al. 1995; Pelegrin 2005, etc.). The main approach is the technological analysis, supported by the concept of chaîne opératoire (Mauss 1998; Leroi-Gourhan 1966, etc.). Together they allow the identification of the production stages of lithic objects, from their conception (mental image – Pelegrin 2005) – culturally determined, selection of raw material, to the completion, use, disposal, and sometimes reuse of them. The chaîne opératoire permits to replace tools, cores and further debitage products hierarchically, in order to organize the pre historic space. The assemblage fundamentally presents beads at different stages of production (technical states), and, more rarely, cores and flakes related to them. Thus, the reconstructions of the production stages were based on the scars left on the beads, taking into account the sequence of the different techniques used (knapping, smoothing, polishing and drilling). Another reference were the results obtained in the study of a collection of silicified kaolinite beads, with 20,000 lithic pieces, from this same river basin, which allowed a better understanding of the entire production chain.

In this article, a bead is an "object usually round with only one central perforation in the axis of rotation of the piece so that it can rotate on itself around this axis" (Barge 1982: 33).

A bead has faces and sides (lateral parts). The faces are the flattest and largest parts, generally parallel and opposite to each other, while the sides are more or less narrow surfaces, which connect the faces (Fig. 2).

### 4.2. The technological analysis of the rounded/flat beads of silicified kaolinite

#### 4.2.1. Quantitative and qualitative presentation of the collection

The collection presented here consists of 11 beads found in the 6 sites studied (Mirim – 1; Bitoca 1 – 4; Bitoca 2 – 1; Pau Preto – 4; Alex – 1). The beads are made in

---

[3] Dates on AP refer to thermoluminescence dating and the present is the year of 2006.

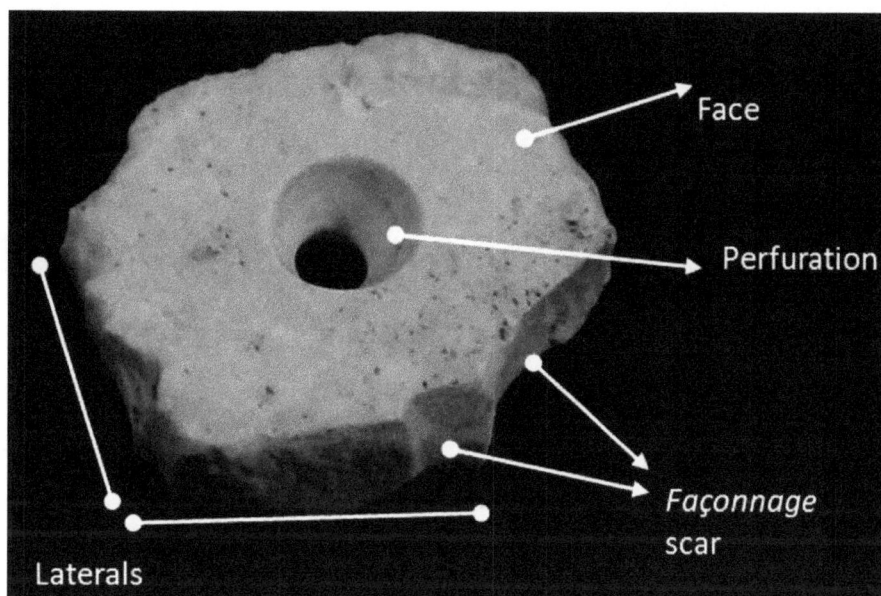

*Figure 2 – Terminology used to describe the parts of the beads*

silicified kaolinite, flat, small, (near 0.8 x 0.7 x 0.3 cm and 3.3 x 3.2 x 1.2 cm), morphology tending to a rounded one, formed by two lat and large faces, parallel to each other, linked by the sides, being slightly thick (0.3 to 1.2 cm). Some of them are perforated with small holes of which the diameter sare between 0.3 and 0.4 cm.

There are also 9 flakes (Botoca 1 – 6; Pau Preto – 1; Alex – 1; Cachorro Cego – 1) and 2 cores (Bitoca 1 – 1; Alex – 1) related to the bead's production. The flakes were knapped with the technique of percussion on the oblique anvil. They are products with low dimensions (close to 2-3 cm), thin, with both faces very flat and few accidents. The directions of the scars presented on the superior faces bound them directly to the cores, wicht have many percution plans, being explored different *débitage* surfaces, or bipolar plans.

The conservation condition of the parts is excellent, what allowed a detailed analysis of the technical gestures and production phases.

### 4.2.2. The raw material

The only raw material used for the production of the beads presented in this article is kaolinite. This was identified based on pieces from two of the sites of the studied basin. It is a kaolinite which has a relatively high hardness (hence the name silicified – or hardened – kaolinite), different from the one commonly found in very low hardness. The hardness of the silicified kaolinite usually takes place because of the thermal action at the time of its formation. The presence of microcrystalline quartz, inter grown with the same, also contributes to this characteristic, resulting in a higher indirect hardness to the set. This type of kaolinite is known as "flint". Quartz was found in several samples and its presence is quite clear forming layers with micro elements that can be seen with the naked eye.

### 4.2.3. Chaîne opératoire *and techniques used*

It's important to stress that the *chaîne opératoire* presented here is an ideal sequence of the production's steps, reconstructed according to the elements found in the analysed collection. In other words, the linear *chaîne opératoire* proposed here is a model, since the knapper can come and go through the production's steps. Knapping, smoothing, polishing and drilling aren't actions restricted to specific phases, unlike, i. e., during the smoothing phase, the pre-historic can knapp again and the opposite can also happens.

Notwithstanding the fewer number of cores, supports and flakes, the *chaîne opératoire* can also be reconstructed by the analysis of the objects themselves. Their different production's satages reveal phases, techniques, methods and products of their production.

Two operational chains were observed for the production of beads: one on flake and the other on kaolinite silicified plaquette (Fig. 3).

The first is with drawal of blanks from a core (*debitage*), rare in the collection, through percussion on the anvil. These flakes can show crushed, linear, smooth or, more rarely, cortical butts, always without abrasion, with prominent bulbs and, many times, hinged-flakes in the distal part. Then, the blank will be transformed into beads through various stages of production and the use of different techniques. You can observe them on several "technical states", *i. e.* the blanks are in different degrees of transformation, closer or farther from the desired product. Three technical states were observed:

In *State 1*, the pieces are far from the sought morphology. The blanks are still flakes that may still have a butt (part of the old striking platform) and or be hinged on the lower face. They are also misshapen, showing no clear

65

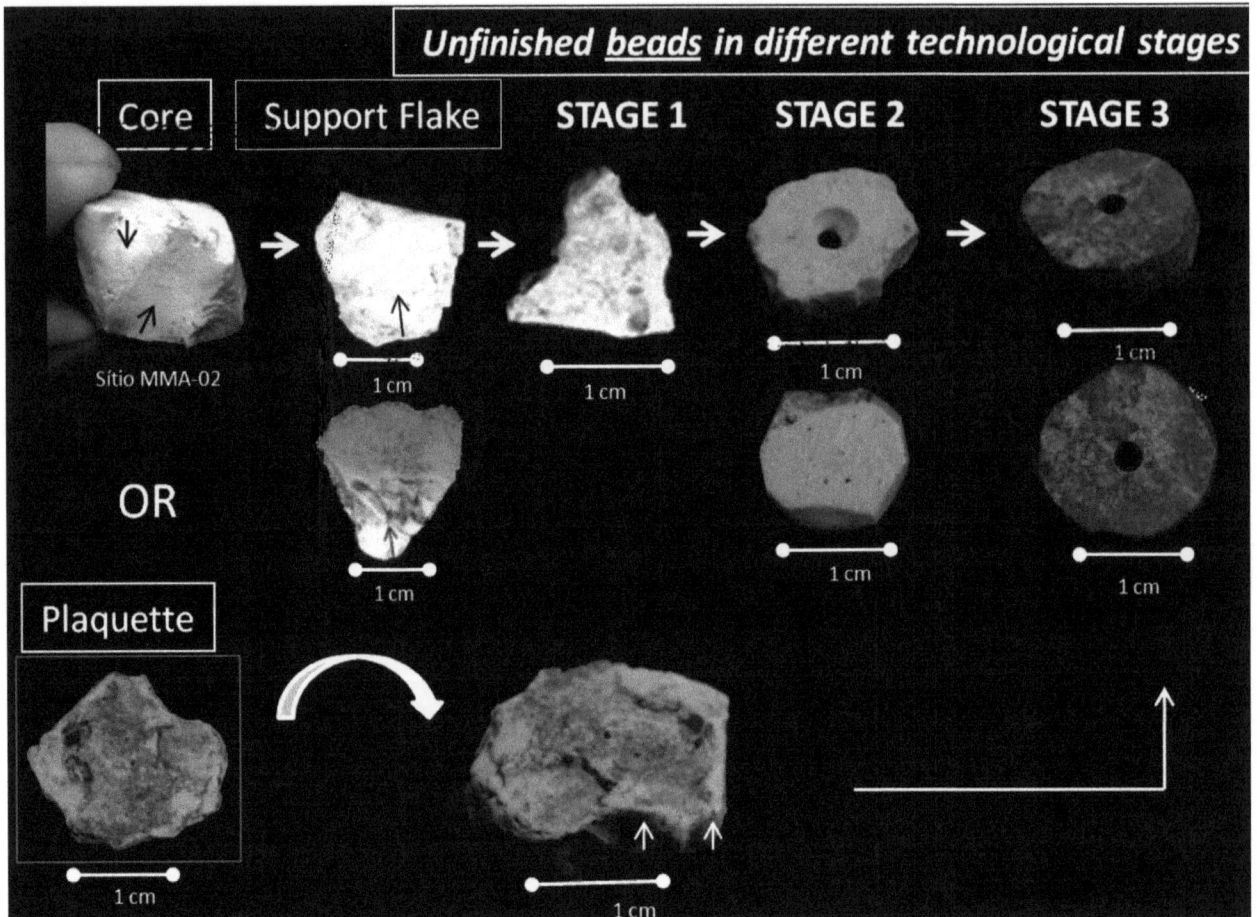

*Figure 3 – The two possible chaînes opératoires observed for the beads production*

evidence of the sought morphology, being easily identified. The pieces may or may not show abrasion marks by smoothing, besides the characteristic cortex of silicified kaolinite.

In this first moment of production, the blanks show some negatives of lateral removals (towards the thickness of the piece), often bipolar, mainly carried out by percussion on the anvil. The procedure of knapping consists in placing the piece on an anvil (wood, stone or other) and hitting it with a hammer with an accurate and firm gesture. The flakes show, on their lower faces, very often, well-marked counter bulbs, crushing just beneath the butt of striking platform, reflections, negatives or small breaks in the distal edges.

This lateral knapping of the bead corresponds to the shaping phase, that is, the beginning of the search for the wished shape and volume. Geometrically, it can be said that it has a faceted shape – hexagonal or octagonal (Walter and Scaglion 1994).

In a more advanced technical state, **State 2**, the beads show a lateral smoothing which aims to soften and round off the edges of the negatives left by the previous phase, with the existence of more or less smoothed pieces. The smoothing can also be on both the largest and most parallel sides of the bead. The piece gets more rounded, closer to the final goal. From this state on the pieces can

be drilled before or after the smoothing phases. The stigmas observed are linear marks resulting from the friction with an abrasive surface. They are thin, generally shallow and parallel to each other, besides the rounding of the edges.

In **State 3**, the bead has already a morphology and thickness very close to the final project: the edges are imperceptible (or almost), the two faces have stretch marks (striae) by smoothing or are partially polished. The bead has a rounded morphology, very symmetrical, generally more or less thick, which is the final products ought by pre-historic groups. At this stage, usually, it is already perforated. However, this is not a rule. Perforations can be already observed in the first stage of production.

The other *chaîne opératoire* uses slightly thick and small cortical plaquettes as blanks. The production steps are, in general, the same already described: shaping on the sides, giving the piece a roughly rounded morphology, the rounding of the edges by smoothing, and sometimes polishing and drilling, not always in that order. The big difference is that the blank will not undergo the process of debitage as the plaquette will be directly transformed.

The techniques used in the production of these beads are: knapping, smoothing, polishing and drilling.

The knapping operation, used for both the removal of the blanks and for shaping the sides, was performed with the technique of percussion on the anvil and, more rarely, with direct percussion with a hard stone hammer. However, in this case, in general, there was not a split fracture (90°). The piece was placed on the anvil slightly oblique in relation to its contact point and the percussion was performed at an angle close to 140°.

This percussion leaves very characteristic marks on the blanks: counter bulbs that can be well marked (depending on the angle of the piece and the angle of percussion), presence of crushing of the lower face near the butt (corresponding to the beginning of the detachment of the flake), a negative or wave on the distal part corresponding to the anvil's counter blow (or it is also possible to see small fractures transversal to the axis of debitage, in this sector).

Techniques for smoothing and polishing operations normally occur on the second technical state, when the bead has already received lateral knapping. The stigmas of these two techniques can be observed both on the sides and on the two faces. Furthermore, they can be observed covering the holes, indicating that it was applied after the perforation. On the largest and flattest faces, the smoothing stigmas (abrasion marks) are thin, linear striae, often shallow, parallel to each other, generally tending to an organization in a single steering axis or slightly transversal to each other, indicating a steady and monotonous come and go, which can reach the edge, making it round. More rarely, the abrasion marks have different directions on each of the faces, pointing to a less ordered movement.

When a person smooths one of the faces, then turns the piece, and smooths the other face, the abrasion marks present in each of the surfaces, when compared to each other, will show completely different axes of movement.

The sides of the pieces are smoothed in movements that have different directions. First one seeks the smoothing of the arrises left by the negatives of the chipping. It is noted slightly transversal striae to the longitudinal axis of these arrises. When these have reached the same thickness (or almost) the negatives present between them, it starts their smoothing, regularizing the surface completely. Striae left on the sides indicate a movement that follows the contour of the piece.

Polishing is the final stage of production, time of completion and final definition of the beads. In technological terms, this technique erases the stigmas of the other phases. Polishing beaches in sectors of some pieces were observed. So far, this technique was observed only in the cylindrical/tubular beads and in other pendants. The flattened beads were not finished with polishing.

These two techniques, although more expensive in terms of time and energy than knapping, are more easily controlled, i.e., in small pieces such as these ones, it is difficult to control the size of the knapping removals in the sense that they can remove more material than wished and deform the piece. Further, in this raw material, silicified kaolinite, less resistant with regard to the process of knapping, polishing is carried out more easily, with lower energy consumption.

The perforation of the pieces is performed in their longitudinal sections. It can be made from one of the faces until reaching the other one, or from both faces, meeting roughly in the centre of the bead. Drilling is probably performed by small drillers. In the collection, there is a possible driller of about 3 to 4 cm long, slightly thick, made of quartz (Mirim site), which fits very well in the hole (0.4 cm – thickness of the driller and diameter of the holes). Or, if we use a collection of 20,000 pieces from another site on the Serra dos Carajás as a reference, where various quartz tools of the same type were found, it is notice a blet hat these drillers also fit the perforations observed in the beads of that collection.

According to the observations of the inside the hole using the electron microscope, it is not possible to know whether the movement during the drilling comprised a complete rotation, or not (M. Alonso personal communication).

The perforations are made at any time of production, without any rule: it was possible to observe its presence in states 2 and 3 (more rarely in state 1). Sometimes the holes interrupt the smoothing striae of one of the faces, i. e., they were made after smoothing. Other times it is noted that the striae are not interrupted, but that the holes have smooth ededges, indicating that smoothing was performed after the hole or at least that the piece was smoothed again after the making of the hole.

Drilling is perhaps the most delicate moment in production. The pieces, slightly thick, performed in a fragile raw material, receive considerable and penetrating pressure, which often causes its fragmentation into two parts.

## 5. FINAL CONSIDERATIONS

The lithic collections located in the Itacaiúnas river basin, if compared with the ceramic vestiges, are few in number, specially the beads. Thus they're not representatives of the site's major function. However, there is a production site related to this type of rounded/flat beads approximately 50 km north (straight line). In that place, a lithic collection of bead production in silicified kaolinite was unearthed, which comprises more than 20,000 pieces (cores, flakes, *cassons*, beads in several technical states, etc.). It is possible that there is a local (or nearby) raw material mine and that the groups made the beads and then they were distributed along the hydrographic network of the sector. This hypothesis becomes more interesting considering that the conception of the bead is the same in both sectors (slightly thick, flat beads, with central hole), besides sharing the same stages of the *chaîne opératoire* and the techniques used in production.

The beads are related to the Tupiguarani ceramic levels and, in general, were collected in dwelling areas. In general, the ceramic material has technological, morphological and stylistic features, related to Tupiguarani Tradition (Figueiredo 1965; Oliveira and Silveira 2009, etc.). However, it was verified the existence of non Tupi sites, with contemporaneous datings and technological and decorative aspects that also refer to the ceramic industries of Incisa Ponteada Tradition, found in the regions of Santarém and Trombetas (Gupindaia 2008, etc.). The data suggest networking and indicate a more complex scenario for the occupation of this area.

## References

ALMEIDA, F.O. de 2008. *O complexo Tupi da Amazônia Oriental.* Dissertação de Mestrado, MAE-USP, São Paulo.

BARGE, H. 1982. *Les parures du Neolithique ancien au début de l'age des metaux en Languedoc.* Paris: Editions du CNRS. 396 p.

BRANDT, Meio Ambiente 1998. Documento integrado dos relatórios de zoneamento ambiental e monitoramento biológico da área de influência do Projeto Salobo. Belo Horizonte: Salobo Metais S.A. 165 p.

BROCHADO, J.P. 1981. Desarrollo de la tradicion ceramica Tupiguarani (AD 500-1800). I Simpósio Nacional de Estudos Missioneiros, 1981, Santa Rosa. *Anais do I Simposio Nacional de Estudos Missioneiros.* p. 76-156.

COUDREAU, H. 1980. *Viagem à Itaboca e ao Itacaiúnas.* Tradução Eugênio Amado. Belo Horizonte: Itatiaia; São Paulo: Edusp. 177 p. (Coleção Reconquista do Brasil, vol. 60).

CVRD – COMPANHIA VALE DO RIO DOCE 1981. *Projeto Ferro Carajás,* CVRD. 134 p.

FIGUEIREDO, N. 1965. A cerâmica arqueológica do rio Itacaiúnas. *Boletim do Museu Paraense Emílio Goeldi.* Belém: Museu Paraense Emílio Goeldi, p. 1-17, (Nova série Antropologia, vol. 27).

FRIKEL, P. 1968. Os Xikrín. Equipamento e técnicas de subsistência. *Publicações Avulsas do Museu Paraense Emílio Goeldi.* Belém: MPEG. 7 p.

GUAPINDAIA, V. 2008. *Além da margem do rio: a ocupação Konduri e Pocó na região de Porto Trombetas, PA.* Thesis (Doutorado) – FFLCH, MAE-USP, São Paulo. 194 p.

INIZIAN, M.-L.; REDURON, M.; ROCHE, H.; TIXIER, J. 1995. *Technologie de la pierre taillée.* Paris, Editions du CREP, 4. 199 p.

KIPNIS, R. *et al.* 2005. Contribuição para a cronologia da colonização Amazônica e suas implicações

teóricas. *Revista de Arqueologia.* São Paulo, v. 18. p. 81-93.

LEROI-GOURHAN, A. 1966. *La préhistoire: problèmes méthodologiques.* Presses Universitaires de France. p. 240-269.

LOPES, D. *et al.* 1988. Levantamento Arqueológico. In *Relatório Final do Projeto Estudo e Preservação de Recursos Humanos e Naturais da Área do Projeto "Ferro Carajás".* Belém: Museu Paraense Emilio Goeldi (vol. 1).

MAGALHÃES, M.P. 1995. *Arqueologia de Carajás. A presença pré-histórica do homem na Amazônia.* Rio de Janeiro: Companhia Vale do Rio Doce, 96 p.

MAUSS, M. 1998. *Manual de Etnografia.* São Paulo: Perspectiva. 431 p.

OLIVEIRA, E.R. de & SILVEIRA, M.I. da 2009. A ocupação de grupos ceramistas pré-coloniais no sudeste do Pará: aspectos do uso do espaço intra e inter sítios. In *Coletânea de Artigos do Prêmio Bolsista Destaque* PCI 2006-2008, p. 61-94 (vol. 1).

PELEGRIN, J. 2005. *Les pierres taillées: un historique de leur apport à l'archéologie.* 8 p.

PEREIRA, E. *et al.* 2008. A tradição Tupiguarani na Amazônia. In *Os ceramistas Tupiguarani.* Sínteses Regionais. A. Prous & T.A. Lima (Eds.). Belo Horizonte: Sigma. p. 49-66. (Vol. 1).

SILVA, M.F. 1989. *Aspectos ecológicos da vegetação que cresce sobre Canga Hematítica em Carajás – PA.* Thesis (Doutorado) – INPA/FUA, Manaus.

SILVEIRA, M.I.; LOPES, D.F.F.; MAGALHÃES, M.P. 1985. Salvamento arqueológico em Carajás (PA). III Congresso da Sociedade de Arqueologia Brasileira, Goiânia. *Caderno de Resumos.*

SILVEIRA, M.I. & RODRIGUES, M.C.L. 2007. *Quinto Relatório do Projeto de Salvamento Arqueológico na área do Projeto Salobo/PA (sítios Alex, Sequeiro, Marcos).* Belém: Museu Paraense Emílio Goeldi. 116 p.

SILVEIRA, M.I. *et al.* 2009. *Relatório Final de Atividades Laboratoriais referentes aos Projetos "Prospecção e Salvamento arqueológico na área do Projeto Salobo – PA.* Belém: Museu Paraense Emilio Goeldi, 343 p.

SIMÕES, M.F.; LOPES, D.F.F.; SILVEIRA, M.I. & MAGALHÃES, M.P. 1985. Nota sobre as pesquisas arqueológicas em Carajás. *American Antiquity (Current Research)* 50 (1): 175 p.

TIXIER, J. 1982. Techniques de débitage: osons ne plus affirmer. *Studia Prehistorica Belgica* 2: 13-22.

WATTERS, D.R. & SCAGLION, R. 1994. Beads and Pendants from Trants, Montserrat: implications for the Prehistoric lapidary industry of Caribbean. *Annals of Carnegie Museum* 63 (3): 215-237. Translated to Portuguese by Vera Guapindaia.

# WEAR TRACES ON BEAVER TEETH:
# THE USE OF TEETH AS TOOLS

Vanesa Esther PARMIGIANI & María Celina ALVAREZ SONCINI

Centro Austral de Investigaciones Científicas – CADIC CONICET, Laboratorio de Antropología,
B. Houssay 200, 9410 Ushuaia, Tierra del Fuego, Argentina
veparmigiani@yahoo.com.ar      mcalvarezson@gmail.com

**Abstract**: *The dental pieces constitute an important part of the archaeological material recovered in numerous sites and with different chronologies. They are a first degree taxonomic indicator but also, at the same time, an excellent raw material for ornaments and tool- making. This last aspect is the one that we are interested in presenting in this work.*

*With this purpose, we carried out an experimental study with teeth of* Castor canadensis, *where incisors were used as tools, for scraping and cutting on different materials.*

*Analysis was carried out by means of stereomicroscope and metallographic microscope, in order to identify traces of use different from natural traces on teeth.*

**Key words**: *Functional analysis, Experimentation, Dental pieces*

**Résumé**: *Les pièces dentaires constituent une partie importante du matériel archéologique récupéré dans de nombreux sites archéologiques, avec des chronologies diverses. Elles sont un indicateur fondamental du point de vue taxonomique, mais en même temps elles constituent une matière première d'excellente qualité pour la confection d'ornements et d'outils. C'est ce dernier aspect que nous considérons dans ce travail.*

*Dans ce but, nous avons développé une étude expérimentale avec des dents de* Castor canadensis, *où nous avons utilisé les incisives comme outils, pour grater et couper différents matériaux. L'analyse a été faite avec loupe binoculare et microscope métallographique, pour identifier des traces d'utilisation, différentes des traces naturelles des dents.*

**Mots-clé**: *Analyse fonctionnelle, Expérimentation, Pieces dentaires*

## 1. INTRODUCTION

There is an extense record of archaeological sites with diverse chronology, in which dental pieces from diverse animal species are represented.

There is general agreement among scholars that analysis of teeth from the archaeological record has a great explanatory potential, since we can extract valuable information from them, such as sex, age and death seasonality. But above all, dental pieces constitute an excellent indicator from the taxonomical point of view.

Moreover, the teeth, along with the rest of the anatomical parts of animals utilized in the archaeological sites, provide information to interpret the subsistence of diverse human groups in the past.

There are also many records of dental pieces revealing that they were used as raw material for the manufacture of ornaments, facts documented in both ethnographic and archaeological studies. (Hasselin, 1986).

Nevertheless, other studies have shown that teeth could perform in ways different from the ones described; they could have been directly used as tools. In some cases, teeth are removed from the jaw and modified while in other cases they are used directly, taking advantage of their morphology (Camps-Fabrer, 1979; Voruz, 1990, 1997; Maigrot, 2001; Clemente *et al.* 2002).

The teeth, the same as bone, constitute an excellent raw material to manufacture tools, ornaments and weapons, due to their remarkable plasticity and resistance. Coming from a live source, they are easily adapted and often do not require a lot of preparation work to use them.

The particular morphology of some dental pieces such as incisives and canines (or fangs) facilitates their transformation into tools, or their direct use.

This direct use is subject to the selection of the dental piece and its size, which in turn will depend on the age of the individual and the selected species

Generally, in the archaeological assemblages where tools are made on a biological support, either bone or tooth, the manufacturing technique and its functionality are scarcely researched upon, contrary to what happens with rocks (Semenov, 1964).

From this point of view, we believe that the analysis of traces of use on dental pieces is an important part in archaeological analysis, and for that reason teeth need to be selected from the archaeofaunistic assemblages and to be analysed separately, as considered as potential tools.

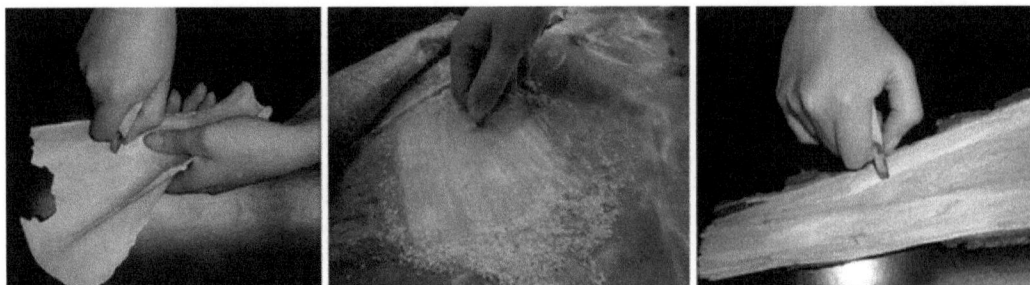

*Figure 1 – From left to right: work on bone, leather work and wood work*

There are both etnographic and archaeological works that present the study of teeth as tools (Clastres, 1972; Leroi-Gourhan, 1973; Pétrequin & Pétrequin, 1988; Tizzer, 1993; Zhilin, 1997; Maigrot, 2001; Delgado *et al.* 2002; Chaix, 2004).

Based on these background and also taking the work published by I. Clemente, E.Y. Gyria, O.V. Lozovzska and V.M. Lozovski (2002) as starting point, we decided to carry out an experimental study with teeth from these animals.

During this work, Dr. Clemente kindly made available for us the results of his experimentation where the instruments recovered in the archaeological site were exactly replicated (I. Clemente & V. Lozovska, 2011); both results will be discussed later.

## 2. MATERIALS AND METHODS

To develop the experiment, a sample of 20 beaver skulls was used, both female and male from several ages belonging to the CADIC Collection. All of them belong to the *Castor canadensis* species, that inhabits the northern hemisphere, except some american beavers that were introduced in Tierra del Fuego in 1946, in the region that corresponds to the area of sample collection.

The incisives from different individuals were selected, both loose and still inserted in the jaw. These dental pieces were not modified for its use.

The materials worked on were: Bone (*Lama guanicoe*), hide (*Castor canadensis*) and wood (*Nothofagus pumillio*) (Figure 1).

### 2.1. The experimental protocol

Experimentation was carried out according to the following experimental protocol:

1. Observation under low magnification (stereomicroscope, 6x to 50x) to see the tooth topography and dentin as well as the enamel surface.

2. Observation under high magnification (metallographic microscope, 50x to 500x) before being utilized, to see and characterize the enamel and dentin aspect in their natural state (Figure 2).

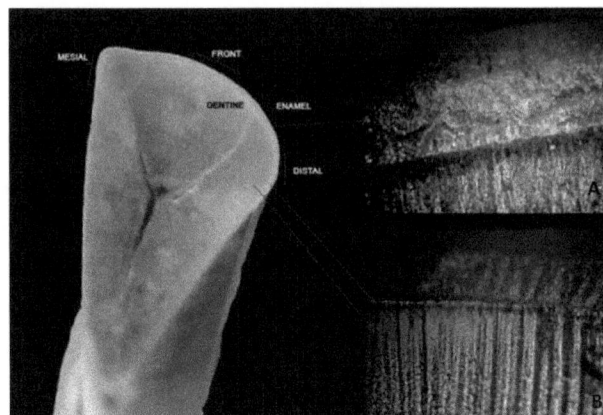

*Figure 2 – Parts of the tooth in its natural condition and detail of a) enamel and b) dentine*

3.- Use of dental pieces on wood (fresh), bone and hide (in dried state) with longitudinal and transversal motion relative to teeth cutting edge. During 5, 10, and 15 minutes with each piece.

4. Image capture at fixed points, before being utilized, and then after use, at intervals of 5', 10'and 15'.

5. Each piece was accompanied by an experimentation file card.

### 2.2. Functional Experimentation

As a reference sample, six dental pieces from the total number of craniums were used. Some of them were used to work on three kinds of materials: bone, hide and wood (Table 1).

Two of the pieces were utilized with their bone support (hemimandibles) working as a support handle (PCC426 Left, PCC426 Right). The other four pieces (1, 2, PCC429 Left, PCC429 Right) were utilized directly applying manual pressure without intermediaries, in this case, they were the upper and lower incisives.

Beavers use their upper and lower incisives to gnaw constantly on wood, since these teeth present continuous growth. Therefore, all incisives in their natural state present traces of use on wood.

It is interesting to point out that the cutting movement produced by this action is in one direction (longitudinal

*Table 1 – Data source of the sample*

| CODE | AGE | SEX | INCISORS |
|---|---|---|---|
| 1 | No data | No data | Upper left |
| 2 | No data | No data | Top right |
| PCC429 | 1 age | Male | Right lower |
| PCC429 | 1 age | Male | Lower left |
| PCC426 | No data | Female | Right lower |
| PCC426 | No data | Female | Lower left |

to the tooth axis) as a consequence of continuous growth, the distal part is being discarded (which is where the natural traces are developed). Because of this, only the last traces of work before the animal's death can be observed.

## 3. RESULTS

### 3.1. Work on wood

Both pieces worked on beech wood (*Nothofagus pumilio*), in fresh state PCC426 Left and PCC426 Right (Table 2). The first piece worked transversally (scraping) and the second worked longitudinally (cutting).

*Table 2 – Experimental data*

| PIECE | MATERIAL WORKED | MOVEMENT | WORKING TIME |
|---|---|---|---|
| 1 | Flat bone | Transversal | 15 min. |
| 2 | Long bone | Transversal | 20 min. |
| PCC429 Right. | Beaver leather | Transversal | 15 min. |
| PCC429 Left. | Beaver leather | Longitudinal | 15 min. |
| PCC426 Right. | Fresh wood | Longitudinal | 15 min. |
| PCC426 Left. | Fresh wood | Transversal | 5 min. |

*Macroscopic observations:*

Piece #PCC426 Left was used for transversal work (scraping). This piece was broken transversally very close to the edge which did not allow to continue with the experiment. Consequently, the results that we present here correspond to the first five minutes of use observation.

For the cutting work (longitudinal) only one incisive #PCC426 Right was used and during the experimentation it did not show fractures although there was some microsplinter release in both the enamel and dentin.

In every case, the work performed showed no difficulty, proving its efficient use for scraping and cutting wood. The main effect of the work on wood, with any of the movements, is the release of microsplinters mainly from enamel and some from dentin, in those areas in contact with the material.

*Microscopic traces:*

During microscopic analysis, the samples show some micropolish with the following characteristics: brilliant, with deep, dark and short striations.

In the longitudinal work (cutting) there was a rounding of both distal and mesial ends (Figures 3a and 3b) and a microsplintering in the central part of the edge of the tooth (Figures 3c and 3d).

In the case of the transversal work (scraping) up until the first five minutes of use there was a microsplintering on the whole working edge. After this initial period, the edge becomes regular and the ends are rounded off.

### 3.2. Work on Bone

For the scraping on bone, two dental pieces were used #1 and #2 (Table 1). Both pieces worked on dried guanaco bone (*Lama guanicoe*).

Piece #1 was used to work on a flat bone (scapula). Piece #2 was used over a long bone (humerus) in which we achieved 20 minutes work time. In both cases, it was a transversal motion (Table 2).

*Macroscopic observations:*

Both incisives behaved in a similar way throughout the experiment. During the first five minutes of scraping, the enamel is coming off easily in both dental pieces, producing a great amount of microsplintering on the edge.

In this first stage of the work, both incisives acquired such a configuration regarding their shape, that remained up until 20 minutes of work, and a follow up to the microsplinters' behaviour could be performed.

*Microscopic traces:*

In the microscopic analysis, the samples show a more brilliant micropolish than the ones observed in the work with wood, the striation is longer and slimmer. The

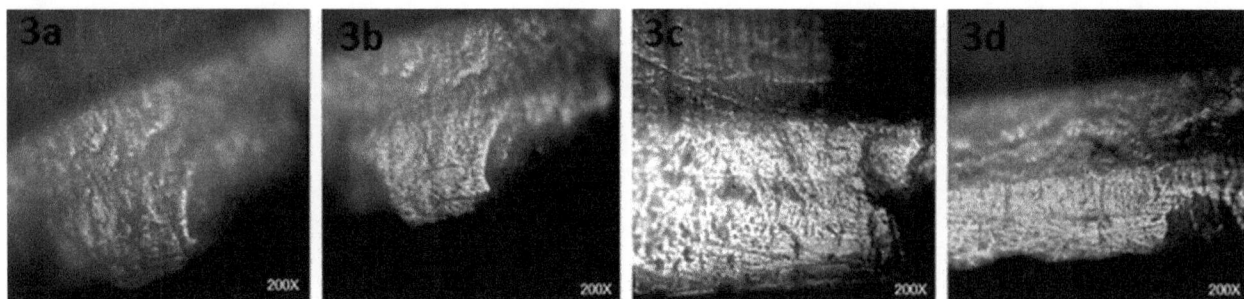

*Figure 3 – Longitudinal work on wood (Code PCC426-Right) from left to right:*
*3a) Mesial 5', 3b) Mesial 15', 3c) Front 5', 3d) Front 15'*

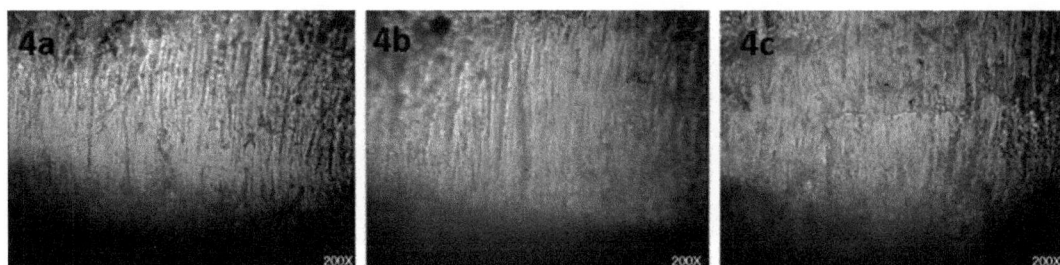

*Figure 4 – Cross work on bone (Code 1) from left to right: 4a) Front 10', 4b) Front 15', 4c) Front 20'*

*Figure 5 – Longitudinal work on hides (Code PCC429-Left) from left to right:*
*5a) Front/Dentin 5', 5b) Front/Dentin 10', 5c) Front/Dentin 15', 5d) Front/Enamel 10'*

microsplintering is produced towards the extremes and the rounding towards the middle part on the edge of the piece. This micropolish is more extended towards the interior of piece compared to that forms on wood (Figures 4a, 4b, 4c).

### 3.3. Work on hides

The dental pieces utilized for the experiment on hide were PCC429 Right and PCC429 Left (Table 2). In this case, the teeth were removed from the jawbone since the rising branch of it would not allow an efficient scraping with the whole edge of the tooth, thus modifying the angle of work. The material on which the work was performed in both cases was beaver hide in a dried state.

The first one of pieces was used for longitudinal work (cut) and the second one for the transversal work (scrape).

*Macroscopic observations:*

Throughout the work on hide, none of the dental pieces showed any dentine nor enamel release. The general configuration of the teeth remained almost the same, and changes could only be witnessed at a microscopic level.

*Microscopic traces:*

In the microscopic analysis, it was possible to see that the micropolish in the pieces used on hide presented a more opaque shine compared to the pieces used on wood or bone, and the striation is long, wide and dark.

The piece modification is conditioned by kinematics. When there is longitudinal movement, the microsplintering is produced on the ends and the center of the tooth is rounded off to become regular. The micropolish develops first in the central area of the tooth, moving towards the ends after 10 minutes of use (Figure 5).

In the transversal movement (scrape), the opposite happens. The ends become regular and there is microsplintering in the center of the piece. The micropolish develops on the ends of piece during the first five minutes while the micropolish in the central part of

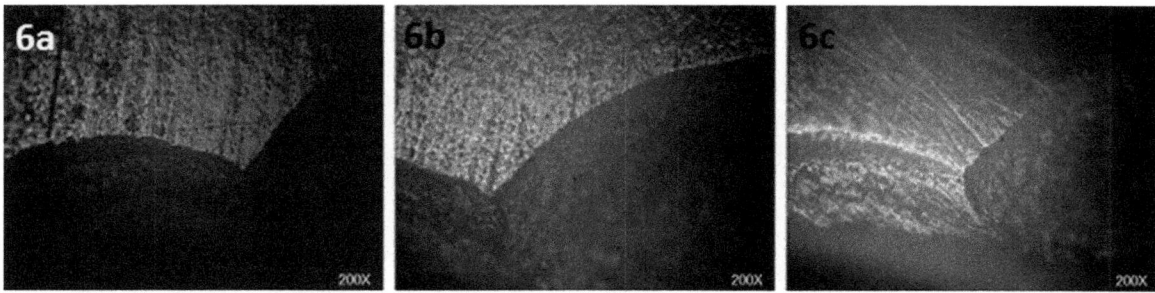

*Figure 6 – Cross work on hides (Code PCC429-Right) from left to right: 6a) Front 5', 6b) Front 10', 6c) Front 15'*

the piece develops once that area becomes regular. That could be observed after ten minutes of work (Figure 6).

## 4. REFLECTIONS ON THE RESULTS OF THE EXPERIMENTS

The results of the experimentation shows us in first instance that it is possible to distinguish if a dental piece with "natural traces" of wood, such as the case of the beaver, was utilized as a tool to perform cutting or scraping activities on different materials, including wood.

In this work, we performed a research on the development of the micropolish in the different dental pieces.

In the pieces used on wood and bone, the modifications occurred within the first five minutes of work and they did not vary greatly on the following stages. An edge stabilization could be observed in those first minutes of use, followed by a gradual development of the micropolish on later stages of use (10, 15, and in some cases 20').

The pieces used on hide behaved in a different way. First, it is necessary to differentiate that edge stabilization in this case occurred by sectors, depending on cinematics (see previous description or micropolish). Besides, the micropolish develops in two stages: one starts at five minutes in those areas where the edge is not splintered, and the second one starts at ten minutes once the edge stabilization occurred.

Regarding microtraces, we could observe that wood and bone show a brilliant micropolish (betweeen them, the bone microwear polish is shinier than the one from wood) while hide microwear polish is opaque. Regarding striations, we also found differences. Those produced by work on bone are long and thin, while the ones produced by wood and hide are wider and deeper.

It is important to emphasize that enamel and dentine behave very differently while working on these materials. The enamel usually comes off forming microsplinters, and dentine is more succeptible to micropolish formation during work. Regarding edge stabilization, it mainly depends on the enamel. In their natural state, beaver teeth present a curved shape with outings towards the edges,

that is why depending on the material used, the angle of work and the cinematics those edges will show a more developed micropolish, as long as there is no microsplintering.

## 5. DISCUSSION

The analysis of teeth as potential tools is still an underdeveloped and marginal study. Except some cases in which this material is taken as such, we could mention some work studies carried out in South America on capibara teeth, on beaver teeth in several groups in North America, from archaeological sites in Russia and on pigs in Indonesia (Clastres, 1972; Leroi-Gourhan, 1973; Stewart, 1973; Pétrequin & Rachez, 1997; Maigrot, 2001; Clemente et al. 2002; Clemente & Lozovzska, 2011 and bibliography cited there). Interpretation of their functionality based on the microscopic analysis is recent, since in many cases this is carried out based on direct etnographic analogies (Petrequín & Petrequín, 1988). It is only in the last decades when the functional analysis on a microscopic basis started to be used to determine their use (Maigrot, 2001; Clemente et. al., 2002, 2011).

Parallel to this investigation, the authors Clemente & Lozovska were developing and experiment with beaver teeth, replicating the tools found in the excavation of the Zatmoje 2 site (Russia). Upon reading the results from the authors, it was possible to see that those results were compatible with ours: The efficiency of the teeth to perform the tasks, the distribution and development of microtraces in two levels. On one side, related to the part of the tooth being observed and on the other side, the formation of traces of use varies according to the work on different materials, due to hardness of the material, kinematics or time spent.

Our experimentation, despite being limited to a small number of samples, resulted very successful regarding the results and conclusions and, at the same time, it opened us new research lines to pursue deeper in the future. In a later work, we will try to expand the reseach on beaver teeth (*Castor canadensis*) and start with other species, such as the incisives from different rodents natives of South America, such as Capibara (*Hidrochoerus hidrochaeris*) and Tucu Tucu (*Ctenomys*), to be able to perform a more american approach to the interpretation of the use of teeth as possible tools.

## Acknowledgments

To Guillermo Deferrari for access to the collection, Ignacio Clemente for access to the bibliography, Hernán De Angelis for the help with the pictures, Gastón Delgado for the translation and María Estela Mansur for her critical reading.

## References

CAMPS-FABRER, H. 1979. L'industrie osseuse néolithique de l'abri Jean-Cros. In: Guilaine J., ed. – L'Abri Jean Cros; essai d'approche d'un groupe humain du Néolithique ancien dans son environnement, edited by: Centre d'Anthropologie des sociétés rurales, Toulouse, pp. 185-196.

CHAIX, L. 2004. Le castor, un animal providentiel pour les Mésolithiques et les Néolithiques de Zamostje (Russie). In: Brugal J.P. y Desse J., eds. – Petits animaux et sociétés humaines. Du complément alimentaire aux ressources utilitaires. XXIVe rencontres internationales d'archéologie et d'histoire d'Antibes. Editions APDCA, pp. 325-336.

CLASTRES, P. 1972. Chroniques des indiens Gwayaki. Collection Terre Humaine, Plon. Paris.

CLEMENTE I; GYRIA, E.Y.; LOZOVZSKA, O.V. and LOZOVSKI, V.M. 2002. Análisis de instrumentos en costilla de alce, mandíbulas de castor y en caparazón de tortuga de Zamostje 2 (Rusia). In: I. Clemente, R. Risch and J.F. Gibaja – eds. Análisis Funcional: su aplicación al estudio de sociedades prehistóricas. BAR International Series 1073. BAR Publishing, Oxford: pp. 187-196.

CLEMENTE CONTE, I. & LOZOVSKA, O.V. 2011. Los incisivos de castor utilizados como instrumentos de trabajo. Rastros de uso experimentales para una aplicación arqueológica: el caso de Zamostje 2 (Rusia). Morgado, A. Baena, J. García, D., eds. – La investigación experimental aplicada a la arqueología, pp. 227-234.

DELGADO, T.; VELASCO, J.; ARNAY DE LA ROSA, M.; GONZÁLEZ, R.; MARTÍN, E. 2002. Huellas de trabajo en piezas dentarias de la población prehispánica de Gran Canaria. In I. Clemente, R. Risch and J.F. Gibaja, eds., – Análisis Funcional: su aplicación al estudio de sociedades prehistóricas. BAR, International Series 1073. BAR Publishing, Oxford: pp. 295-305.

HASSELIN, M. 1986. Contribution à l'étude du site néolithique des Prises à Machecoul (Loire-Atlantique) l'Industrie osseuse. In: Mémoire de maîtrise, université de Nantes, vol. 2.

LEROI-GOURHAN, A. 1973. L'Homme et la matière, évolution et technique. T.1 collection – Sciences d'aujourd'hui, ed. Albin Michel, Paris.

MAIGROT, Y. 2001. Technical and functional study of ethnographic (Irian Jaya, Indonesia) and archaeological (Chalain and Clairvaux, Jura, France 30th century BC) tools made from boars'tusks. In: S. Beyries, P. Pétrequin, eds. – Ethno-archaeology and its transfers. BAR International Series. BAR Publishing, Oxford: pp. 67-80.

PÉTREQUIN, A.M. and PÉTREQUIN, P. 1988. Le néolithique des lacs, Préhistoire des lacs de Chalain et de Clairvaux (4000-2000 av. J.-C.), Ed. Errance, Paris.

PÉTREQUIN, P. and RACHEZ, E. 1997. Un biseau naturel: l'incisive de castor, In P. Pétrequin ed. – Les sites littoraux néolithiques de Clarivaux et de Chalain (Jura), III, Chalain station 3, 3200-2900 av. J.-C., Editions: Maison des Sciences de l'Homme, Paris, pp. 523-528.

SEMENOV, S.A. 1964. Prehistoric Technology. Moonraker Press. Wiltshire.

STEWART, H. 1973. Artifacts of the northwest coast Indian. Haucock House Publishers.

TYZZER, T.T. 1993. Animal Tooth implements from shell heaps of maine. American Antiquity, Vol. 8, No. 4, pp. 354-362. Society for American Archaeology.

VORUZ, J.L. 1990. L'outillage en os et en bois de cerf. In: Le Néolithique moyen, II, les sites littoraux de Clairvaux-les Lacs (Jura)- Pétrequin P. ed.,- editions de la Maison des sciences de l'homme, Paris, pp. 313-348.

VORUZ, J.L. 1997. L'outillage en os et en bois de cerf de Chalain 3. In: Les sites littoraux néolithiques de Clairvaux-les Lacs et de Chalain (Jura), III, Chalain station 3, 3200-2900 av. J.C. Pétrequin P. (ed) vol. 2, editions de la Maison des sciences de l'homme, Paris, pp. 467-510.

ZHILIN, M.G. 1997. Beaver mandible tools from Veretje 1. In: Oshibkina S.V. Veretje 1. Poselenije borealnogo vremeni na severe Vostochnoy Evropy. Moscow. (in Russian), pp. 191-192.

# MICROSCOPIC USE-WEAR ANALYSIS IN LATIN AMERICA ITS CONTRIBUTION TO NEW PROBLEMS, RAW MATERIALS AND TAPHONOMIC CONTEXTS

María Estela MANSUR, Hernán DE ANGELIS
Centro Austral de Investigaciones Científicas – CADIC CONICET, Laboratorio de Antropología,
B. Houssay 200, 9410 Ushuaia, Tierra del Fuego, Argentina
estelamansur@gmail.com      hernandeangelis@yahoo.com.ar

Marcio ALONSO LIMA
UFMG – Setor de Arqueologia do Museu de História Natural, SETE – Soluções e Tecnologia Ambiental, Brasil
mg.alonso@gmail.com

**Abstract**: *Since the publication of S. Semenov's Prehistoric Technology in Europe in 1964, microscopic analysis of archaeological materials has developed continuously, although it has followed an uneven rhythm. In Latin America, microscopic analysis started at about the same time and developed in a parallel way as in Europe and North America. Nevertheless it had its own course to follow, as it tried to solve different methodological problems, mainly concerning raw materials used, different depositional contexts, etc. But besides methodology, it was also singular because of its theoretical-methodological approach in relation with the type of ethnographic and archaeological problems investigated.*

*Different reasons led it to be little known, not only in the Old World but also in North America. We believe that this first meeting of the Commission* Tools function and socio-economical reconstructions of the past, *which takes place in a Latin American country, is an excellent opportunity to attempt to dress a preliminary synthesis of the principal investigations and lines of research developed, as well as their contribution to micro wear analysis as a whole.*

**Key words**: *Bibliography, Use-wear traces, Functional Analysis*

**Résumé**: *Depuis la publication en Europe de PrehistoricTechnology par S. Semenov en 1964, l'analyse microscopique des matériaux archéologiques s'est développée en permanence, même si elle a suivi un rythme inégal. En Amérique Latine, l'analyse microscopique est commencée à la même époque qu'en Europe et en Amérique du Nord et s'est développée de façon parallèle. Néanmoins, elle avait sa propre voie à suivre, car elle a essayé de résoudre différents problèmes méthodologiques, concernant principalement les matières premières utilisées, les différents contextes dépositionnels, etc. Mais au-delà de la méthodologie, elle a également été singulière en raison de son approche théorique et méthodologique en relation avec le type de problèmes ethnographiques et archéologiques étudiés.*

*Différentes raisons ont conduit à ce que ces recherches soient peu connues, non seulement dans l'Ancien Monde mais aussi en Amérique du Nord. Nous croyons que cette première réunion de la Commission sur la fonction des outils et les reconstituions socio-économiques du passé, qui a lieu dans un pays d'Amérique latine, est une excellente occasion pour établir une synthèse préliminaire des principales investigations et axes de recherche développés, ainsi que leur contribution à la recherche sur les micro traces dans son ensemble.*

**Mots-clé**: *Bibliographie, Traces d'utilisation, Analyse fonctionnelle*

## INTRODUCTION

The publication of the English translation of S. Semenov's Prehistoric Technology in 1964 can be considered as the real starting point of functional analysis in archaeological studies in the West. From that time on, microscopic analysis of archaeological materials has developed continuously, although it has followed an uneven rhythm, sometimes more rapid and sometimes slower. Nowadays, since it was established as a formal discipline, use-wear analysis has acquired the position of a routine practice in archaeological research. Its methods have become ever more sophisticated, with improvement in optical equipment, new observation as well as analysis and recording techniques, better photography of use-wear, etc.

This type of study receives different names, sometimes used indistinctively, such as functional analysis, traceology, micro-wear analysis, etc. Anyhow, it is basically focused towards the functional interpretation of artifacts and their correlates in the socio-economical analysis of past societies.

In Latin America, microscopic analysis started at about the same time -and developed in a parallel way- as in Europe and North America. Nevertheless it had its own course to follow, as it tried to solve different methodological problems, mainly concerning raw materials used, depositional contexts, etc. But besides methodology, it was also singular because of its theoretical-methodological approach in relation with the type of ethnographic and archaeological problems investigated.

Different reasons led it to be little known, not only in the Old World but also in North America. We believe that this first meeting of the Commission *Tools function and socio-economical reconstructions of the past,* which takes place in a Latin American country, is an excellent opportunity to attempt to dress a preliminary synthesis of the principal investigations and lines of research developed, as well as their contribution to micro wear analysis as a whole. Here we are presenting a preliminary list of publications concerning microwear analysis produced in Latin America, as well as of publications produced in the old world but concerning Latin American archaeology. Number of publications, as well as geographical distribution of papers, show its increasing tendency along the last decades. We know that the list is not complete, there are certainly many publications that we do not know, and that we will be grateful to receive. Consequently, we hope that this first attempt will help us as an approach to an exhaustive bibliography in the future.

## BIBLIOGRAPHIC SUMMARY OF PUBLICATIONS ABOUT FUNCTIONAL ANALYSIS IN LATIN AMERICA

### 1970-1979

YACOBACCIO, H. 1978. Aportes para una tipología de los rastros de utilización en instrumentos líticos. Ponencia presentada en *V Congreso Nacional de Arqueología Argentina,* San Juan.

### 1980-1989

ALONSO LIMA, M. y MANSUR, M.E. 1986/90. Estudo traceológico de instrumentos em quartzo e quartzito de Santana do Riacho (Minas Gerais). *Revista do Museu de Historia Natural,* 11: 173-190, Belo Horizonte, Brasil.

CARDICH, A.; MANSUR-FRANCHOMME, M.E.; GIESSO, M. y DURAN, V. 1981-1982. "Arqueología de las Cuevas de 'El Ceibo', provincia de Santa Cruz, Argentina". *Relaciones,* Revista de la Sociedad Argentina de Antropología, Buenos Aires (1982). T. XIV, n° 2 N.S: 173-209.

CASTRO DE AGUILAR, A. 1987/88. Análisis microscópico de huellas de utilización en artefactos líticos de Fortín Necochea. *Paleoetnológica* Vol. 4: 65-77.

LEWENSTEIN, S. 1981a. El uso de métodos cuantitativos en el análisis de la lítica. En: *Nuevos Enfoques en el estudio de la lítica,* Simposio realizado en el Inst. Invest. Antrop. de la UNAM, publicado por M.D. Soto de Arechavaleta (Ed.) 1990.

LEWENSTEIN, S. 1981b. La función de los artefactos líticos por medio de análisis de huellas de uso. En: *Nuevos Enfoques en el estudio de la lítica,* Simposio realizado en el Inst. Invest. Antrop. de la UNAM, publicado por M.D. Soto de Arechavaleta (Ed.) 1990.

LEWENSTEIN, S. 1981c. Mesoamerican Obsidian Blades: an Experimental Approach to Function. *Journal of Field Archaeology* 8: 2, 1981, pp. 175-188 (14).

LEWENSTEIN, S. 1987. *Stone tool use at Cerros: The ethnoarchaeological and use-wear evidence.* The University of Texas Press, Austin.

LUMLEY, H. de; LUMLEY, M.-A. de; BELTRÃO, M.; YOKOYAMA, Y.; LAYBERIE, J.; DELIBRIAS, G.; FALGUERES, C. y BISCHOFF, J.L. 1987. Presence d'outils taillés associes a une faune quartenaire datée du pléistocène moyen dans la Toca da Esperança, État de Bahia, Brésil. In: *L'Anthropologie,* Paris, 1987, 91(4):917-942.

LUMLEY, H. de; LUMLEY, M.-A. de: BELTRÃO, M. de; YOKOYAMA, Y.: LAYBERIE, J., DANON, J.; DELIBRIAS, G.; FALGUÈRES, C. y BISCHOFF, J.L. 1988. Découvertes d'outils taillés associes a une faune quartenaire datée du pléistocène moyen dans la Toca da Esperança, État de Bahia, Brésil. In: *CR. Acad. Sc. Paris,* 1988, T.306. série II, pp. 241-247.

MANSUR, M.E. 1980. Las estrías como microrrastros de utilización: mecanismos de formación y clasificación. *Antropología y Paleoecología Humana* 1: 21-41. Granada.

MANSUR, M.E. 1986/1990. Instrumentos líticos: Aspectos da análise funcional. *Arquivos do Museu de História Natural,* vol. 11: 115-169. Belo Horizonte, Brasil.

MANSUR-FRANCHOMME, M.E. 1982. Microwear analysis of natural and use striations: new clues to the mechanisms of striation formation. *Studia Praehistorica Belgica* 2: 23-233.

MANSUR-FRANCHOMME, M.E. 1983a. *Traces d'utilisation et technologie lithique: examples de la Patagonie.* Tesis de Doctorado, Universidad de Bordeaux I, Bordeaux.

MANSUR-FRANCHOMME, M.E. 1983b. Scanning electron microscopy of dry hide working tools: the role of abrasives and humidity in microwear polish formation. *Journal of Archaeological Science* 10: 223-230.

MANSUR-FRANCHOMME, M.E. 1984. *Préhistorien de Patagonie: L'industrie "Nivel 11" Technologie lithique et traces d'utilisation.* BAR International Series 216. BAR Publishing, Oxford.

MANSUR-FRANCHOMME, M.E. 1986. Microscopie du matériel lithique préhistorique: traces d'utilisation, alterations naturelles, accidentelles et technologiques. *Cahiers du Quaternarie* 9, CNRS, Bordeaux, Francia.

MANSUR-FRANCHOMME, M.E. 1987a. *El análisis funcional de artefactos líticos.* Cuadernos Serie Técnica 1, Instituto Nacional de Antropología. 86 p.

MANSUR-FRANCHOMME, M.E. 1987b. Outils ethnographiques de Patagonie. Emmanchement et traces d'utilisation. *La main et l'outil: manches et emmanchements préhistoriques,* TMO 15, Lyon.

MANSUR-FRANCHOMME, M.E. 1988. Tracéologie et technologie: quelques données sur l'obsidienne. En:

*Industries Lithiques. Tracéologie et Technologie.* Sylvie Beyries, Ed. BAR Int. Ser. 411. BAR Publishing.

MANSUR-FRANCHOMME, M.E.; ORQUERA, L.A. y PIANA, E. 1987/1988. El alisamiento de la piedra entre cazadores-recolectores: el caso de Tierra del Fuego. *Runa*, XVII-XVIII, Buenos Aires. p. 111-205.

NAMI, H. 1984. Análisis de microdesgaste de algunos artefactos líticos del sitio Casa de Piedra 1. En: *Investigaciones arqueológicas en el área de Casa de Piedra.* Pp. 66-87.

SUSSMAN, C. 1985. Microwear in quartz: fact or fiction? *World Archaeology* Vol. 17 (1).

SUSSMAN, C.1986. *Functional studies of experimental quartz artefacts using microscopic analysis of use-wear and polish formation.* PhD Thesis, UC Berkeley, Department of Anthropology.

SUSSMAN, C. 1988a. *A microscopic analysis of use-wear and polish formation on experimental quartz tools.* BAR, Int. Series, 395. BAR Publishing, Oxford.

SUSSMAN, C. 1988b. Aspects of microwear as applied to quartz. Industries Lithiques. *Tracéologie et technologie. Volume 2: Aspects méthodologiques.* Beyries, S. Ed. BAR, International Series, 411 (ii). BAR Publishing, Oxford.

YACOBACCIO, H. 1981. Sobre los rastros de utilización del material lítico del Alero Los Sauces. En: *Trabajos de Prehistoria* 1: 53-59.

YACOBACCIO, H. 1984. Los raspadores de Patagonia: un problema de multifunción. *Actas de las I Jornadas de Arqueología de la Patagonia*, Trelew.

YACOBACCIO, H. 1988. Multifunction and morphological homogeneity: a Patagonian case study. *Industries Lithiques. Tracéologie et technologie*, vol. 1: 53-68. Beyries, Ed. BAR International Series 411 (ii). BAR Publishing, Oxford.

**1990-1999**

ÁLVAREZ, M.R.; FIORE, D.; FAVRET, E. y CASTILLO GUERRA, R. 1998. Microwear analysis of experimental tools used for making rock art engravings by using scanning electron microscope. *Electron Microscopy: Proceedings of 14th International Congress on Electron Microscopy* Vol. III: 261-262. 1998. H.A Calderón Benavides y M.J. Yacamán (Eds).

ÁLVAREZ, M. y FIORE, D. 1999. How were the images made? Finding the artifact in connection to engraving techniques. An experimental program. *Proceedings of NEWS95 International Rock Art Congress.* Turín, Italia.

ÁLVAREZ, M.R.; FIORE, D.; FAVRET, E. y CASTILLO GUERRA, R. 1999. El uso de artefactos líticos para la ejecución de grabados rupestres: observación y análisis de los rastros de utilización mediante las técnicas de microscopía óptica. *Actas del XII Congreso Nacional de Arqueología Argentina.* Tomo I: 327-335. Editorial de la Universidad de La Plata. La Plata. Editado por Cristina Diez Marín.

AOYAMA, K. 1993. Experimental microwear analysis on Maya obsidian tools: case study of the La Entrada Region, Honduras. En: *Traces et fonction: Les gestes retrouvés* (S. Beyries ed.) ERAUL 50, 2: 423-432. Liége.

ARIET, I. 1991. Tratamiento térmico en grupos tempranos de la Región Pampeana. *Shincal 3.*

CASTRO DE AGUILAR, A. 1994. *Estudios de Análisis Funcional de material lítico: Un modelo alternativo de clasificación tipológica.* Tesis Doctoral Inédita. Facultad de Ciencias Naturales y Museo, UNLP.

CASTRO, A. 1996. El análisis funcional de material lítico: un punto de vista. *Revista del Museo de La Plata* (NS) IX: 318-326.

CASTRO, A. y MORENO, E. 1993-1994. Determinación de enmangues en instrumentos líticos por medio del análisis de huellas de utilización. *Paleoetnológica* 7: 7-20.

CLEMENTE, I. 1995. *Instrumentos de trabajo líticos de los Yámanas (Canoeros nómades de la Tierra del Fuego): una perspectiva desde el análisis funcional.* Tesis de Doctorado. Departement d'Historia de les Societats Precapitalistes i d'Antropologia Social. Universitat Autónoma de Barcelona. Edición microfotográfica.

CLEMENTE CONTE, I. 1997. Los instrumentos líticos de Túnel VII: una aproximación etnoarqueológica. *Treballs D'Etnoarqueologia* 2, CSIC-UAB, Madrid.

CLEMENTE, I. y TERRADAS, X. 1993. Matières premières et fonctions: l'exemple de l'outillage lithique des Yamana (Terre de Feu). En: *Traces et fonction: les gestes retrouvés.* P.C. Anderson *et al.* (Eds). ERAUL 50 (II): 513-521.

CLEMENTE, I.; MANSUR, M.E.; TERRADAS, X. y VILA MITJA, A. 1996. Al César lo que es del César: los "instrumentos" líticos como instrumentos de trabajo. En: *Arqueología. Sólo Patagonia. Actas de las II Jornadas de Arqueología de la Patagonia.* Coord. Julieta Gómez Otero. Publicación del CENPAT, Puerto Madryn, pp. 319-332.

FIEDEL, S. 1996. Blood from stones? Some methodological and interpretative problems in blood residue analysis. *Journal of Archaeological Science* 23: 139-147.

LEIPUS, M. 1997. Manufactura y uso de los artefactos líticos del sitio Arroyo Seco 2, partido de Tres Arroyos, provincia de Buenos Aires. *Libro de Resúmenes del XII Congreso Nacional de Arqueología Argentina*, Pp. 24, La Plata.

LEIPUS, M. 1999. Análisis funcional: caracterización de los microrrastros de uso en materias primas líticas de la región pampeana. *Actas del XII Congreso Nacional de Arqueología Argentina*, Tomo I: 345-354, La Plata.

MADRID, P.; POLITIS, G.; LEIPUS, M. y LANDINI, C. 1991. Estado actual de las investigaciones en el sitio 1 de la Laguna de Tres Reyes: Análisis lítico tecno-morfológico y procesos de formación del sitio.

*Boletín del Centro de Registro del Patrimonio Arqueológico y Paleontológico* 2: 112-122. Dirección de Museos Monumentos y Sitios Históricos de la Provincia de Buenos Aires.

MANSUR, M.E. 1991. Microwear on quartz crystals and obsidian: its contribution to use wear analysis on heterogeneous materials. Presented at *VI International Flint Symposium*. Madrid.

MANSUR, M.E. 1997. Functional analysis of polished stone-tools: some considerations about the nature of polishing. En: *Siliceous rocks and Culture,* M.A. Bustillo y A. Ramos Millán (Eds.), Universidad de Granada, pp. 465-486.

MANSUR, M.E. 1999. Análisis Funcional de instrumentos líticos: problemas de formación y defor-mación de rastros de uso. *Actas del XII Congreso Nacional de Arqueología Argentina,* T I. La Plata.

MANSUR-FRANCHOMME, M.E. 1990. Quelques observations sur les altérations naturelles des microtraces d'usage des outillages lithiques. In: Le silex, de sa genèse á l'outil. *Cahiers du Quaternaire* 17. Bordeaux.

MANSUR, M.E. y LEIPUS, M. 1999. Materias primas, tecnología y función en el Sudeste de la Región Pampeana. *Libro de Resúmenes del XIII Congreso Nacional de Arqueología Argentina,* Pp. Córdoba.

MANSUR M.E.; ALONSO LIMA, M. y PROUS, A. 1991. Traceologia revela uso de artefatos pré-históricos. *Ciência Hoje,* vol. 13, n° 73: 20-22. Brasil.

MANSUR, M.E. y SREHNISKY, R. 1996. El alisador basáltico de Shamakush I: microrrastros de uso mediante el análisis de imágenes digitalizadas. *Relaciones de la Sociedad Argentina de Antropología* Tomo XXI: 267-288.

MANSUR, M.E. y VILA MITJA, A. 1993. L'analyse du matériel litique dans la caractérisation archéologique d'une unité sociale. *Traces et Fonctions: les gestes retrouvés. Colloque International de Liège.* Editions, ERAUL, Vol. 50: 501-512.

SREHNISKY, R. 1999. Caracterización de los rastros de uso en riolitas, cineritas e ignimbritas de Tierra del Fuego. *Actas del XII Congreso Nacional de Arqueología Argentina,* Tomo I: 401-409. La Plata.

NAMI, H. y SCHEINSOHN, V.G. 1997. Use-wear patterns on bone experimental flakers: a preliminary report. En: *Proceedings of the 1993. Bone Modifica-tion Conference, Hot Springs, South Dakota,* L.A. Hannus, L. Rossum y R.P. Winhan (Eds), pp. 256-264, Archaeology Laboratory, Agustana College, Sio-ux Falls, South Dakota, Occasional Publication N° 1.

NAVARRO HARRIS, X. 1991. Análisis comparativo de microhuellas de uso en artefactos de basalto experimentales y arqueológicos del sitio Quillén 1, IX Región, Chile. *Actas del XI Congreso Nacional de Arqueología Chilena:* Pp. 189-195.

OLIVA, F. y LEIPUS, M. 1999. Vías alternativas de estudio aplicadas a reservorios de materias primas líticas: análisis de rastros de uso en artefactos del sitio

Laguna de Puan 1. *Libro de Resúmenes del XIII Congreso Nacional de Arqueología Argentina,* Pp. 22-23. Córdoba.

OWEN, L. 1993. Materials worked by hunter-gatherer groups of northern North America: implications for use-wear analysis. En: *Traces et fonction: les gestes retrouvés.* P. Anderson, S. Beyries, M. Otte y H. Plisson Eds. Editions ERAUL, Vol. 50: 1-11. Lieja.

PÉREZ, S. 1993. Informe de los primeros ensayos experimentales sobre azadas y/o palas líticas (Antofagasta de la Sierra – Catamarca". *Palimpsesto – Revista de Arqueología,* N° 3: 139-149, Buenos Aires.

PÉREZ, S. 1994. Proyecto y primeros pasos en la investigación: Análisis tecno-funcional a través de microdesgaste de azadas y/o palas líticas de Antofagasta de la Sierra – Catamarca: una aproximación experimental. *Los primeros pasos* (213-221). Eds. Asociación de Amigos del Instituto Nacional de Antropología, 251 pág., Buenos Aires.

PRIETO, A.; MORELLO, F.; CARDENAS, R et CHRISTENSEN, M. 1998. Cañadón Leona: a sensenta años de su descubrimiento. *Anales del Instituto de la Patagonia,* Serie Ciencias Humanas, vol. 26, p. 83-105.

PROUS, A.; MOURA, M.T. de; ALONSO, M. 1991. Indústria Lítica de Santana do Riacho: Tecnologia, Tipologia e Traceologia. *Arquivos do Museu de História Natural,* UFMG, Belo Horizonte, vol. 12, p. 275-284.

PROUS, A.; FOGAÇA, E.; ALONSO, M. 1994/95. As últimas indústrias líticas do Vale do Peruaçu (MG – Brasil). *Revista de Arqueologia,* São Paulo, vol. 8, n°2, p. 49-64.

PROUS, A.; COSTA, F.; ALONSO, M. 1996/1997. Arqueologia da Lapa do Dragão – Análise Funcional de Peças da Lapa do Dragão. *Arquivos do Museu de História Natural,* UFMG, Belo Horizonte, vol. 17-18, p. 184-191.

RIBEIRO, L.; ALONSO, M.; FOGAÇA, E. 1995. Produção e Utilização de Artefatos Líticos: Uma reconstituição do espaço ocupado no início do Holoceno na Lapa do Boquete (Minas Gerais – Brasil). In: *Anais da VIII Reunião Científica da Sociedade de Arqueologia Brasileira,* Porto Alegre, p. 17-30.

SCHEINSOHN, V.G. 1997a. Use-wear patterns on bark removers. En: *Proceedings of the 1993 Bone Modification Conference,* Hot Springs, South Dakota. L.A. Hannus, L. Rossum y R.P. Winhan (Eds), pp. 265-276, Archaeology Laboratory, Agustana College, Sioux Falls, South Dakota, Occasional Publication N° 1.

TERRADAS, X.; VILA, A.; CLEMENTE, I. y MANSUR, M.E. 1999. Etno-neglect or the contradiction between etnohistorical sources and the archaeological record: the case of stone tools of the Yamana People (Tierra del Fuego-Argentina). En: *Ethno-analogy and the reconstruction of prehistoric artefact use and production.* Tübingen. Urgeschichtliche Materialhefte 14: 87-99.

VILA, A.; TERRADAS, X.; CLEMENTE, I.; MANSUR, M.E. 1995. La larga marcha: de roca a instrumento. *In: Encuentros en los conchales fueguinos.* Coord.: J. Estévez Escalera y A. Vila Mitja, Treballs d'Etnoarqueología 1, CSIC y UAB, Barcelona. pp. 261-273.

**2000-2011**

ALONSO, M. 2008. *Estudo traceológico de indústrias líticas do Brasil Central.* Dissertação de Mestrado, FAFICH/UFMG, Belo Horizonte.

ÁLVAREZ, M. 2000. La explotación de recursos líticos en las ocupaciones tempranas del Canal Beagle: el caso de Túnel I. *Desde el País de los Gigantes. Perspectivas arqueológicas en Patagonia,* Tomo I: 73-85. Universidad Nacional de la Patagonia Austral. Río Gallegos.

ÁLVAREZ, M. 2000/2002. El trabajo del hueso en la costa norte del canal Beagle: técnicas de manufactura de a través del análisis funcional de instrumentos líticos. *Cuadernos del Instituto Nacional de Antropología y Pensamiento Latinoamericano* 19:49-70. INAPL.

ALVAREZ, M. 2001. Diseño y función. Variabilidad instrumental en la costa Norte del Canal Beagle. *Libro de Resúmenes del XIV Congreso Nacional de Arqueología Argentina,* Pp. 194-195. Rosario.

ALVAREZ, M. 2003. *Organización tecnológica en el Canal Beagle. El caso de Túnel I (Tierra delFuego, Argentina).* Tesis Doctoral. Facultad de Filosofía y Letras, Universidad de Buenos Aires. MS.

ÁLVAREZ, M. 2004. ¿A qué responde la diversidad instrumental? Algunas reflexiones a partir del análisis funcional de materiales líticos de la costa norte del canal Beagle. *Contra viento y marea. Arqueología de la Patagonia.* Editado por Civalero, T.; Fernández, P. y Guráieb, P. 29-43.

ÁLVAREZ, M. 2004. El uso de materias primas vegetales en la costa norte del canal Beagle a través del análisis funcional de base microscópica. *Contra viento y marea. Arqueología de la Patagonia.* Editado por Civalero, T.; Fernández, P. y Guráieb, P. 279-294.

ÁLVAREZ, M. 2004. Estrategias tecnológicas en los grupos canoeros tempranos del área Fuego-Patagónica. *Magallania,* 32:191-208. Chile. Con referato.

ÁLVAREZ, M. 2005. Organización tecnológica en la costa norte del canal Beagle: estrategias de uso de materiales líticos de los cazadores litorales del extremo sur de Patagonia. *Relaciones de la Sociedad Argentina de Antropología XXX:* 33-57. SAA.

ÁLVAREZ, M. 2007. Procesos de producción y uso de instrumentos bifaciales entre los grupos canoeros del canal Beagle. En *Arqueología de Fuego-Patagonia. Levantando piedras, desenterrando huesos... y develando arcanos*: 247-255 Ediciones CEQUA. Chile.

ÁLVAREZ, M. 2009. Diversidad tecnológica en el extremo sur de Patagonia: tendencias y continuidades

en el diseño y uso de materiales líticos. En *Perspectivas actuales en arqueología argentina,* 243-267. Editado por Barberena, R.; K. Borrazo y L. Borrero. CONICET.

ÁLVAREZ, M. 2009. Tendencias y cambios en las prácticas tecnológicas de los grupos cazadores-recolectores del extremo Sur sudamericano. *Arqueología de Patagonia: Una mirada desde el último confín,* 19-33. Editado por M. Salemme, F. Santiago, M. Álvarez, E. Piana, M. Vázquez y M. Mansur. Editorial Utopías.

ALVAREZ, M. Diseño y función. Variabilidad instrumental en la costa Norte del Canal Beagle. En prensa en: *Actas del XIV Congreso Nacional de Arqueología Argentina,* Rosario.

ÁLVAREZ, M. y BRIZ, I. 2004. Divergencias y vigencias en la tecnología lítica de las sociedades canoeras fueguinas: Túnel I y Túnel VII, extremos de 6.000 años de ocupación. *Actes del I Congrés Catalunya-Amèrica. Fonts i documents de recerca. Col·lecció Amer y Cat,* 12: 310-318. Editado por A. Vidal-Folch y G. Dalla-Corte Caballero. Institut Català de Cooperació Iberoamericana.

ÁLVAREZ, M. y BRIZ, I. 2006. Organización tecnológica en el proceso de poblamiento del extremo sur de Sudamérica. *Revista Habitus, Goiânia* 4 (2) 771-795. Universidad Católica de Goiás. Brasil.

ÁLVAREZ, M.; LASA, A. y MANSUR, M. 2000. La explotación de recursos naturales perecederos: análisis funcional de los raspadores de la costa norte del canal Beagle. *Relaciones de la Sociedad Argentina de Antropología* 25: 275-295. SAA. Buenos Aires.

ÁLVAREZ, M.; VAZQUEZ, M. y PIANA, E. 2008. Prácticas mortuorias entre los cazadores-recolectores del canal Beagle: el caso de Shamakush entierro. *Magallania* 36 (2): 107-124. Chile.

ÁLVAREZ, M.; BRIZ, I.; PAL, N. y SALVATELLI, L. 2010. Contextos de uso y diseños: una propuesta metodológica para el análisis de la variabilidad de los conjuntos. *XVII Congreso Nacional de Arqueología Argentina.* Mendoza, Argentina. 11 al 15 de Octubre de 2010. Facultad de Filosofía y Letras, UNCuyo. Instituto de Ciencias Humanas, Sociales y Ambientales, CRICYT-CONICET.

ÁLVAREZ, M.; FIORE, D.; FAVRET, E. y CASTILLO GUERRA, R. 2001. The use of lithic artefacts for making rock art engravings: observation and analysis of use-wear traces through optical microscopy and SEM. *Journal of Archaeological Science* 28: 457-464. Academic Press.

ÁLVAREZ, M.; ZURRO, D.; BRIZ, I.; MADELLA, M.; OSTERRIETH, M. y BORRELLI, N. 2009. Análisis de los procesos productivos en las sociedades cazadoras-recolectoras-pescadoras de la costa norte del canal Beagle (Argentina): el sitio Lanashuaia. *Arqueología de Patagonia: Una mirada desde el último confín,* 903-917. Editado por M. Salemme, F. Santiago, M. Álvarez, E. Piana, M. Vázquez y M. Mansur. Editorial Utopías.

BABOT, M.; MAZZIA, N. y BAYÓN, C. 2005. Potencialidad de los análisis sobre artefactos de molienda. *Libro de Resúmenes del IV Congreso de Arqueología de la Región Pampeana Argentina*, Pp. 105-106. Bahía Blanca.

BABOT, P.; CATTÁNEO, R.; HOCSMAN, S. 2010. ¿Puntas de proyectil o cuchillos? múltiples técnicas analíticas para una caracterización funcional de artefactos arqueológicos. *La Arqueometría en Argentina y Latinoamérica* pp. 127-134. Córdoba.

BELTRÃO, M.C. 2000. *Ensaio de Arqueogeologia. Uma abordagem transdisciplinar*. Rio de Janeiro.

BORELLA, F. y BUC, N. 2009. Ópticas y ópticos. Una aproximación a la tecnología ósea en la Bahía de San Antonio (Río Negro), Argentina. En M. Salemme, F. Santiago, M. Alvarez, E. Piana, M. Vazquez y M.E. Mansur *(eds) Arqueología de Patagonia: una mirada desde el último confín*, editado por, Editorial Utopías (Ushuaia): 421-432.

BRIZ, I.; ZURRO, D.; ÁLVAREZ, M. y MADELLA, M. 2009. Ethnoarchaeology and residue analysis in fisher–hunter-gatherer analysis sites: a pilot study. In *The Cultural Dynamics of Shell Middens and Shell Mounds: A worldwide perspective*. Edited by Roksandic, M.; Mendoça de Souza, S.M.F.; Eggers, S.; Burchell, M. y Klokler, D. University of New Mexico Press. Alburquerque. En prensa.

BRIZ, I.; ÁLVAREZ, M.; SPIKINS, P. y NEEDHAM, A. 2009. 'Durable Residues': Addressing the use of microwear, a case study from March Hill. *Internet Archaeology* 26.

BRIZ, I.; ÁLVAREZ, M.; ZURRO, D.; BALBO, A.; MADELLA, M.; VILLAGRÁN, X. y FRENCH, C. High-resolution shell midden archaeology: experimental ethnoarchaeology on Tierra del Fuego (Argentina). *Quaternary International*.

BUC, N. 2005. Ser o no ser: arpones y arpones B en el Humedal del Paraná inferior. *Libro de Resúmenes del IV Congreso de Arqueología de la Región Pampeana Argentina*, Pp. 15, Bahía Blanca.

BUC, N. 2007. Ser o no ser: arpones y "arpones B" en el humedal del Paraná inferior. En C. Bayón, A. Pupio, M.I. González, N. Flegenheimer y M. Frère (eds.) *Arqueología en las Pampas*. SAA, Buenos Aires. Tomo I: 325-342.

BUC, N. 2008. *Análisis de microdesgaste en tecnología ósea. El caso de punzones y alisadores en el noreste de la provincia de Buenos Aires (humedal del Paraná inferior)*. Tesis de Licenciatura del Departamento de Ciencias Antropológicas II, M. Woods (ed.). Fac. Filosofía y Letras-UBA. CDROM

BUC, N. 2010a. Bone Bi-points: Testing Functional Hypothesis. En A. Legrand-Pineau, I. Sidéra, N. Buc, E. David y V. Scheinsohn, *Ancient and Modern Bone Artefacts from America to Russia. Cultural, technological and functional signature*. BAR International Series 2136: 217-225. BAR Publishing.

BUC, N. 2010b. Microscopic Analysis on Bone Archaeological Tools. The case of Low Paraná Wetland, Argentina. 17 *International Microscopy Congress*, 19-24 de septiembre, Rio de Janeiro. CD ROM.

BUC, N. 2011. Experimental Series and Use-Wear in Bone Tools. *Journal of Archaeological Science* 38: 546-557.

BUC, N. y LOPONTE, D. 2007. Bone tool types and microwear patterns: Some examples from the Pampa region, South America. En C. Gates St-Pierre y R.B. Walker (eds.) *Bones as Tools: Current Methods and Interpretations in Worked Bone Studies*, BAR International Series 1622: 143-157. BAR Publishing.

BUC, N. y PÉREZ JIMENO, L. 2010. Puntas para la comparación. Tecnología ósea en el Paraná Inferior y Medio. En *Zooarqueología a principios del siglo XXI: aportes teóricos, metodológicos y casos de estudio*, M. De Nigris, P.M. Fernández, M. Giardina, A.F. Gil, M.A. Gutiérrez, A. Izeta, G. Neme y H.D. Yacobaccio (Eds.), pp. 439-451.

BUC, N. y SILVESTRE, R. 2006 Funcionalidad y complementariedad de los conjuntos líticos y óseos en el humedal del nordeste de la Pcia. de Buenos Aires: Anahí, un caso de estudio. *Intersecciones en Antropología*: 7: 129-146.

BUC, N. y SILVESTRE, R. 2010. Distribución de artefactos líticos y óseos en el humedal del Paraná inferior. En: *Arqueología de Cazadores-Recolectores en la Cuenca del Plata* G. Cocco y R. Feulliet Terzaghi (Eds.). Santa Fé, Centro de Estudios Hispanoamericanos.

BUC, N.; SILVESTRE, R. y LOPONTE, D. 2009. What about shells? Analysis of shell and lithic cut-marks. The case of Paraná's wetland, Argentina. En E. Álvarez Fernández y D. Carvajal Contreras (eds) *Not only food: Marine terrestrial and freshwater mollusks in archaeological sites. MUNIBE* 31: 252-261. Donostia, San Sebastián.

BURRONI, D.; R. DONAHUE, A.; POLLARD, M. y MUSSI, M. 2002. The surface alteration features of flint artifacts as a record of environmental processes. *Journal of Archaeological Science* 29 (11): 1277-1287.

LANDA, Carlos G.; MONTANARI, Emanuel G.; GÓMEZ ROMERO, Facundo; de ROSA, Horacio; CIARLO, Nicolás C. and CLEMENTE CONTE, Ignacio 2010. Not all were spears and *facones*: firearms from Otamendi fortlet (1858–1869), Buenos Aires province, Argentina. *Journal of Conflict Archaeology* 10, LandaMontari. proef 1. 14-1-2010:16.19, pp. 183-200.

CATTÁNEO, G.R. 2004. Conjuntos instrumentales líticos durante la transición Pleistoceno / Holoceno en el Macizo del Deseado. *Contra viento y marea. Arqueología de Patagonia*. Argentina; p. 71-88.

CATTÁNEO, G.R; GUZMAN, G.; DI LELLO C.; CALO, M.; AGUERRE, A.M. 2009. Análisis por FT-IR de residuos orgánicos en instrumentos líticos provenientes del sitio cueva de las manos, capa 6, Río pinturas (Santa Cruz, Argentina). *Arqueometría Latinoamericana*. Buenos Aires; p. 176-181.

CATTÁNEO, G.R.; MEILÁN, P.; GULICH, D.; GARAVAGLIA, M. 2009. Microscopia Láser Confocal de Barrido (CLSM) y software de reconocimiento de imágenes aplicada al estudio funcional de artefactos líticos: una perspectiva cuantitativa. *Arqueometría Latinoamericana*. Buenos Aires; p. 89-95.

CATTÁNEO, G.R.; FERNÁNDEZ ORDOÑEZ, M. 2008. Programa de observación de microhuellas de uso en instrumentos líticos y su aporte a la discusión de la funcionalidad de sitios. Datos experimentales y arqueológicos. *Problemáticas de la Arqueología Contemporánea*. Rio Cuarto; p. 449-456.

CATTANEO, R.; AGUERRE, A.M. 2009. Estudios funcionales de artefactos líticos de Cueva de las Manos, Río Pinturas, Santa Cruz, Argentina. *Revista del Museo de Antropologia*; Cordoba; vol. 2: p. 3-22.

CATTANEO, G.R.; MEILÁN, P.; GULICH, D.; FERNÁNDEZ, M.; GARAVAGLIA, M. 2007. Microscopia laser confocal de barrido (clsm) aplicada al estudio de microhuellas de utilizacion en instrumentos liticos experimentales: una perspectiva cuantitativa. *Arqueología de Fuego-Patagonia*. Punta Arenas, Chile; p. 327-342.

CHRISTENSEN, M. 2003. Analyse fonctionnelle de l'outillage en pierre taillée. Análisis funcional de las herramientas de piedra tallada. In: D. Legoupil, *Les chasseurs-cueilleurs de Ponsonby (Patagonie australe) et leur environnement du VIème au IIIème mil. Av. J.C.* Cazadores-recolectores de Ponsonby (Patagonia Austral) y su paleoambiente des de VI al III milenio A.C., Magallania Tirada Especial (Documentos), vol. 31. p. 205-213.

CLEMENTE CONTE, I. 2005. Hide processing by Yamana people: working activities and consumption goods according to the ethnohistorical sources and their reflection in the lithic tool assemblage from the site Tunel VII (Tierra del Fuego, Argentina). In: Xavier Terradas (ed.), *Lithic Toolkits in Ethnoarchaeological Contexts*. Acts of the XIVth UISPP Congress, pp. 41-45. BAR International Series, 1370. BAR Publishing, Oxford.

CLEMENTE CONTE, I. y GÓMEZ ROMERO, F. 2006. Análisis de vidrios "retocados" del Fortín Miñana (Azul, Provincia de Buenos Aires) In *A.H. Tapia, M. Ramos y C. Baldassarre (eds.), Estudios de Arqueología Histórica. Investigaciones argentinas pluridisciplinarias*, pp. 109-124. Museo de la Ciudad de Río Grande, Tierra del Fuego.

CLEMENTE CONTE, I. y GÓMEZ ROMERO, F. 2008. Analysis of 'retouched' glass fragments from Fortlet Miñana (Azul, Argentina Pampas). *International Journal of Historical Archaeology* vol 12 (3): 248-262.

CLEMENTE CONTE, I. y TERRADAS BATLLE, X. 2009. Igneous and metamorphical rocks exploitation by the last aboriginal from Fuegian Channels. En: M. de Araujo Igreja y I. Clemente Conte (coords), *Recent functional studies on non flint stone tools: methodological improvements and archaeological inferences,* pp. 65-87. Fundação para a Ciencia e Tecnologia (Ministerio da Ciencia e da Tecnologia) IGESPAR Ministerio da Cultura Portugal.

CLEMENTE CONTE, I., GASSIOT BALLBÈ, E. y GARCÍA DÍAZ, V. 2010. Distribución espacial de estructuras y actividades productivas en el conchero nº 4 de Karoline (KH4), Kukra Hill RASS, Nicaragua. En: *The Diversity of Caribbean Archaeology*. XXII Conference of the International Association for Caribbean Archaeology (IACA). Publisher: The Jamaica Nacional Heritage Trust, pp. 660-675.

CLEMENTE CONTE, I.; GASSIOT BALLBÈ, E. y LECHADOS RÍOS, L. 2009. Shellmiddens of the Atlantic coast of Nicaragua: something more than mounds. In: M. Coutinho Afonso y G. Bailey (eds) *Evolutions and Environment – C62- Coastal geoarchaeology: the research of shellmounds*. UISPP, Procedings of the XV World Congress (Lisbon 4-9 September 2006). Serie Editor: Luiz Oosterbeek. BAR International Series, pp. 119-125. BAR Publishing, Oxford.

CLEMENTE CONTE, I.; GASSIOT BALLBÈ, E. y TERRADAS BATLLE, X. 2008. Manufacture and use of stone tools in the Caribbean Coast of Nicaragua. The analysis of the last phase of the shell midden KH-4 at Karoline (250-350 cal AD). En: L. Longo y N. Skakun (ed.) *Prehstoric Technology 40 years later: functional studies and the Russian Legacy. BAR International Series* 1783: 285-293. BAR Publishing, Oxford.

CLEMENTE CONTE, I.; MORENO RUDOLPH, F.; LÓPEZ MAZZ, J.; CABRERA PÉREZ, L. 2010. Manufactura y uso de instrumentos en hueso en sitios prehistóricos del Este de Uruguay. *En: Revista Atlántica Mediterránea de Prehistoria y Arqueología Social nº 12*, pp. 77-95.

CUENCA, D.; GUTIÉRREZ-ZUGASTI, I. y CLEMENTE, I. 2011. The use of molluscs as tools by coastal human groups: contribution of ethnographical studies to research on Mesolithic and early Neolithic contexts in Northern Spain. *Journal of Anthropological Research* 67, 1: 77-102.

DE ANGELIS, H.; LASA, A.; MANSUR, M.E.; SOSA, L.; VALDEZ, G. 2009. Análisis tecnomorfológico y funcional de artefactos de vidrio: Resultados de un programa de experimentación". En: *Arqueometría latinoamericana. Segundo Congreso Argentino y Primero Latinoamericano.*T. Palacios *et al.* (eds). Buenos Aires: Comisión Nacional de Energía Atómica. pp. 134-141.

DE ANGELIS, H. & MANSUR, M.E. 2010. Artefactos de vidrio en contextos cazadores-recolectores. Consideraciones a partir del análisis tecnológico y funcional. En: RAMPAS, *Revista Atlántica-Mediterránea de Prehistoria y Arqueología Social, Nº 12*, pp. 59-73.

FAVRET, E.; FUENTES, N. y ÁLVAREZ, M. 2004. RIMAPS and Variogram analysis of Microwear Traces in Experimental Stone Tools. *Microscopy and Microanalysis*. *10* (Suppl. 2) 968-969. Microscopy Society of America. Cambridge University Press. New York. USA.

FRANCO, N.V.; CASTRO, A.; CARDILLO, M. y CHARLIN, J. 2009. La importancia de las variables morfológicas, métricas y de microdesgaste para evaluar las diferencias en diseños de puntas de proyectil bifaciales pedunculadas: un ejemplo del sur de Patagonia continental. *Magallania* 37(1):99-112.

FRANCO, N.V.; CASTRO, A.; CIRIGLIANO, N.; MARTUCCI, M. y ACEVEDO, A. 2011. On cache recognition: an example from the area of the Chico river (Patagonia, Argentina). *Lithic Technology* 36 (1): 39-55.

GUIDON, N. 2008. Pedra Furada: uma revisão. In: *FUMDHAMentos, Piauí*, v.VII, p. 380-403.

JOHNSON, E.; POLITIS, G. y GUTIERREZ, M.A. 2000. Early Holocene bone technology at the La Olla site, Atlantic Coast of the Argentine Pampas. *Journal of Archaeological Science* 27: 463-477.

LEIPUS, M. 2001. El uso de artefactos líticos manufacturados por talla en el procesamiento de recursos vegetales en la región pampeana: evidencias a partir de la aplicación del análisis funcional. *Libro de Resúmenes del XIV Congreso Nacional de Arqueología Argentina*, Pp. 199-200. Rosario.

LEIPUS, M. 2002a. Evidencias del uso sobre vegetales de artefactos líticos manufacturados por talla en la Región Pampeana: el aporte del Análisis Funcional. *Libro de Resúmenes del III Congreso de Arqueología de la Región Pampeana Argentina*, Pp. Olavarría.

LEIPUS, M. 2002b. *Análisis Funcional de instrumentos líticos de los sitios Cerro La China y Cerro El Sombrero, provincia de Buenos Aires: resultados preliminares y perspectivas*. Informe de investigación de proyecto, MS.

LEIPUS, M. 2003. Los reservorios de materia prima lítica del sitio Laguna de Puan 1: resultados y perspectivas a partir del análisis funcional de base microscópica. *Libro de Resúmenes de las III Jornadas Arqueológicas Regionales*, Pigué.

LEIPUS, M. 2004. Tendencias en el uso de artefactos líticos de la Subregión Pampa Húmeda: relación entre morfología y función a partir del análisis de rastros de utilización. En: *La Región Pampeana, su pasado arqueológico*. C. Gradin y F. Oliva Eds. Laborde Editor.

LEIPUS, M. 2006. *Análisis de los modos de uso prehispánicos de las materias primas líticas del Sudeste de la Región Pampeana: una aproximación funcional*. Tesis de Doctorado. Facultad de Ciencias Naturales y Museo, Universidad Nacional de La Plata.

LEIPUS, M. y LANDINI, M.C. 2000. Revisión de la tecnología del sitio Arroyo Seco 2 (partido de Tres Arroyos, provincia de Buenos Aires). *Libro de Resúmenes del II Congreso de Arqueología de la Región Pampeana Argentina*, Mar del Plata.

LEIPUS, M. y. MANSUR, M.E. 2005. El análisis funcional de base microscópica aplicado a materiales heterogéneos. Perspectivas metodológicas para el estudio de las cuarcitas de la Región Pampeana. *Libro de Resúmenes del IV Congreso de Arqueología de la Región Pampeana Argentina*, Pp. 20-21, Bahía Blanca.

LYNCH, V.; HERMO, D. y ÁLVAREZ, M. 2010. El uso de la forma: análisis funcional del componente inferior de Piedra Museo (Santa Cruz, Argentina). Presentado en *V International Symposium "Early man in America"*. *En prensa.*

MANSUR, M.E. 2007. Confección y uso de artefactos discoides en contextos de cazadores-recolectores de Patagonia meridional: pesas para redes en el sitio HST01AM (prov. Santa Cruz, Argentina). En: *Arqueología de Fuego-Patagonia. Levantando piedras, desenterrando huesos... y develando arcanos*. Pp. 701-707. Morello, F.; M. Matinic, A. Prieto y G. Bahamonde eds. Ediciones CEQUA. Punta Arenas, Chile.

MANSUR, M.E. 2007. Arqueología de la zona de Punta Bustamante (Prov. de Santa Cruz, Argentina). En: *Arqueología de la costa Patagónica. Perspectivas para la conservación*. Pp. 173-193. Cap. 11. Editoras I. Cruz y M.S. Caracotche. UNPA.

MANSUR, M.E. y CLEMENTE, I. 2009. ¿Tecnologías invisibles? Confección, uso y conservación de instrumentos de valva en Tierra del Fuego. *EN Arqueología Argentina en los inicios de un nuevo siglo*. Publicación del XIV Congreso Nacional de Arqueología Argentina. F. Oliva, N. de Grandis y J. Rodríguez (Eds). Tomo II, pp. 359-367. Universidad Nacional de Rosario. Laborde editor.

MANSUR, M.E. y LASA, A. 2004. Tecnología y Función en el IV Componente de Túnel I (Tierra del Fuego). En prensa en *Actas del XV Congreso Nacional de Arqueología Argentina*, Río Cuarto.

MANSUR, M.E. y LASA, A. 2005. Diversidad artefactual vs. especialización funcional Análisis del IV Componente de Túnel I (Tierra del Fuego, Argentina). *Magallania* Vol. 33 N° 2: 69-91, Punta Arenas, Chile.

MANSUR, M.E.; MARTINIONI, D. y LASA, A. 2000. La gestión de los recursos líticos en el sitio Marina 1 (Zona central de Tierra del Fuego, Argentina). *Desde el País de los Gigantes. Perspectivas arqueológicas en Patagonia*. Tomo I, p. 57-72. Argentina.

MANSUR, M.E.; CASTRO, A. y ALVAREZ, M. 2005b. Perspectivas en el análisis de conjuntos líticos. Teoría, metodología, nuevas tendencias. En prensa en *Actas del XV Congreso Nacional de Arqueología Argentina*, Río Cuarto.

MANSUR, M.E.; LASA, A. y MAZZANTI, D. 2005a. Análisis tecnofuncional de pigmentos provenientes de reparos rocosos de Tandilia: estudio arqueológico y experimental. *Libro de Resúmenes del IV Congreso de Arqueología de la Región Pampeana Argentina*, Pp. 175-176. Bahía Blanca.

MANSUR, M.E.; LASA, A. y VAZQUEZ, M. 2004. Investigaciones arqueológicas en Punta Bustamante, Prov. de Santa Cruz: el sitio RD01BK. *Contra Viento y Marea Arqueología de Patagonia*. Buenos Aires. p. 755-775.

MANSUR, M.E.; MAZZANTI, D. y LASA, A. 2004. Análisis microscópico de pigmentos e instrumentos líticos provenientes de reparos rocosos de Tandilia (provincia de Buenos Aires). En Prensa en: *Actas del XV Congreso Nacional de Arqueología Argentina*, Río Cuarto.

MARTUCCI, M. y CASTRO, A. 2009. Análisis funcional de piezas experimentales en dacitas. Manuscrito en preparación.

MORENO RUDOLPH, F.; CLEMENTE CONTE, I. 2010. Functional Analysis of Prehistoric Bone Instruments from the Uruguayan Atlantic COSAT. En: *Ancient and Modern Bone Artefacts from America to Russia Cultural, technological and functional signatura*. Edited by A. Legrand-Pineau, I. Sidéra, N. Buc, E. David, V. Scheinsohn. BAR International Series 2136, pp. 287-293. BAR Publishing, Oxford.

MUSALI, J.; BUC, N. El uso de armas vinculadas a la pesca entre los aborígenes que habitaron el humedal del Río Paraná inferior. Una aproximación experimental. In: Martínez, J., Bozutto, D. (Eds.) *Armas prehispánicas: múltiples enfoques para su estudio en Sudamérica*. Fundación Azara, Buenos Aires, in press.

ORQUERA, L.A.; PIANA, E.L.; ÁLVAREZ, M.; FIORE, D.; VÁZQUEZ, M.; ZANGRANDO, A.F.; TESSONE, A. y TIVOLI, A.M. 2006. El Proyecto Arqueológico Canal Beagle. En *Arqueología de la Costa Patagónica. Perspectivas para la conservación*. Editado por Cruz I y Caracotche S. 266-290. Universidad Nacional de la Patagonia Austral y Secretaría de Cultura de la provincia de Chubut.

PAUNERO, R. y CASTRO, A. 2001. Análisis lítico y funcionalidad del Componte Inferior del sitio Cueva 1, localida arqueológica Cerro Tres Tetas, provincia de Santa Cruz, Argentina. *Anales del Instituto de la Patagonia*, Serie Ciencias Sociales, Vol. 29: 189-206.

PÉREZ, S. 2003a. Aproximación experimental aplicada a la determinación funcional de palas y/o azadas líticas. *Hombre y Desierto. Una Perspectiva cultural* N° 11: 85-113. Instituto de Investigaciones Antropológicas, Facultad de Educación y Ciencias Humanas. Universidad de Antofagasta. Antofagasta, Chile.

PÉREZ, S. 2003b. *Experimentación y análisis de microdesgaste de 'palas y/o azadas' líticas de Antofagasta de la Sierra (Catamarca)*. Tesis de Licenciatura en Ciencias Antropológicas (orientación Arqueología), 208 pág., (inédita). Facultad de Filosofía y Letras, Universidad de Buenos Aires.

PÉREZ, S. 2004. Experimentación de uso con palas y/o azadas líticas. *Intersecciones en Antropología* N° 5: 105-117. Facultad de Ciencias Sociales, UNCPBA, Olavarría, Buenos Aires.

PÉREZ, S. 2005. Análisis de microdesgaste por uso de palas y/o azadas líticas de Antofagasta de la Sierra (Pcia. de Catamarca.) Aportes para su interpretación funcional. *Hombre y Desierto. Una Perspectiva Cultural* N° 12: 23-46. Instituto de Investigaciones Antropológicas, Facultad de Educación y Ciencias Humanas, Universidad de Antofagasta, Chile.

PÉREZ, S. 2006-2007. Experimentación de enmangue de palas y/o azadas líticas. *Boletín de Arqueología Experimental* N° 7: 73-85. Edición on-line, Depto. de Prehistoria y Arqueología de la UAM, Museo Reg. de la Comunidad de Madrid, Servicio de Public. de la Universidad Autónoma de Madrid (España).

PÉREZ, S. 2008a. Análisis de microdesgaste por uso de palas y/o azadas líticas de Antofagasta de la Sierra (Pcia. de Catamarca.) Aportes para su interpretación funcional. *Problemáticas de la Arqueología Contemporánea*, Tomo II: 279-283. A. Austral y M. Tamagnini (Eds.), Universidad Nacional de Río Cuarto (Córdoba, Argentina). (Artículo breve con evaluación científica)

PÉREZ, S. 2008b. Experimentación de enmangue de palas y/o azadas líticas. *Problemáticas de la Arqueología Contemporánea*, Tomo II: 285-288. A. Austral y M. Tamagnini (Eds.), Universidad Nacional de Río Cuarto (Córdoba, Argentina). (Artículo breve con evaluación científica)

PÉREZ, S. 2008c. La organización de la tecnología lítica en el Noroeste Argentino. Aproximación a través de experimentación, análisis tecno-morfológico y de microdesgaste por uso de palas y/o azadas líticas. *Comechingonia Virtual. Revista Electrónica de Arqueología*, Vol II, N°3, Invierno 2008: 186-222.

PÉREZ, S. 2009. ¿Tecnología conservada o expeditiva? Análisis de un caso de estudio: palas y/o azadas líticas de Antofagasta de la Sierra (Catamarca – Puna Meridional Argentina). *Memorias del Primer Simposio sobre Tecnología Lítica en el Área Centro Sur Andino 2006*, pp. 63-69. Editores K. Aranda Alvarez y J.L. Paz Soria. Inst. de Investig. Antrop. y Arqueol., Universidad Mayor de San Andrés (UMSA). Impreso en Producciones CIMA, La Paz, Bolivia. (Artículo breve con evaluación científica).

PÉREZ, S. 2010. Estrategias tecnológicas conservadas en contextos agropastoriles tempranos de la Puna Meridional Argentina. *Chungara – Revista de Antropología Chilena*, Vol. 42, N°2: 405-418.

PÉREZ, S. y CÉSAR ÁVALOS, J. 2010. 'Formas Típicas' de artefactos agrícolas de la Puna Oriental de Jujuy: Producción experimental de filos. *Arqueología Argentina en el Bicentenario de la Revolución de Mayo*. XVII CNAA, Tomo III/V, Capítulo 25, Simposio 25: 1237-1242. Mendoza, 2010. (Artículo breve con evaluación científica).

PIANA, E.; ÁLVAREZ, M. y RÚA, N. 2006. Sea nomads of The Beagle Channel and surrounding areas. *Proceedings of Otto Nordenskjöld's Antartic Expedition of 1901-1903 and Swedish Scientists in Patagonia: A Symposium.* Editado por Jorge Rabassa y María Laura Borla: 195-214. Editorial Taylor y Francis. The Netherlands, Lisse. Swets y Zeitlinger Publishers.

PIANA, E.; VAZQUEZ, M. y ÁLVAREZ, M. 2008. Nuevos resultados del estudio del sitio Ajej I: un aporte a la variabilidad de estrategias de los canoeros fueguinos. *Runa* 29:102-212.

PIANA, E.; VÁZQUEZ, M.; ÁLVAREZ, M. y RÚA, N. 2007. El sitio Ajej I: excavación de rescate en la costa del canal Beagle. En *Arqueología Argentina en los inicios de un nuevo siglo,* tomo I, 345-356. Compilado por F. Oliva, N. de Grandis y J. Rodriguez. Editorial Laborde. Rosario.

PROUS, A.; ALONSO, M.; PILÓ, H.; XAVIER, L.; LIMA, Â.; SOUZA, G.N. de 2002. Os machados pré-históricos no Brasil – descrição de coleções brasileiras e trabalhos experimentais: fabricação de lâminas, cabos, encabamento e utilização. *CANINDÉ – Revista do Museu de Arqueologia de Xingó*, UFS. Xingó, n°2, p. 161-236.

REYES, M.; CASTRO, A. y ALFARO, M. 2004. Análisis microscópico de rastros de uso en instrumentos de basalto: factibilidad, potencialidad y limitaciones. *Libro de Resúmenes del XV Congreso Nacional de Arqueología Argentina*, Pp. 129. Río Cuarto.

SILVESTRE, R. 2004. Análisis de rastros de uso en lascas de filo natural del sitio arqueológico Anahí. En: *Aproximaciones contemporáneas a la arqueología Pampeana. Perspectivas teóricas, metodológicas, analíticas y casos de estudio,* G. Martínez, M.A. Gutierrez, R. Curtoni, M. Berón y P. Madrid (Eds), pp. 183-201. Olavarría, Facultad de Ciencias Sociales, UNCPBA.

SILVESTRE, R. 2010. *Análisis Funcional de Artefactos Líticos del Humedal del Paraná Inferior: El Sitio Túmulo de Campana Como Caso de Estudio.* Tesis de Licenciatura, FFyL, UBA. Buenos Aires MS.

www.ingramcontent.com/pod-product-compliance
Lightning Source LLC
Chambersburg PA
CBHW061010030426
42334CB00033B/3436